The 40-Day Challenge:

From the Cross to the Heart of Man

Second Edition

LaWanda Nall

<u>Exterior and Interior Design of the book by</u>: *Called-Out Ministries Publishing*

<u>eBook conversion by</u>: *Called-Out Ministries Publishing*

The 40-Day Challenge by LaWanda Nall
Called-Out Ministries, Inc.
P O Box 323
Repton, AL 36475-0323
Called-out@minister.com

CALLED-OUT
MINISTRIES INC

Called-Out Ministries, Inc. (Publishing Imprint)
P O Box 323
Repton, AL 36475 USA
Fax: 251-248-2709
Email: called-out@minister.com

Library of Congress Number: 202020202020

Kindle eBook ISBN: 978-1-7351626-4-5
Paperback ISBN: 978-1-7351626-5-2
ePub ebook ISBN: 978-1-953239-28-0
Mobi eBook ISBN: 978-1-953239-29-7

Printed in the United States of America

Paperback Book Cover and eBook cover designed by:
Called-Out Ministries Publishing.

First Edition of *The 40-Day Challenge: From the Cross to the Heart of Man*

Copyright: © 2009 LaWanda Nall

Library of Congress Control Number: 2007904734

Paperback ISBN: 978-1-4257-7911-3

Xlibris Corporation
Indianapolis, IN

Exterior and Interior Design of the book by: *LaWanda Nall*
eBook conversion by: *Xlibris Publishing.*

LAWANDA NALL

DEDICATION

This book version is dedicated to all the inmates
that were at the following jails, prisons, and camps
during 2004, 2005, & 2006:

Escambia County Detention Center,
Pensacola, FL

Wakulla County Jail
Wakulla, FL

Tallahassee Federal Correctional Institute
Tallahassee, FL

Mariana Prison Camp
Mariana, FL

Federal Half-Way House
Spanish Fort, AL

LAWANDA NALL

ACKNOWLEDGMENTS

The second edition of this 40-day devotional's design provides updated resources, expands topics, and adds information on humility and the fruits of the spirit throughout this book. Since it has been 15 years, technology changes have impacted the resources available to authors, family members, and inmates. If you read the first edition, you remember the following acknowledgments. However, I want to make one addition. This second edition has been made possible by my parents and my husband. Their encouragement to update this devotional is part of our celebration of over 60,000 inmates completing this 40-day challenge in state and federal correctional facilities across the United States. We praise God for the 33,000(+) souls won to Christ due to this book and ministry outreach. Some prisons have incorporated this devotional into one of the life skills courses, utilizing it as a textbook.

LAWANDA NALL

TABLE OF CONTENTS

BOOK INTRODUCTION

You may ask why I chose the topic, *the 40-Day Challenge,* or why I selected the devotional book format for this challenge, but there was a strategic plan for this design. I chose the number of forty due to the number of crucial topics that I found to cover with the inmates I was teaching. Also, 40 is a number God uses in the Bible in several ways. The Bible is full of examples of 40-days as an anointed time with God. Below is a list of examples of 40-days, 40-weeks, 40-months, and 40-years used in the Bible. Hopefully, this introduction will explain to you why the Lord made 40-days so crucial to me.

40-Days:

1) Ezekiel fasted for 40-days.
2) Ezekiel lay for 40-days on his left side as penance for the 40-years of the iniquity of the children of Israel.
3) Jesus fasted 40-days in the wilderness and was tempted by Satan before starting his ministry
4) It rained upon the earth 40-days when Noah and his family went into the ark.
5) The Egyptians embalmed Joseph, and the people mourned 40-days as per their custom for him.
6) Moses in Exodus went up on the mount and was before the Lord for 40-days, and the Lord gave him the laws and the ten commandments.
7) The 12 spies checked out the land of Canaan for 40-days then brought Moses their report.
8) Moses went back upon the mount for another 40-days of prayer and fasting in the Old Testament book of Deuteronomy for the second set of tablets.
9) Goliath, the Philistine giant, presented himself morning & evening for 40-days before the children of Israel, tempting them to send a man to fight him.
10) In I Kings, the prophet rose, ate, drank, and went 40-days on the strength of that meal unto Mount Horeb.
11) Jonah preached, "Yet 40-days and I will destroy this city, saith the Lord."

12) Jesus was on earth 40-days after his resurrection from the dead before he ascended to heaven.

40-Weeks:

1) The expected delivery time of a baby is 40-weeks. The mother carries the baby an average of 36-40-weeks. That is for nine to ten months.
2) 40-wks stood for a new life/birth in the Old Testament.
3) Old Testament prophecy refers to 40-weeks in several scriptures.
4) In the Old Testament, 40 weeks is noted in prophecy many times. Plus, 40 years is considered a generation in the Old Testament.

40-Months:

1) Each time the Lord sent a word of warning to the children of Israel to clean up their ways, turn from their idols and return to Bethel, he gave them 40-months of words from the prophets and challenges to change. When they did not turn their hearts toward God, he sent them into captivity.
2) 40-months is the probationary period of God.

40-Years:

1) Moses was 40-years old when he killed the Egyptian and fled to the wilderness.
2) Moses remained for 40-years in the wilderness before returning to Egypt to lead Israel's children out of bondage. He was 80 years old.
3) The children of Israel wandered around in the wilderness, then came to Jordan and refused to cross over. Their faith was weak. God sent them back into the wilderness to ramble some more. For a total of 40-years, they wandered in the wilderness. Then God took Moses on his 120th birthday. Because their faith was so weak, they were sent back out to walk another 40-years, and that generation did not see the promised land.
4) After wandering around for 40 years in the wilderness, then Joshua led the children of Israel across Jordan and took Jericho.
5) Isaac was 40-years old when he took Rebekah to be his wife
6) Esau was 40-years old when he took the Hittite wife

7) Joshua was 40-years old when Moses assigned him to go into Jericho as a spy
8) 40-years later, Joshua led the Israelites into Jericho
9) In Judges, the land had rest 40-years
10) Also, in Judges, the land was in peace for 40-years.
11) When the children of Israel did not obey God in Judges, he delivered them up to the Philistines control for 40-yrs
12) Samuel judged Israel forty years
13) King David was 30 years old when he began to reign as king. He reigned for 40-years.
14) King Solomon reigned for 40-years over Israel.
15) King Solomon's son was 40-years old when he began to reign as king, and he reigned for two years.
16) In the 7th year of Jehu's reign over Israel (from Samaria), Jehoash began to reign in Jerusalem and reigned 40-years.
17) The land laid waste or desolate for 40-years. (Ezekiel).
18) **40-years** in the Old Testament is a generation.

While I was in the Escambia County Jail, waiting for sentencing, the Lord spoke to me and told me to study the "40s" of the Bible. I had never paid any attention to the time frames in the Old Testament. As I begin to examine each of the incidents listed, I began to see that 40 was a number that God used. Forty is as significant with God as the number seven. In the Bible, the number seven represents "completion."

I began to ask God the significance of the 40-days, weeks, months, and years to me personally. In response to my prayers and studying, God told me to set down the events' key dates. As I wrote down the date of the burglary, the date State Farm made their claim, the date I was arrested, the date of the trial, the date of the verdict, etc., I began to count the days between each set of dates. I counted 40-days before each date and after each date. I was shocked to see the events on these dates. The Lord had witnessed what was going to happen either to me or someone else each time.

It was 40-days from one of these dates that a lady minister named Carolyn Williams (from Pensacola) was driving her car down Fairfield Drive. The Lord spoke to her while at the Fairfield and Hwy 29, intersection red-light. God told her to come to the jail, go to the fourth floor, east wing female housing unit, and bring a word to a red-headed lady. Sister Williams had no idea who I was, but she knew that God had given her a word for me.

I heard the most challenging words from the Lord that day that anyone could bring me. Sister Williams told me that the Lord had sent her to tell me to get ready (this was on a Saturday), that I would be sentenced on Wednesday, and that I was going to prison! That the Lord had something special that he wanted me to do for him there. He would show me when I arrived. But that I was to be a witness to him, and I was to write a book out of that experience, and it would be called "*Living a Christian Life in Prison.*" I shared with Sis. Williams, what the Lord had spoken about the "40s" of the Bible. She told me to study it because God might want another book out of me or at least a study or sermon. I counted back 40-days from that word of prophecy, and it was the date of my beating and sexual assault. I counted 40-days forward, and it was the day that I was transported to prison. I knew God was speaking to me. I begin to study the significance of each of the Bible's events that dealt with 40-days and 40-years. I turned 40-years old while in the county jail, waiting to go to prison after being sentenced!

Without consideration for the list of 40, I began working on my list of things to teach to the ladies I had Bible study with at the prison. Miraculously that list had 40 items on it. That is how this 40-day challenge was developed. These 40 lessons/devotionals were the topics that I felt moved upon by the Holy Spirit to teach. These topics gave these ladies something to stand on when they got out of prison. Some were not saved when we started this course/program of study. But they were when we finished. It became my greatest witnessing tool. Give God 40-days; if he does not change you, walk away! I will not ever ask you again to be a Christian or trust God if you will just give him this chance. God's offer is better than any 30-day money-back guarantee that you could every purchase.

Praise the Lord, I saw 89 people get saved and 19 filled with the Holy Spirit during this horrible trial of my life and test of my faith. God sent me on a mission for souls for him. Some key people needed reaching! God sent me to help them. I did not feel worthy of this mission assignment. I feel honored that God chose to use me but humbled at the same time.

I counted back 40-weeks from the date I went to prison. On that day, written on the inside back cover of my Bible was a word of prophecy given by Rev. Jerry Trotter. This word was given at a revival I had attended at Rabun Church of God in Rabun, AL. He called me out one night and said the Lord told him to tell me that I needed to choose whether it was a career or ministry for my future. I said, "ministry." Then Rev. Trotter said, "the Lord told me to ask you a second time. 'Are you sure you are willing to go wherever the Lord wants to send you?' Are you, Sister?" I replied, "Yes."

I thought this line of questioning from God was because I only want to go to certain countries on missions. Even though I had felt pulled to other countries at times, I had rejected the offers to go. I just knew that God was going to send me to one of those remote areas of Africa or an Asian Country that I had turned down in the past! Rev. Trotters' next words were confusing, and I did not understand them at all. Even my parents and the church's pastor were baffled by the words. The pastor, after the service, said to me, "I do not know what it means, but Sister, there must be something important that God wants you to do." Then Rev. Trotter said, "Sister, the Lord said he was going to send you on a mission, where you would not take, coat, cloak, purse or script, but he would provide all that you needed."

After much discussion regarding this prophecy, we were still baffled. Full-time missionaries need sponsors, and they take Bibles, study materials, books, money, and clothes with them. However, when I counted these 40-weeks back and saw that prophecy, I knew what it meant. Even months before I was arrested and charged, God knew the outcome of the trial. He had already set the wheels in motion the night I said, "Yes, Lord, send me!" He was sending me to prison. I could not take anything with me, no money, no books or Bibles, and no clothes. All of that was provided for me there! See how wonderful our Lord is by warning us what he is going to do!

God always prepares us if we listen! All the warnings, dreams, prophecies, and the study on the "40s" warned me and gave me strength during this trial. God knew I would need something to stand on (a faith boost) when things got tough on the inside. It helped me knowing that I was in God's will, on a mission for my heavenly Father! The *40-Day Challenge: From the Cross to the Heart of Man* was borne out of this mission experience. Even on the outside, this challenge has had powerful results for drawing people to God in the real world. I had a lady who was an agnostic buy this book and read it. Her husband was also a believer in many gods, and all ways lead to Heaven. One day in the process of moving, something was said that reminded her of my book. She began to unpack, looking for this book. She panicked when she realized she had lost her copy. She immediately ordered a second book and, after reading it, accepted Jesus as her Savior. Praise God. A seed took root! She told me that after the book came, and she read it a second time, she began explaining Christianity and salvation to her husband. Even though he refused to change, she gave her heart to God. She asked us to pray that she could lead her husband to the Lord. It is miraculous what a word from God can do in a person's heart, even years later!

As you read this section, you will see how to use this study guide to get the most out of this book. If you are not a Christian, it tells you how to use it for its maximum potential in your lives too. If you are a prison or jail chaplain, write to us, and we will send you the 45-day Life Skills Course outline (preferred by most jails) or the 40-45-week Life Skills Course outline (preferred by most prisons). Most county jails give the inmates 45-days of "good time" for completing the course and all assignments. They allow 45 days instead of 40 to spend the first two days covering the introduction, commitment, and why this course is significant. On day three, they start lesson number one. On day 43 and 44, they begin reviewing what is learned, getting into Bible studies, etc. They answer all questions, help the inmates make commitments to Christ, and the final day is a day for testimonies, certificates being issued, and a celebration party for the program's inmates.

The prisons that use this book for a Life Skills course give anywhere from 45 days to 4 months of "good time." The 40-45-week version requires completing a journal and prayer journal in addition to the course and assignments. Spreading this course out over 40 weeks helps the instructors have more time with the inmates to ensure that they have a solid foundation spiritually. The multiple options for using this course as a textbook for these life skills courses has made this book extremely popular. Whether you are incarnated or not, I pray that this book impacts your life forever!

READ AND ENJOY...THEN SHARE

THIS BOOK WITH OTHERS.......

PLEASE KEEP THIS BOOK MOVING!

USING THIS BOOK AS A STUDY GUIDE

Whether or not you are a Christian does not matter. This book is designed to show people of all faiths and walks of life the true God of heaven. This book aims to take Christ's passion from the cross and instill it into the hearts of men and women and changing their hearts. This 40-day challenge will become a way of life for you if you choose to follow Jesus Christ.

If you are not a Christian but want to study these materials, by all means, continue reading. Study about the God of the Christian faith. Learn why we love him so much. Learn why it is so easy for us to lean on him and let him carry our burdens. If you are someone searching, but you do not know if you want to be a Christian or not, please give this 40-day challenge your sincere and honest efforts. Give the challenge the ultimate test. See if my Jesus will come through for you as he did for me.

If you have been taught all of your life that there is no God or just Allah or Buddha, keep reading. You will find answers to those nagging questions that have bugged you for years. If you are not sure that you want to do this study or take this challenge, let me ask you one question. "What if you do not accept this challenge and my God is the one true God? What are you going to do when he returns and takes us to heaven? What will you do if you die tomorrow, and I was right, and you were wrong? Then you will wish that you had tried this simple 40-day challenge! If I am wrong and my Jesus is not the savior of the world, and his father, God, is not the creator of heaven and earth, and if I am entirely wrong and there is no heaven or hell, what have you got to lose? You will have lost one hour per day for 40-days. You will have gained some sound moral principles to live by and found happiness, peace, and contentment. So, what do you have to lose?

This challenge is not hard because the Christian walk is simple and easy. Some people make it hard because they give you a list of dos and do not's, but all God wants is YOU…. ALL OF YOU …. not a part of you, part of the time. He wants ALL of you, ALL of the time. He wants you to fall in love with him and keep falling in love with him each day. This is the best love affair you will ever have in my life! See, my Jesus is not like earthly lovers; he never changes his mind about us. Jesus will always love us, no matter what we do! Where can you find that kind of love?

To take this 40-day challenge, you need to decide what day you will start it, hopefully today! Then set aside a period of 30-minutes to one hour each day to get by yourself and read the devotion for that day. At the end of the devotion, there will be an assignment for each day. Complete that assignment and keep your notes in a 3-ring binder or composition book, or note pad, so that you will not lose the notes you take. Write the date at the top of the page and the day in the book. This process will help keep you organized and on track. Throughout this study, you will refer back to things you have written down in previous lessons. It will make it easier for you to locate your notes if you have the day listed beside the date. (For example, *28 May 2020, Day One*). You will be able to find the lesson when you look back.

Items you will need:

1) A three-ring binder with plenty of notebook paper or a composition book or note pad
2) Pencils or pens, and a highlighter pen if you have access
3) A pocket dictionary or desk dictionary
4) A Bible. Preferably a King James Version, New King James, or New International Version of the Bible. This book quotes the King James Version (KJV).

Now follow these steps:

1) Lay aside or temporarily forget all preconceived ideas about Christianity, church, Christians, and Jesus Christ.
2) Come each day with an open mind and heart that is willing to learn to your study place.
3) Begin each day with a simple prayer that says, "Lord, I have agreed to this 40-day challenge. I am coming to this study with an open mind and heart that is willing to learn. Please show me what you want me to know about you. Teach me your ways. Show me in these 40-days how great you are and how wonderful are your mercies."

4) Lay aside or temporarily forget any traditions that you have learned in the past that are church rituals like those used in non-protestant churches.

5) Promise yourself not to worry about what people will think of you for doing this study or what they will think of you if you are changed at the end of this study; leave this problem to God to handle.

6) Come as a blank tablet or book before God and ask him to write in your heart what he wants you to know about him.

7) Take this challenge sincerely and honestly. Give this challenge your best! Follow each day's assignments, no matter how simple and stupid they may appear to you. Even if you do not think that you have a problem with a topic, still follow the devotion and the exercise/assignment at the end. It is always great to refresh our minds with what God wants from us.

My Pledge to You: "If at the end of this 40-day challenge you are not closer to God (if you are already a Christian), or if you have not found my God, the Lord God Jehovah, to be the one true and living God who gave his Son, Jesus to die in your place, then you can walk away, and I will never bug you again. God has a purpose and plan for your life; he wants to help you and prove to you that he is God!"

God wants to have a relationship with you so that he will reveal himself to you in this challenge. Read the lessons and complete the assignments. I promise you that this book will build your faith and renew your zeal to win souls if you are already a Christian. If you are not a Christian, accept Christ as your savior today, and God will change your evil heart to a good heart. You will be more Christ-like by the completion of this challenge. You will find more peace and contentment in your life, and if you follow the step thoroughly, you will discover God's purpose for your life in this study. You will find yourself falling in love with Jesus more and more each day. Read and study and enjoy the blessing of the Lord! Do not let anything or anyone stop you; complete all 40-days, one day at a time! Do not read ahead. There is a purpose for taking one topic per day and giving yourself time to adjust to the changes that God will make in you and your life.

If you are in a prison that utilizes this book as the textbook for a 40-week Life Skills Course, the instructor will explain to you the agenda and purpose of one lesson per week versus one per day. You will have daily journaling assignments and daily prayer journal assignments added to each lesson. So, your course and challenge become a 40-week challenge, but it only takes 30-minutes per day.

I pray you enjoy this book or course and that you write to us with wonderful news. We want to know if you have accepted Jesus as your Lord and Savior if you felt closer to him after completing this book. If you were already a Christian when you read this book, let us know if this helped you. We would also appreciate your feedback and recommendations for future changes in this book.

Feel free to write to me with your prayer request, questions, etc. We have a group of prayer partners that work with us that will take your prayer request seriously. There is power in corporate prayer. Let us help you fight your spiritual battles. We do not ask for money from individuals. We will not try to take you away from your church or encourage you to divert your tithes to us. We are only concerned with winning as many people to Christ as possible!

Your prayer partner and Sister in Christ,

LaWanda Nall

LaWanda Nall
Called-Out Ministries, Inc.
P. O. Box 323
Repton, AL 36475-0323

Email: called-out@minister.com
Fax #: 1-251-248-2709

DAY ONE:

A RELATIONSHIP WITH GOD, *A Heart Transplant*

Are you happy with your relationship with God and your family? Do you get along with your friends and work well with your Colleagues? What is your relationship with your church family? Are you satisfied with these relationships, or do your children and grand-children hate you? **Contentment** is a condition or state whereby a person feels happy with his/her surroundings. They think that their life is satisfying to them. Paul said, "I will be content in whatsoever state I am in." (Philippians 4:11, KJV, 2020). The most challenging things to deal with in prison is contentment and patience because of your circumstances. I quoted this scripture to myself thousands of times while incarcerated. I thought it would get better once I was released, but I found this lesson more crucial on the outside than inside because of people's adverse reactions to the fact I had been in prison.

We all understand that life is not fair at times. However, when you are wrongfully accused, that lesson is harder to swallow. You will have to remind yourself that if the apostle Paul was able to adjust for the many years he was incarcerated and transferred between so many prisons, we could adapt. We have Jesus with us, and he has given us the Holy Spirit to comfort us. We only have to accept these gifts to experience the gift of contentment! Once you are released, you will experience a melting pot of emotions. Things will not be the same at home, because your friends may not accept you. Employers may turn you away. So, you must take more time in prayer to obtain contentment and patience. Remember, if you wait on God with the right attitude, you will see incredible results in your life!

Satisfied is a condition or state where you are happy with what you have done, where you live, what you have, and what you are doing. You are comfortable with your surroundings. You can only have a **SATISFIED** Life through Jesus Christ. We are made in the image of God, created by him to honor and worship him. We were not designed to make us look good or make us feel great or make us famous, but we were created for HIS purpose.

11

As we learn to love and honor God, we see the beginnings of change in our lives as we become more like him. During this transition, God becomes proud of us and pleased to call us his children. His magnificent grace and mercy reaches out to us, showing us more love than we deserve. He reaches down to bless and anoints our lives. As we witness of his love and mercy, we honor him even more! Then we realize the true contentment!

If you are not content with your life or satisfied with how things have turned out, this book is definitely for you! You need to commit today to stick with this book for 40-days and see if you like the changes that will occur in your life and home. If you are not a Christian, it is OK. For this 40-day challenge, you can accept God and accept this challenge and be honest about that fact. You may not know whether this is something that you want to do. Maybe the thought of being a Christian is something overwhelming to you. Perhaps it is against everything you were taught as a child, especially if you were raised in a family that worshipped many gods as most eastern religions do, or you are a Muslim or Jehovah's Witness. Whatever the circumstances that make you hesitate to commit to trying a relationship with Jesus today, lay it aside. Do not let it hinder you. All you need to do is give God a chance, and he will prove to you that he loves you, that God created you to worship him, and that he delights in loving, caring for, and giving gifts to his children, just like you do for your children or grandchildren.

New Heart versus Evil Heart

We are born with the "Adam" nature that is an evil heart. Even though God created us to love and worship him, sin has caused our hearts to be corrupted. That is why God wants us to come to him, repent of our sins and accept his gift of salvation and a new pure, clean heart!

An **evil heart's spiritual characteristics** (a heart before salvation) are very specific, yet the same in each person. Some individuals may experience more dramatic displays of these characteristics, but we are all plagued with them. The first characteristic that we will discuss is stubbornness. We have all experienced this in our lives! **Stubbornness** is defined by Google.com (2020) as a "dogged [persistent] determination not to change one's attitude or position on something."

Ecclesiastes 8:11: *"Because sentence against an evil work is not executed speedily; therefore, the heart of the sons of men is fully set in them to do evil."* (KJV, 2020).

In this verse, King Solomon (the author of this book of the Bible) gives the reason why men and women continue to sin and rebel against God. It is their evil hearts. In the Old Testament, the penalty for sin or breaking their laws was swift. If you are caught committing a crime in the Middle East, you are taken before the officials on Friday. If you are condemned to lose a hand for stealing, or your life for dealing drugs, then you are beheaded in the town square on Friday. The punishment is swift. The penalty for crimes is severe. That is why they have less than 11 percent crime rate in Saudi Arabia. If the penalty for breaking the laws were quicker here in the United States, like in some Middle Eastern countries, people would not feel that they could escape the punishment of their sins and not continue to do evil. The *Adam Nature* of our sinful hearts is in control until we ask God to forgive our sins and lead us. God can change all of that for you!

Madness is defined by Google.com (2020) defines it as "the state of mind of having a serious mental illness…. Foolish….or wild and chaotic activity [behavior]." Merriam-Webster online (2020) defines madness as "the quality or state of being mad: such as a state of severe mental illness." Non-technically it means "fortifications against inner darkness, for example: 'the threat of madness that crouched above him throughout his life' describes a person with madness."

Ecclesiastes 9:3 says: *"This is an evil among all things that are done under the sun, that there is one event unto all: yea, also the heart of the sons of men is full of evil, and madness is in their heart while they live, and after that, they go to the dead."* (KJV, 2020).

As humans who are not saved and given a new heart are evil, and we are driven with the madness of this world to possess things and have fame or fortune. We feel like this is a race that we are running, and the person who wins is the one who at retirement has the most toys and things accumulated! But things cost us. They wear us out physically. Things make us work more; to keep up those things we have purchased and drive us even harder. It is the madness of materialism and idolatry. We will discuss these in more detail in the lesson for Day-24. We need to forget this madness and strive for the peace and contentment that God gives and for a new heart.

Depravity: According to Google.com (2020), depravity is defined as "moral corruption; wickedness."   It lists synonyms for depravity as corruption, perversions, deviances, degeneracy, degradation, immorality, shamelessness, brutality, debauchery, dissipation, dissoluteness, turpitude, lewdness, lasciviousness, obscenity, indecency, libertinism, sordidness, wickedness, sinfulness, vileness, iniquity, criminality, viciousness, etc. Merriam-Webster (2020) defines depravity as "a corrupt act or practice (depravities of war); the quality or state of being corrupt, evil, or perverted: state of being deprived."

Jeremiah 17:9: *"The heart is deceitful above all things, and desperately wicked: who can know it?"* (KJV, 2020).

The writer of this book, Jeremiah, the prophet, is trying to explain to the children of Israel that their heart has desperately searched for things to make them happy. They went so far in their acquisition of "things" as to let deceit come into their hearts. They allowed their deceitful hearts to desire and commit evil actions to secure the things that they wanted. Here Jeremiah is saying that the heart is the most deceitful organ of the body. That the heart will do wickedly and take control, leaving us without the power to stop it. Because of this nature of our human hearts, we must have a spiritual heart transplant. We need God's new, good heart, a heart that is not deceitful.

SOURCE OF UNBELIEF & COVETOUSNESS:

Unbelief is defined by Google.com (2020) as a "lack of religious belief; an absence of faith."   Synonyms listed are atheism, nonbelief, agnosticism, heresy, apostasy, etc.   Merriam-Webster online (2020) defines unbelief as "incredulity or skepticism, especially in matters of religious faith." **Covetousness** is defined by Google.com (2020) as "eager or excessive desire, especially for wealth or possessions: Social media often encourages us to compare ourselves to others, inspiring covetousness." Merriam-Webster online (2020) defines it as "being covetous, [jealous], greedy, acquisitive, grasping, avaricious, mean having or showing a strong desire for especially material possessions. It is an inordinate desire for another's possessions."

Hebrews 3:12: *"Take heed, brethren, lest there be in any of you an evil heart of unbelief, in departing from the living God."* (KJV, 2020).

14

The Hebrew writer warned the Christians to beware that they did not let unbelief come into their hearts. It would make their hearts evil and separate them from the one true living God. When God gives us a new heart, that new heart's characteristics and actions will differ from the old heart. When we accept Christ as our personal Lord and Savior, and we confess our sins to him, asking for forgiveness, then he gives us a spiritual heart transplant. He takes that old, stoney, hard heart of ours, and he replaces it with a new, clean heart.

NEW HEART CHARACTERISTICS

Throughout the Old and New Testaments, we read numerous scriptures that remind us that we should fear God and keep his commandments. The ten commandment's first command is to have no other God's before our Lord God Jehovah. God must be in first place in our hearts and lives. If we have him in first place in our lives, we will want to keep his commandments!

A HEART THAT FEARS GOD:

Deuteronomy 5:29: *"O that there were such an heart in them, that they would fear me, and keep all my commandments always, that it might be well with them, and with their children forever!"* (KJV, 2020).

God wants to give us a new heart by exchanging our evil heart for a new, loving heart. God is a God of love. To serve him, we must have a caring heart that can forgive and forget the wrong done to us. We have to love like we have never been hurt before and love our neighbors as we love ourselves.

Luke 10:27: *And he answering said, thou shalt love the Lord thy God with all thy heart, and with all thy soul, and with all thy strength, and with all thy mind; and thy neighbour as thyself.* (KJV, 2020).

When you accept Jesus Christ as your Savior, you accept his mercy and grace. God forgives you of your sins, exchanging your old sinful, evil heart with a new heart. He instills within us a new attitude, outlook on life, and a new way of thinking. No, you do not have to undergo open-heart surgery or receive blood transfusions to change. We simply ask God to help us to follow his commandments and to be more Christ-like each day. We are not perfect, and we will never do everything right 100% of the time. However, we can do better each day with the help of the Holy Spirit. The Holy Spirit is one of the gifts that God gives to us when we accept Jesus!

I do not encourage fear in people's lives. I believe that when we have perfect love toward God, we are reading and praying each day that God will remove the spirit of fear from our lives. However, a "fear of God" is a respectful fear that protects us. It keeps us seeking to obey all of God's commandments in our lives. It will help you make choices that will impact your future and your end of life destination (heaven or hell). If I do not have a fear (or respect) for God, then I will not be concerned with the consequences of my choices. Without this concern or fear, my life will take on a different purpose. That is not what God wants from us in our lives. He wants us to be obedient to his commandments in the Bible and our purpose in life, which can only be accomplished if we allow God to exchange our evil hearts for a new heart. A heart with a new focus and purpose!

A HEART THAT SERVES GOD:

If we give God our heart, ask him to forgive our sins, and openly confess that we are a Christian, then we are proclaiming that we will be God's forever. To remain God's forever, then we must fix our eyes on Christ and focus on the prize at the end (heaven).

Psalms 57:7: *"My heart is fixed, O God, my heart is fixed: I will sing and give praise."* *(KJV, 2020).*

These were the words of the psalmist King David as he sang his praises to God. David knew that his heart was FIXED permanently on God. King David knew that God had given him a new heart and that he would never turn away from God as long as he kept his heart on God and his word. The new heart God gives us will love him and be dedicated to him forever!

The most important part of our relationship with God is giving him our whole heart. This process may seem impossible to you. However, once you accept Jesus Christ as your personal Lord and Savior, it will become easier for you to accomplish this task. The more you read God's word and learn of him, you will find that your heart longs to know even more! As you grow in the wisdom and knowledge of God's word, you will begin to see changes occurring in your attitude, personality, lifestyle, and actions. These changes will happen automatically. In the future, you will look back and wonder when this change occurred. You will notice that you not only desire to spend time with God's word but that you will never turn back from following Jesus. Do not be discouraged if this step takes time. But it will occur if you keep reading and praying.

Once you accept him as your Savior, God's gift to you will be to give you a new heart and a new spirit. The prophet Ezekiel tells us in **Ezekiel 11:19** that God's promise to us is this new heart. God will also take our stony heart and give us a soft, receptive heart, which is a heart that can receive God's word and process it. Without the Holy Spirit making this spiritual heart transplant in our lives, we would not understand the Bible. It is difficult to make sense of the Bible without divine intervention and anointing.

God loves to redeem, restore, and rejuvenate our hearts and lives! He loves giving these gifts to those who turn their hearts to him! God desires that we also be content with what he blesses while remaining honest to God and ourselves. At times people will not understand us or accept the changes or choices we make once you go home. We only have to worry about is whether our choices are in God's will and according to his word (the Bible).

Luke 8:15: *"But that on the good ground are they, which in an honest and good heart, having heard the word, keep it, and bring forth fruit with patience." (KJV, 2020).*

Make your commitment today to God and watch as he changes you from the inside out, one day at a time! Accept him, then begin reading his word, praying, and completing Bible Studies.

THE FIRST STEP: RECEIVING A NEW HEART

Tell God, "Yes, I will give this 40-day challenge a try…a sincere try." Then ask God to forgive you of your sins and to come into your heart. You can tell him that you know that you are just "trying him out for 40-days" and that his money-back type guarantee is that he will never again ask you to serve him if this does not work for you. You must be sincere, but what do you have to lose? What is 40-days? You have wasted more than six weeks of your life before on stupid projects that cost you money and left you sad, so what do you have to lose? NOTHING!!

THE SECOND STEP: RECEIVING A NEW HEART

Ask God for a **spiritual heart transplant**. You will not undergo open-heart surgery; you are merely going to ask God to give you a new heart that no longer has a sinful nature. Your new heart will be one that is not defiled with the world or the evil of this world. You will be a new man or new woman; your sinful nature is gone. You will be more like Jesus every day that you walk this new path. You will not be perfect, you will make mistakes, even sin, but forgiveness is a prayer away!

Ezra 11:19: *"I will give them one heart, and I will put a new spirit within you, and I will take the stoney (old) heart out of your life and give you a heart of flesh (a new heart)."* (KJV, 2020).

II Corinthians 5:17: *"If any man be in Christ, he is a new creature, old things are passed away: behold old things are become new."* (KJV, 2020).

Ephesians 4:24: *"And that ye put on the new man, which after God is created in righteousness and true holiness."* (KJV, 2020).

Reading these scriptures will remind you that God made provisions for your heart transplant over 3000 years ago in the Old Testament. Over 2000 years ago, he gave his life so that you could go free. There is not a more generous gift than the sacrifice Jesus made for us. There is not a greater friend to have on your side during this time of your life! God has got you! He will keep you in the palm of his hand if you do not rebel and walk away! Now, you are ready for the **New Heart Blessing**!

THE NEW HEART BLESSING

When Jacob wrestled with the angel (Genesis), he asked to be blessed. Jacob had prayed earlier and asked God to give him a new heart. God took his request seriously and gave him a new heart and a new name. Jacob met his brother Esau the next day and was blessed at this meeting, in response to God's new heart. Jacob's new heart was one without deceit, and it endowed him with his meeting with his brother, Esau, the next day. (Remember, Esau is the one that Jacob beat out of his birthright and blessing because he deceived their father. Esau had searched to kill Jacob ever since). When the angel blessed him, he also changed his name and called ISRAEL. God completely changed Jacob, including his name!

When Jesus met Saul on the road to Damascus and blinded him with a light, Saul prayed. When God finished working on Saul (three days Saul was blind), God gave Saul a new heart and a new name, Paul. God changed Saul from a murdering salvage to one of the greatest apostles the Christian world has ever known. Paul wrote the majority of the books of the New Testament. This change in Paul resulted in churches being established, not destroyed. Paul's new heart and humility changed him to the point that he could allow God control in his life. God used Paul to witness to men and women worldwide, including kings and great leaders. It is incredible what God can do with a person when he replaces the old *Stoney Heart*!

Let our Heavenly Father prove to you that he is the ONE and only God. He gave his only son, Jesus, to die on the cross in our place so that we would not have to die the death that we deserve. That we would not have to be punished for the sins of our lives, but that we could have everlasting life in heaven with him FOREVER! What a tremendous promise! See, our faith is the only faith with a risen Savior. Our Jesus is alive and sitting at the right hand of the Father, interceding on our behalf. Jesus is our defense attorney, on our side, always believing in us! Jesus went a step further than any defense attorney I know; he took our place on Calvary, dying in our place.

I do not know about you, but I have never met a man other than my father, who loved me enough to give his life for me until I met my husband. Most people never know an earthly love this strong. However, Jesus died on the cross for you and me, then rose from the grave, so you could have life eternal. That is caring enough to be bothered with our lives' details and loving enough to give me this challenge and meet me there! Where will you ever find a religion with a Savior like my Jesus? You will not! Give him a try today and start this challenge with the commitment to give this study a 40-day trial and accept this new heart he wants to provide you with; then, you will have a chance to succeed in this study.

DAY ONE ASSIGNMENT

For each day of this challenge, there will be an assignment to complete. Please do not skip around, but complete the lessons in order. The order is specific, with each topic building upon each other. Some things have to be deal with first. It is crucial!

ASSIGNMENT FOR TODAY:

Make notes, and list thoughts you want to remember from today's lesson in your notebook. Then I want you to complete the assignment below, using a separate sheet or page of paper for each list. Different sheets will allow you to add to this list as you go through this book. No one will see this list but YOU & GOD, so be honest. You will use these lists in lessons later.

On each side of the paper, write one of the questions below at the top of the page. Use the front and back of the paper.

What I hate about my life   What I like about my life
What I hate about my marriage   What I love about my church
What I hate about my church   What I love about my marriage
What my children do that irritates me most
What I wish my children would do
Ten things I wish my spouse would change
Ten things I am willing to change about myself for my spouse.
Three dreams that I had, but I never had the chance to do or complete.
Three dreams that I had, and I have had the chance to complete them.
Ten weaknesses/faults that you possess
Ten talents or strong points that you possess

When you make your lists, they do not need to be formal, typed, or extensive. Do not make it complicated; keep it simple. But be honest with yourself. God will meet you during this study. He will help you to address each and everything that we put on our list. Trust God. He will surprise you.

DAY TWO:

COMMITTING TO GOD

Sometimes in life, we look over our lists or search our thoughts when they drift to topics like we discussed yesterday and feel *depressed*, and we feel like failures. It looks like nothing we ever started has turned outright or that whatever we did was a flop. If you looked at your list yesterday and felt that way, do not worry. We are going to talk about those feelings and lists today.

The number one reason for feeling like there is a great void in our lives is because we left God out or decided to serve other gods. God is a jealous God. He wants us to worship only him. God created us for the sole purpose of honoring and glorifying him. He created us to worship him continually in all that we do. The more things we do to honor God, the more he wants to give and do for us. God knows that he will get more glory and honor from our lives as we share the miracles he has given to us.

We cannot desire to follow the world and God too. We have to make a choice today who we will serve. If you are unsure, but you want to give this challenge your best, then choose to serve God today, commit and give God the 40-days of this study. Walk away from evil, from the things that you know are wrong, and stand up and say, "I am going to serve the Lord God Jehovah!"

JOSHUA'S CHOICE:

Joshua's story is beautiful. It is about a young man who loves the Lord, even though somewhat overzealous at times; he never turns away from the opportunity to help Moses. Joshua was there when Moses led the children of Israel from Egypt. Joshua stayed close to Moses, learning from him. I believe that Joshua felt there was something "big" for his life. He felt that God had a special purpose and plan for him. He had no idea that one day a "Moses" would enter his life and turn it upside down.

When Moses showed up in Egypt with a word from God that he would deliver Israel's children from Egypt's bondage, Moses completely upset every Jew's entire life and careers. The future changed for them too.

It is incredible how one person can cross your path and change your life. It can be good or bad. Most of you reading this book are in prison because of a person entering your life and influencing it. It is so easy to let other people convince us that it will not hurt anyone for you to smoke a joint. It is not something that hurts anyone else! They forget to tell you how the addiction will ruin your life, cost you your children, destroy your career, and in some cases, cost you your home, car, family, marriage, and everything that you own.

When Moses entered Joshua's life, it changed it for good. That is God's desire for each of us. He wants us to have men and women with God's favor on their lives, pass on the *New Heart Blessing,* and the favor of God to us! Joshua not only caught Moses' eye, but he caught God's attention too. God chose Joshua to be Moses' successor. Since God would not allow Moses to enter into Canaan after he disobeyed the Lord and smote the rock in the wilderness, God told Moses to prep and train Joshua to take his place.

Joshua came to the position of leader of Israel as a young man. Joshua was a man with a heart that was sold out to God. There was no question in Joshua's mind, whether he would serve God or not. When Joshua selected a wife, I am confident that he insisted she was firm in her commitment to God. There was no other option for Joshua's family and house. Like Joshua, every man and woman are free to choose eternal life or eternal damnation. We can also decide what we want, what we will do, what we will be, or determine what we will not do each day of our lives. God does not make us choose to do right or to serve him; it is our choice. However, he created us to love and worship him with all of our hearts, soul, mind, and strength. He desires for us to want him more than anything or anyone!

Joshua issued a challenge to the children of Israel in this verse in **Joshua 24:15.** When some of the children of Israel desired to serve the Amorite and Canaanite gods, Joshua knew that this would anger God and bring his wrath on them. He knew that God would not allow his gift, *this new land,* to turn his people from him. Joshua knew that God would take away this land he had given to them for their inheritance before he would allow it to destroy them. God had moved for the children of Israel and had delivered them from their enemies, parted Jordan so they could cross on dry land, and given them Jericho without even a battle. But look at how quickly they forgot what God had done for them. The children of Israel's desire to follow the other inhabitants in their idol worship caused God's wrath to come on them. They became captives (slaves) to other countries.

Joshua 24:15: *"And if it seems evil unto you to serve the Lord, choose you this day whom ye will serve; whether the gods which your fathers served that were on the other side of the flood or the gods of the Amorites, in whose land ye dwell:* **but as for me and my house, we will serve the Lord."** *(KJV, 2020).*

So today, join me and agree to serve God and him only. No other Gods, no other faiths. Give him a wholehearted chance to prove himself to you. Take this pledge. Write it out in your notebook and sign it. If this is your book, you can sign this page. This will be your prayer and promise to God for the next 38 days of this challenge.

"Jesus, I promise to love, honor, and adore you. I promise today to give you my ALL. Take all that I am, no matter how small or bad, but all of me. Take me and use me; however, you think best. I do not know if you can do anything with me, but I trust you, and I know that you can make something beautiful of my life. Just know that as for me and my house, I am going to serve you, Lord. Today, I pledge to serve you for the rest of my life!"

DAY TWO ASSIGNMENT

This is the assignment for today, just like the lists that you made yesterday. Each day you will have an assignment. Some are not as long as the one we had yesterday, but each one is important. **DO NOT SKIP** this part of the lesson!

ASSIGNMENT FOR TODAY:

In addition to any notes or thoughts you had about today's lesson, I want you to make a list in your notebook of all the dilemmas you face that seem to hinder you from getting where you need to be in life. You can list things, circumstances, or people.

Below is a list of categories that will trigger your memory. If you are having a problem with anything or anyone in one of these categories, then write it out. Be specific. Let this be your prayer for today. God will help you with all of these areas and give you the wisdom to know how to handle each one.

1) Family—extended family, immediate family, in-laws
2) Church family, Community, or Neighbors
3) Colleagues/Career/Finances
4) Legal Issues, co-defendants, anyone who makes you angry
5) Addictions, other areas, desires for revenge, and hate

DAY THREE:

PRAYER

Prayer is a request or petition that one makes to God. According to Google.com (2020), prayer is defined as "a solemn request for help or expression of thanks addressed to God or another deity." Dictionary.com (2020) describes prayer as "a devout petition to God …. spiritual communion with God as in supplication, thanksgiving, adoration, or confession. The act or practice of praying to God. [Example: The Lord's Prayer]." When you pray, you do not have to look at the person or idol (object) to pray. It is not necessary to be in church or kneeling at an altar to pray. A prayer is voiced or said silently. A prayer can be written down and read to God.

There are many ways to pray. The critical component is that you pray like you are talking directly to God. When I pray, I talk to God just like I would my husband or best friend. A prayer can be a request, comments, praise, thanks, please, requests for a blessing, or just a simple *Thank You.* I strongly recommend you talk to God as you would talk to a close friend. This makes it easier; no need to make praying harder. Prayer is your communication with God. Reading God's word is his communication back to you. All conversations require two or more people; one talks and one listens. After the first person finishes, the second person talks. Praying works the same way; it may sound overly simple, but it works! You can say a prayer in your mind, under your breath, as a whisper, or even as an audible conversation. It does not matter how you say the prayer, choice of words, or delivery method. What counts is the frame of mind, the attitude which we possess when we go to God in prayer.

We must come humbly come before our Heavenly Father when we pray like we would approach the Queen of England or the United States president. It must be done with humility and respect. When we pray, we are honoring God. We are trusting him with our problems and needs. We are telling God that we know he is capable of handling all situations for us. This level of trust is required in a successful marriage, and it works the same in communication with God.

Is praying everyday essential? Yes, each day, you should pray at least two times. Look at it this way. Each day you desire for your spouse or significant other to greet you in the morning with a pleasant comment, hopefully. You want the last thing he/she says at night to be something sweet, thoughtful, and romantic. If your spouse went for days upon end without talking to you, you would get upset. If your spouse decided to talk to you only on Sunday mornings when other people were around, eliminating the chance for quiet, quality time with you, how would you react? After enough weeks of this, you would file for divorce. You cannot survive in a marriage without communication. It is the same with a relationship with God. You have to talk to him. He wants to know your most secret thoughts. He wants to know how you feel, what you think, even if it is not pleasant! God is your best friend! He wants to share everything with you. Do not shut him out. Do not turn over in bed and go to sleep without saying good night and telling him how much you love him. Please do not rush out to face the day without asking for his help. Do not rush past him and ignore his presence. He is your best friend!

The more you talk with God, the easier it becomes. After a while, you will find yourself talking to God in your car, in the shower, in the bathroom, or whispering a prayer at work. Talking with God about issues will become so natural that you can talk to God anytime, anywhere, without anyone else knowing it!

I Thessalonians 5:17: *"Pray without ceasing." (KJV, 2020).*

Do not worry about the myth that you are losing your mind because you are talking to yourself. Know that all intelligent individuals classified at the genius level like Einstein talked to themselves. It was a way of keeping themselves organized and focused on the task at hand.

You need to begin praying now. As you complete this 40-day challenge, you will need to make prayer a vital part of your morning and nighttime rituals. If you start praying now, then it will be a habit by the time you are through with this study. Most teachers will tell you that it will become a habit if you practice something for at least 21 days. By the time you have been praying twice per day for 40 days, you will not even have to think or plan; praying will be second nature to you.

Make it a part of your challenge to pray a minimum of two times per day. You can feel free to pray more if you desire. Even if the desire is born out of frustration, confusion, pain, or agony, pray! The more you practice talking to God during this challenge, the easier it will be for you to automatically turn to him after the study is over, and I am not here to remind you each day to pray.

HOW CAN I PRAY WHEN I DO NOT KNOW HOW?

Do not worry. There is no specific way to pray or specific words that have to be said. Yes, the Bible has several model prayers. We will talk about two of those in this study on other days. However, you do not have to follow any particular model. Just simply say what is on your heart. You are talking to your best friend when you talk to God. Talk to him like you do your best friend. Do not make praying a challenging task.

WHAT IS THE PURPOSE OF PRAYING?

The purpose of praying is for us to communicate with God. He wants to hear from us, just like family. He wants to know what we need, how we feel, and what we need him to do for us. Have you ever turned your children away when they came to you asking for help? **NO.** You want to help them. You want to be a part of their lives. You want to know what is going on in their "little worlds." God feels the same about us. We are his children. When we pray, we talk to him. When we read his word (the Bible), he talks back to us, giving us instructions.

Praying does the same thing for our relationship with God that communicating with our spouse does for our marriages. Communication makes trust grow, closeness to improve, and the overall feeling of completeness is felt. The more you pray, the easier it becomes to go to God with all of your problems. If you decide that you will not pray or feel that this is unnecessary, let me remind you of one thing. Just like your spouse, God determines that you are no longer interested in him when you refuse to talk to him. God will decide that you have changed your mind about your commitment to him. When you stop praying, your actions demonstrate to God that you do not desire a relationship with him. God is long-suffering; he hangs around longer than the average person will in a relationship.

However, God can get tired of waiting for us and walk away too. Then we find ourselves a product of a spiritual divorce from God, no longer his child, and cut off from his promises and blessings. As a direct result, things start to fall apart until you once again return to God.

What should I keep in mind when I pray? Humility! Remorse and Contriteness! You are nothing, nobody without God. He is your creator. If you live another day, it depends upon whether or not he wills it. He is the ultimate power. His power is greater than any king, queen, president, or prime minister. He is in total control. So, come humbly before him with a repentant heart that is committed to serve and love him. Talk to God like a friend. Open your heart to God. Open your prayers with what you are thankful for, pray for others, and close with your requests.

God knows everything, so be honest in your prayers. Tell God the truth, regardless of how ugly or nasty you look. Remember, God knows everything. There is no need for you to lie to God or try to be deceitful when you pray. God sees everything we do; he hears everything that we say. God already knows the rest of your story, so no need to lie to him. If you are honest in your talks with him, then he can help you. God wants to lead you, guide you, teach you how to behave and what to say or do. God is not some superpower in the sky that has a lightning rod in his hand and wants to hit you over the head with it or jolt you every time you have a terrible thought or do something terrible. He is not Zeus, passing instant judgment, killing his subjects for mire misaddress, or inappropriate words. Our God is a loving, kind, and merciful God. He wants each of us to learn his ways, and with our new hearts he has given us, he will teach us what we need to know.

The Christian walk is not a hard one. It is a good, clean, moral walk that will not generate any evil in our lives if we follow God's plan. It does not guarantee us that bad things may not happen to us. There is evil in the world all around us every day. Sometimes, something evil may touch our lives, but God is there to help us with those trials, tests, and struggles. God wants it to be easy for us to serve him. He desires that we love him more than anything or anyone else in our lives. God expects us to honor and adore him more than our spouses, children, families, and earthly possessions. Here are promises God has given us to pray:

John 15:7: *If ye abide in me, and my words abide in you, ye shall ask what ye will, and it shall be done unto you. (KJV, 2020).*

Mark 11:24: *Therefore, I say unto you, what things soever ye desire, when ye pray, believe that ye receive, and ye shall have them. (KJV, 2020).*

Luke 11:9: *And I say unto you, Ask, and it shall be given you; seek, and ye shall find; knock, and it shall be opened unto you. (KJV, 2020).*

DAY THREE ASSIGNMENT

ASSIGNMENT FOR TODAY:

In addition to any notes or thoughts that you had about today's lesson, I want you to make a list of the following things in your notebook and pray this list to God:

1) A list of at least ten things that you would like for God to do for you during this 40-day challenge

2) A list of at least ten things that you would like for God to do for your family during this 40-day challenge

3) List any unanswered prayers that you had before coming to prison or walking into the trial you are in on the outside.

DAY FOUR:

ANSWERED PRAYER & INTERCESSORY PRAYER

Do you have problems praying or feel that you do not know what to say? When you pray that no one hears those prayers? Maybe this Christian walk is new to you, or you do not even know how to pray. Read on; this lesson will help you. I realize we have discussed the need to pray, what happens when you pray, and how to pray by just talking with God in a previous lesson. However, another effective way to communicate with God or to pray is to write out your prayer, like writing a letter.

Sometimes it is hard for me to pray about some of the things I experience. However, if I pick up paper and pen or go to the computer and begin to type, I am amazed at how the words will flow from my mind to the paper or the screen. Sometimes, it is hard to voice words, but easier to write them. It is OK to write God a letter. It is OK to be specific to him. It is OK to give God details, ask questions, and then give your petition. Do not forget to praise him and thank him for all that he has done for you before you start asking for favors. No one likes to be the *fairy god-mother* without any thanks!

Here are a few facts about prayer that may help you understand more about the importance of prayer and why Satan does not want us to pray. As long as we do not pray, then we cannot get an answer or have results. Without success or results, we become discouraged and despondent. Satan wants us discouraged, so we will not pray. He wants us to give up and let go of the best thing in our lives! Jesus!

PRAYER

The first time that prayer is mentioned in the Bible is in the Old Testament, in Genesis's first book. This first scripture talks about Enos' relationship with God. Enos was a man that called upon the Lord and experienced answered prayer to the point that it received honorable mention in the scriptures.

Genesis 4:26: *"And to Seth to him also there was born a son, and he called his name Enos; then began men to call upon the name of the Lord." (KJV, 2020).*

There are many types of prayers and different prayer concepts for prayer that you can utilize in this study and your everyday life. There is no one way to pray. I always tell people to choose the type of prayer and the delivery method of praying that feels the most comfortable. You may choose to pray silently. Others pray out loud. You may choose to kneel and pray in the Chapel or by your bed. Or you may choose to pray in the shower, so no one sees you. How, when, and where does not matter. You need to determine what works best for you and your living arrangements. Just make sure you pray at least twice per day.

You need to be aware of the various types of prayer to respect them when you see them in use by others. You also need to be aware of them to utilize the different delivery methods, depending on your need or request before God. You could offer a prayer of thanksgiving to God. Request forgiveness in prayer. Offer a prayer of a petition before God. Or recite a spiritual warfare prayer as you take control over evil in your life. Let us start with reviewing answered prayers. Prayers that are accepted by God and answered is what we all desire. There are ways to ensure your prayers are answered prayers.

ANSWERED PRAYER

There are examples of all types of prayers being answered by God in the Bible. We will discuss some examples of men in the Old Testament and New Testament that had answered prayers. I cannot cover all of the scriptures. There are too many of them.

MOSES:

During his wilderness experience, Moses learned after killing the Egyptians and fleeing to the wilderness to trust God in every circumstance of his life. Moses was 40-years old when he killed the Egyptian. Moses was in the wilderness for 40-years when he returned to Egypt to free Israel's children from bondage. Moses had 40-years to draw close to the Lord and learn of his commandments. Moses understood that humility, sincerity, trust, and faith were essential for putting a petition before God. Moses mastered this skill of praying with faith. Moses had lots of answered prayers.

Exodus 15:24: "*And the people murmured against Moses, saying what shall we drink? And he cried unto the Lord, and the Lord showed him a tree, which when he had cast into the waters, the waters were made sweet.*" *(KJV, 2020).*

In this particular scripture, Moses asked for drinkable water from God for the children of Israel. God answered this prayer. Moses has numerous prayers answered in the book of Genesis that you can read to build your faith. God delivered the children of Israel from Egypt, protected their firstborn children during the plaques, healed Miriam of leprosy, and parted the Red Sea, allowing the children of Israel to cross on dry grown. Finally, the people's healing after being bitten by the snakes, and many more prayers!

GIDEON:

Gideon was a simple man who felt that he, not a hero or man who was honored by God. It was Gideon's spirit of humility and contrition when he came before God with his petitions that drew God to answer Gideon's prayers. Gideon *fleeced* the Lord several times, trying to discern if it was God who had spoken to him or something he thought of in his mind. God answered Gideon's request/fleece each time he prayed.

<u>**Judges 6:39**</u>: *"And Gideon said unto God. Let not thine anger be hot against me, and I will speak but this once: Let me prove, I pray thee, but this once with the fleece; let it now be dry only upon the fleece, and upon all the ground there be dew. And God did so that night: for it was dry upon the fleece only, and there was dew on all the ground." (KJV, 2020).*

Most pastors will tell you not to fleece God, as Gideon did in this scripture. However, there are times when I pray about something, and I think that I know the answer. I search the scriptures and try to answer the question. When I have finished my searching of the scriptures and still feel confused, I may fleece the Lord. If you decide to place a fleece before God, make sure that it is something that man could not do. Gideon asked for the impossible from man's perspective. There was no doubt that it was God who answered, not his eyes playing tricks on him or his wisdom resolving the dilemma. God cares about the smallest of decisions in your life. You can pray and ask him about anything you desire to know spiritually, and God will answer you.

HANNAH:

For years, Hannah had desired a child. She was barren and could not have children. She had been made "fun of" by the other women in her camp/area. She was distraught that it seemed that God had not granted her the one wish she had had for years. Hannah went with her husband to the Temple that year to pray and offer sacrifices for their sins; she fasted and prayed before the Lord. Hannah went to the Temple steps and knelt and stayed before the Lord crying and praying. She begged God to give her a son. Hannah even *bargained* with God. She promised God that if he would just remove her shame and give her a son that she would give him back to the Lord as soon as he was weaned. God heard her prayer and answered it.

I Samuel 1:27: *"For this child I prayed; and the Lord hath given me my petition which I asked of him:"* (KJV, 2020).

Hannah prayed sincerely, making promises to God. I encourage you to reach the entire story of how Hannah prayed, trained Samuel, and her commitment to holding up her end of this bargain. God also rewarded her with more children after Samuel was born. God wants to give us the desires of our hearts. He is our heavenly father. But first, we must give him our hearts, change our ways, and pledge to serve him for the rest of our lives!

SOLOMON:

Solomon built a temple for the Lord so that the Ark of the Covenant and the Holy of Holies would no longer have to be in a tent. On the day that the Temple was ready, Solomon made a ceremony or service to dedicate this new building to the Lord. At this dedication service, Solomon offered sacrifices to the Lord and prayed that God would accept his sacrifice & offerings, thereby accepting the new temple as his house/home. The Lord answered Solomon's prayer and spoke unto him.

I Kings 9:3: *"And the Lord said unto him, I have heard thy prayer and thy supplication that thou hast made before me: I have hallowed this house, which thou has built to put my name there forever and mine eyes and mine heart shall be there perpetually."* (KJV, 2020).

ELIJAH:

Elijah was a prophet of God. He had an extremely close relationship with God. When Elijah prayed, God answered. On the day that Elijah challenged the 300 prophets of Baal to a contest to see whose god would answer by fire, Elijah knew that the God of heaven was alive and would answer his prayers. He was trying to prove to the children of Israel that the god Baal was just an idol. It was a statue that they were praying to and offered sacrifices. It was a dead statute, with no life in it.

The prophets of Baal agreed to Elijah's challenge. They prayed all day and begged their god to answer them. Some priests even cut themselves and inflicted personal pain, trying to get their gods to answer them. There was no answer. Well, Elijah had them drench the altar and the sacrifice with water. He had them feel the trench around the altar with water. Elijah wanted no *excuses* for how it was burnt. He did not want anyone accusing him of a magic trick of setting it on fire. He wanted there to be *NO DOUBT* in Israel's children's minds, which god answered this petition. After all, the water was placed upon the altar and the trench filled, then Elijah made a straightforward prayer. Here is Elijah's prayer that God heard and answered.

<u>**I King 18:37**</u>: *"Hear me, O Lord, hear me, that this people may know that thou art the Lord God and that thou hast turned their heart back again. Then the fire of the Lord fell and consumed the burnt sacrifice and the wood and the stones and the dust and licked up the water that was in the trench." (KJV, 2020).*

God answered Elijah's pray precisely as he requested. God proved to the children of Israel on Mount Carmel that he was the one true God and that they were to serve only him! You can have answered prayers of this magnitude if you dedicate your life to Christ and do your best to live for him. If you are reading and praying, God will help you. We all make mistakes, but God understands our weaknesses and that we are human. God understands our weaknesses. His mercy and grace are awesome that it will deal with us and draw us near to him to be chastised and corrected. God will help you to live for him. You cannot do this on your own!

THE EARLY CHURCH:

The disciples and others had gathered together to pray and seek God. They prayed with sincerity and humility. When they prayed, God answered.

<u>Acts 4:31</u>: *"And when they had prayed, the place was shaken where they were assembled together; and they were all filled with the Holy Ghost, and they spoke the word of God with boldness." (KJV, 2020).*

The early church in the New Testament enjoyed the same favor with God as the Old Testament's prophets. They could go directly to God, and not through a priest with their request. The early church set an example for us to follow in our daily lives. God has given us the Holy Spirit to help us, lead us, and guide us through the Bible and what God desires for us!

CONDITIONS FOR

ANSWERED PRAYER

Many issues can make a difference in whether or not our prayers are answered. There are conditions that one must meet before God answers a prayer or request. I will discuss with you the conditions for answered prayer that will affect your life while incarcerated. There are other conditions that you will learn about once you go home and begin attending church.

HUMILITY

We must pray with a contrite/humble spirit daily, just as Hezekiah prayed when the Lord spoke. Humility is an essential requirement that we must possess in our lives if we want to approach God through prayer with our request. God will not listen to us if we have sin in our lives or approach him with an attitude that does not exhibit humility and contriteness (compassion & meekness).

II Chronicles 7:14: *"If my people, which are called by my name, shall humble themselves and pray and seek my face and turn from their wicked ways; then I will hear from heaven, and I will forgive their sins, and I will heal their land." (KJV, 2020).*

However, I want you to understand that humility is a non-negotiable condition for God's favor and answered prayers. You must have humility in your life to be presentable before the King of Kings, your Heavenly Father! Do not worry; we are going to talk more about humility in a future lesson. Humility is a Christian, new heart character trait that takes time to build in your life.

WHOLEHEARTEDNESS

Jeremiah: 29:13: *"And ye shall seek me and ye shall find me when ye shall search for me with all of your heart." (KJV, 2020).*

We must pray with all of our hearts and be sincere when we pray. This type of commitment is called whole-heartedness. God is an all or nothing God. There are no partial commitments to God. You may know people who are Sunday only Christians but look at their lives. Do they have answered prayers? Are their miracles occurring in their lives? You must remember, God will not accept part of us to serve him and the rest to go its way in the world. We must commit as Joshua did, with our whole heart!

RIGHTEOUSNESS:

James 5:16: *"confess your faults one to another and pray one for another that ye may be healed. The effectual fervent prayer of a righteous man availeth much." (KJV, 2020).*

We are promised that we will have answered prayers if we are righteous through Christ. We obtain righteousness through Jesus Christ by confessing our sins. James says that if we confess our sins, we will be healed, and God will answer our prayers. The essential key to righteousness is the confession of your sins: followed by obedience.

OBEDIENCE:

<u>I John 3:22</u>: *"And whatsoever we ask, we receive of him because we keep his commandments and do those things that are pleasing in his sight."* *(KJV, 2020).*

We are promised that we will have answered prayers if we are obedient to God's will. If we follow the commandments of God (the Ten commandments), we love our neighbor as ourselves (New Testament command of Jesus), we have the fruits of the spirit (Galatians 5), none of the works of the flesh (Galatians 5) in our lives, that we can go to our Heavenly Father and ask what we need, it shall be according to **John 15:7.**

<u>John 15:7</u>: *"If ye abide in me, and my words abide in you, ye shall ask what ye will, and it shall be done unto you."* *(KJV, 2020).*

Obedience comes easy if you read and pray each day. If you do not read and pray, you will find that obedience to God's word is problematic. This is not a walk that we can make by ourselves. To live a Christian life, we must have God's help, leadership, and guidance. We need the help of the Holy Spirit to keep us on track and focused. Without the Holy Spirit, we will not understand what God expects of us, might less how or when to do it.

FAITH:

<u>Mark 11:24</u>: *"Therefore, I say unto you, whatsoever things ye desire, when ye pray, believe that ye receive them and ye shall have them."* *(KJV, 2020).*

This is the last point of this section. It is the most crucial point following the confession of your sins. The Bible says that it is impossible to please God without faith. Faith brings answered prayers and miracles in our lives. Our faith in God touches his heart and makes him long to give to us. When you pray and quote scripture to support your prayer request, you turn God's eyes toward you. You warm his heart, just like a love letter or card warms your heart. We must pray with faith, believing that God will answer our prayers. The easiest way to keep your faith positive is to search for a scripture that talks about what you need from God or a story from the Bible where someone received what they needed that is similar to your request.

For example, if you want a child. Go to the book of I Samuel and read the story of Hannah. (We discussed her a couple of lessons back). Remind God of Hannah's prayer and how he granted that to her. Remind God that you, like Hannah, want a child. This helps you keep your faith pumped, and it speaks to God's heart because you are using his word for your petition. When you pray like this, God cannot turn his eyes away!

OTHER THINGS AFFECTING ANSWERED PRAYER:

The most crucial factor to consider is what is God's will for us. If we pray for something that is not what God had planned for us, he will not answer that request. We could also pray and ask for something that would bring us harm or sorrow, and God may deny that request. Remember, God is like a father. If your children came into the house crying and begging you for a snake (poisonous snake) for a pet versus a puppy or other harmless animal, would you give him/her that snake just because they asked? *NO!* You know that if he/she played with that poisonous snake long enough, that eventually they would get bitten. You would not want your child to die. So, no matter how upset the child was, no matter how angry they were at you, you would not care; their safety is your primary concern.

Well, sometimes, God can see things that we do not. God can see everything. He knows all things at all times. God can be everywhere at once and can see what we are going through. He even knows the future. He can look ahead and see what will happen to us if he grants that request. So sometimes God will not answer a prayer, or he will say *NO*. When he does, it is for our good; usually our safety. We have to learn to pray and ask God for his will for our lives. We have to put our petitions and request before him and tell him what we want, then tell him, "However, Lord, your will be done." Most important, we must be willing to accept his final decision without grumbling or complaining!

Another hard concept to understand at times with God is his timing. We go to God in prayer and ask for a new job wanting him to send the job the next day or the following week at the latest. We do not know or understand God's timing. He may have a fantastic job or promotion where you are currently working. However, there is someone else in the position that God has set aside for you. You have to be patient and give God time to move or promote the other person so that the position is vacant for you to fill. Or maybe the position has to be created, and God knows the time in which that new position will be created; therefore, you must wait awhile.

Remember, we do not have to lose faith in God. Do not fall into this trap! God's timing is perfect even if we think God is dragging around; he is right on time. If you do not grumble, complain, or become discouraged with God when things do not happen when you think they should; but give God time to work on others or change circumstances to fulfill our request. God knows what is best, and when the proper time is to move. Trust him; he will never lead you wrong.

WHAT IS INTERCESSORY PRAYER?

Intercessory prayer is a sincere, honest prayer that is prayed with a humble, open heart before the Lord. It is a prayer that is so open and honest that you do not hide any of your feelings or emotions on the subject (both good and bad) from God. Intercessory prayer is usually prayers that are prayed when you are by yourself in your *special place* where you go to read and pray each day. A place you can go where no one else is around, where you can pray, scream, cry, or just sit there and meditate without any interruptions. It is a special time for you and God to communicate. There is no music in the background, no kids, no TV, or anyone talking to you. This special place that you select, whether in your bedroom, breakfast nook, patio, sunroom, or your favorite workroom in your house, should be your "quiet" place. It is in this special place with your mind totally on God that you can sincerely talk with God and release all of your troubles to him in prayer to resolve them for you. You can also pray and wait on God for an answer!

You may be wondering how to enter into intercessory prayer? Once you are alone, you can open up to God and tell him your heart. It is ok to be emotional and to cry. Once you have received the Holy Ghost/Holy Spirit in your life, you will find that you have a prayer language (some people call it speaking in tongues). This prayer language sometimes takes over when you are crying and praying before the Lord. It prays for you. It just opens you up to God. Sometimes, I feel like I do not even know what to say to God. I know I need help or an answer, but I do not even know which direction to go. It is times like these when my prayer language takes over and prays for me. There have been times when I was so hurt and wounded that I could not even pray. My prayer language would pray for me directly to the throne, without any interference or interruptions. It is a prayer that goes straight to the Father.

As you grow more in your walk with Christ and get into a Bible-believing church, you will learn more about the Holy Spirit. There is a book by Benny Hinn, which I would like to recommend to you called, "***Good Morning, Holy Spirit.***" It is one of the best books to explain the Holy Ghost/Holy Spirit and what it does for us. Once you have completed this 40-day challenge, read this book. It will change your lives even more!

I hope that today's lesson has helped you understand the importance of intercessory prayer and answered prayers. It is a promise God gave to us. It is not a pipe dream out there that is not obtainable. God wants us to have answered prayers!

Pray Each Day—do not miss a day!

DAY FOUR ASSIGNMENT

ASSIGNMENT FOR TODAY:

In addition to any notes or thoughts that you had about today's lesson, I want you to make a list of the following things in your notebook and pray this list to God:

1) You made a list of people who had hurt you. Today, I want you to take that list and select one person off that list and begin writing a letter to God about what that person did to you and why you feel the way you do. Then ask God to help you to forgive him/her. Ask the Lord to show you what you need to do for that person so that you can forgive them. Pray sincerely over that letter when you go to your special place of prayer today.

2) Each day until you have written a letter to God about each one of the people or events on your list that have hurt you, I want you to write a letter as described in # 1 above. This process may take several days or a couple of weeks, depending upon your list. Just do not forget to keep writing until you have told God about each one.

DAY FIVE:

UNANSWERED PRAYER

Have you ever felt that you were doing everything that you knew to do, but still, you could not get an answer to your prayers? Have you ever been in a place where you knew you were in God's will, there was no sin in your life, you had not been disobedient, yet something was hindering your prayers from being answered? Sometimes, we think that we have not received an answer when, in fact, we have already gotten the answer! You are probably wondering what I am rambling about; well, sometimes, NO ANSWER is an answer from God.

For example, you have prayed to know whether to put your house up for sale and move to a different neighborhood. You do not want to move your children to a worse area, but you need a house with cheaper payments or a house outside of the city limits with a larger yard for the children. However, you are afraid to move without knowing if this new place you have found or searching for is God's will. So maybe you have prayed for months over this request, not getting an answer. Yet you know that it would be a wise real-estate move or a smart choice for your family as the world's standards are concerned. So, you wonder why God would be opposed.

It is not that God is opposed, objecting, or refusing to answer your prayers. No answer from God is an answer! *It means, not now, just wait a while!* I have the perfect place for you; It is just not ready for you yet! Sometimes, God holds up our answer to test us. God wants to see if we trust and love him. Before blessing us, he must know that we are serving him because we love him and not because of what he is giving to us!

Yesterday we discussed what causes unanswered prayers. We discussed how to look for things that might be hindering our answered prayers. I will not recap those thoughts today; however, you need to know that you have looked at each of those issues and know that you are not doing anything to hinder you from having answered prayers. We did not discuss one topic yesterday; that is a critical issue that we will discuss on Day-15 and Day-34 devotions. It is a broad topic and cannot all be discussed in one or two days. However, let me give you a summary of that component.

Bitter water and sweet water cannot flow from the same fountain. You will never find saltwater and freshwater in the same body of water. Once the saltwater begins to mix with the freshwater, it all becomes contaminated with the Salt. Your mouth is your fountain. Your mouth is how you praise God and give him Honor and Glory. You cannot speak good things one minute, praising God, and grumble and complain the next minute. If you grumble because God has not dealt with an issue or answered prayer as you desired, then you have bitter and sweet water flowing from your fountain (your mouth). Therefore, it is all contaminated. God will not hear your prayers nor answer them until you repent.

God cannot stand a discontented person who grumbles, complains, and grips about everything. If you are one of these people who is always negative and nothing fits you, then you need to find an altar and pray through! Get someone to help you pray until you have deliverance from this spirit in your life. You can never grow in God or have answered prayers. You can never succeed in life, either. People cannot stand to be around, especially to work in close settings with negative, hateful people. We all want peace, especially at home and at work. (These are the two places where we spend most of our lives). There must be peace and harmony in our homes and our workplaces to prevent stress and stress-related illnesses in our lives.

Remember how we talked about God inhabiting the praises of his people? How he desired to give us the desires of our hearts? God wants to! But he will refuse to bless a negative person. That individual will not be able to give God glory, honor, and praise for his blessings. Instead, they will probably find something to grumble about or complain about in the blessing! God will not waste his time; He will give the blessing to someone who deserves it and will provide him with the honor for it! So, if you are letting bitter and sweet water flow from your fountain (your mouth), STOP NOW!!

CAUSES OF UNANSWERED PRAYERS

Several areas cause failure in our prayer life. So many times, we pray and ask God for things that are not according to his will or plan for our lives. It is easy to desire something because we think that it will make us happy. The first thing you must learn about unanswered prayers is that God may not answer prayer because that answer would take us further from him. God is not going to give you a snake if it will hurt you! He will not let you get a promotion on your job if that promotion takes you away from your family every week and church every weekend.

Most of these topics have already been discussed. However, I feel that it is essential that we take a more in-depth look at them in this chapter. These are definite "deal breakers" with God answering your prayers.

DISOBEDIENCE:

When we are disobedient or sinned, we must go before the Lord and repent of the sins we have committed. Weeping and crying is not always a sign of repentance. It may just be an emotional reaction that a person has to *being caught.* Sometimes it is just a manifestation of frustration for experiencing defeat! Disobedience is a spirit or act of rebellion against God. It is a statement from us to God that we think we know more than him, that we feel that our ways are better than his and that we no longer trust him to be in control of our lives. So, know that God knows the intent of your heart; he knows everything. You must be truly repentant and remorseful of your sins to have forgiveness. You must desire to be obedient to his word and his commandments. Otherwise, you will be like the children of Israel.

Deuteronomy 1:45: *"And ye returned and wept before the Lord, but the Lord would not hearken to your voice, nor give ear unto you." (KJV, 2020).*

I Samuel 14:37: *"And Saul asked counsel of God, Shall I go down after the Philistines? Wilt thou deliver them into the hand of Israel? But he answered him not that day." (KJV, 2020).*

King Saul initially trusted the Lord with everything in his life and career. He went to God in prayer or sought the prophet Samuel to offer sacrifices for him and put his petitions before the Lord. However, after a while, King Saul became lifted in pride. He let his anger, ego, and a spirit of revenge against David cause all types of spirits to come into his life. He then began to disobey various commandments of God whenever they interfered with his choices or preferences. In this scripture, King Saul went to the Lord to pray about going into battle against the Philistines. He wanted to know if he would have the blessing of the Lord upon his army and if he would be victorious in this war. So, he prayed and prayed, but God did not answer. God chose not to answer King Saul because of the disobedience and rebellion in King Saul's life.

On another occasion, King Saul sought God for an answer. This time of seeking came after he continued to rebel against God. King Saul hunted David with a murderous spirit in his heart toward David. Murder or murderous spirit is one of the works of the flesh that God will not allow into heaven—see the glossary. The Bible states that God removed all communications from King Saul, including dreams at this point.

I Samuel 28:6: *"And when Saul inquired of the Lord, the Lord refused to answer him, neither by dreams nor by Urim, nor by prophets." (KJV, 2020).*

God refused to answer King Saul by any means. King Saul had sinned and angered God, so God cut him off. When you reach a place where God refuses to talk to you, then you are doomed. That is a place that you never want to reach in your relationship with God. King Saul could not get answers from any of the prophets or have dreams as he had in the past. So, he consulted the "witches/warlocks." The lady that King Saul went to visit one-night practiced seances or other actions where she called the dead's spirits back to earth. She was not initially able to call the prophet Samuel up, as King Saul requested. But a demon spirit representing Samuel spoke damnation to Saul. This scared the witch more than King Saul.

SECRET SINS:

Secret sins are those things that we do that no one else knows. Sometimes a secret sin can be a thought, desire, or feeling. If you smile each time you see your colleagues or the people you work with, but in your heart, as you are walking away, wish that they would quit or die, then you have a secret sin of hate. We cannot have secret sins or un-confessed sins in our lives. God will not overlook iniquity. (See glossary). An unclean heart or evil heart will prevent answers to our prayers.

Psalms 66:18: *"If I regard iniquity in my heart, the Lord will not hear me." (KJV, 2020).*

Here, the writer of this passage tells us that if we know that we have sinned and elect to overlook it and do not confess it with genuine humility and Godly sorrow, then the Lord will not hear us when we pray. God will not give us his help, support, or answer prayers for us, because he cannot even look upon us to hear our prayers when there is sin in our lives.

I John 3:20-22: *For if our heart condemns us, God is greater than our heart, and knoweth all things, beloved, if our heart condemns us not, then have we confidence toward God. And whatsoever we ask, we receive of him because we keep his commandments and do those things that are pleasing in his sight. (KJV, 2020).*

I John 5:14-15: *And this is the confidence that we have in him, that, if we ask anything according to his will, he heareth us. And if we know that he hears us, whatsoever we ask, we know that we have the petitions that we desired of him. (KJV, 2020).*

NEGLECT OF MERCY:

According to Google.com (2020), mercy is defined as "compassion or forgiveness that is shown toward someone whom it is within one's power to punish or harm." The synonyms are leniency, clemency, compassion, grace, pity.

Proverbs 21:13: *"Whoso stoppeth his ears at the cry of the poor, he also shall cry himself, but shall not be heard." (KJV, 2020).*

The Bible is very specific on several principles. One of the main principles that you must learn at the beginning of this walk with Christ is to show mercy. The man who hardens his heart to the poor will reap what he sows. The person who does not give mercy cannot receive mercy from God.

Galatians 6:7-8: *Be not deceived; God is not mocked; for whatsoever a man soweth, that shall he also reap. For he that soweth to his flesh shall of the flesh reap corruption, but he that soweth to the Spirit shall of the Spirit reap life everlasting. (KJV, 2020).*

Matthew 25:41-45: *Then shall he say also unto them on the left hand, depart from me ye cursed, into everlasting fire, prepared for the devil and his angels. For I was an hungered, and ye gave me no meat: I was thirsty, and ye gave me no drink: I was a stranger, and ye took me not in: naked, and ye clothed me not: sick, and in prison, and ye visited me not. Then shall they also answer him, saying Lord, when saw we thee an hungered or athirst, or a stranger, or naked, or sick, or in prison, and did not minister unto thee? Then shall he answer them, saying, verily I say unto you, inasmuch as ye did it not to one of the least of these, ye did it not to me. (KJV, 2020).*

Luke 11:13: *If ye then, being evil, know how to give good gifts unto your children; how much more shall your heavenly Father give the Holy Spirit to them that ask? (KJV, 2020).*

BLOOD-GUILTINESS:

Merriam-Webster's online dictionary (2020) defines blood-guiltiness as the guilt a person feels from the shedding of innocent blood. For people who have killed, murdered, and destroyed with their hands, God would not allow them to go into the *Holy of Holies* and offer sacrifices before the Lord. Just because you have been in a war and killed people or even been a murderer does not block you from praying to God. However, your hands are guilty of blood or sin until you have sought forgiveness.

We are under grace now, and not the Old Testament law. So, this verse has a different meaning now. It means that no one with sin upon their lives or hands can offer praise or petitions to the Lord. He will not hear if we have sin in our lives. Even though a person with sin in their lives may pray and pray, not giving up till they get an answer to their prayers, it will not be their persistence in prayer that gets the answer through for them. It will be their prayers of repentance and their change to a Godly life that results in God answering their prayers.

Isaiah 1:15: "*And when ye spread forth your hands, I will hide mine eyes from you: yea, when ye make many prayers, I will not hear: your hands are full of blood.*" *(KJV, 2020).*

Matthew 6:5-8: "*And when thou prayest, thou shalt not be as the hypocrites are: for they love to pray standing in the synagogues and in the corners of the streets, that they may be seen of men. Verily, I say unto you; they have their reward.*" *(KJV, 2020).*

I Timothy 2:8: "*I will, therefore, that men pray everywhere, lifting up holy hands, without wrath and doubting.*" *(KJV, 2020).*

DESPISING THE LAW:

The word despise is defined by Google.com (2020) as "to feel contempt or a deep repugnance [disgust or hate] for [the topic or person]."

Proverbs 28:9: "*He that turneth away from his ear from hearing the law, even his prayer shall be an abomination.*" *(KJV, 2020).*

To despise the Bible or God's instructions to us is to feel disgust or hate toward God's commandments. When we voluntarily sin, we are making a statement to God that we despise his commandments. If we despise them, how can we expect his blessings? If you hate the laws of God and his truths or commandments, God will not answer your prayers. (This is also the same as refusing to listen to truth or reason).

Listed below are other topics that I will not go into today's lesson due to time constraints, but I will discuss them in more detail in this book's other lessons. I am listing these topics here so you can study them this week. If you review this list and see areas where you have difficulty, read and meditate on these scriptures. All of these topics are discussed in more detail later, but it never hurts to begin researching problem areas of your life in God's word as we go through each lesson.

1) Refusing to accept God—forsaking him and truth
     II Chronicles 15:2
2) Provoking God: Deuteronomy 3:26
3) Hardening your heart against God's will--Stubbornness:
     Zechariah 7:12-13
4) Doubting God—Instability—Double mindedness:
     James 1:5-8
5) Wrong motives in your heart or self-indulgence: James 4:3

6) Un-confessed sins—iniquity:
James 4:1-5, John 9:31, Isaiah 59:2, Micah 3:4
7) Unbelief—lack of faith: Matthew 17:20-21 and 21:22)
8) Dishonor of spouse or family: I Peter 3:7
9) Unforgiveness: Matthew 6: 14-15 and Mark 11:25-26
10) Worry and anxiety: Philippians 4:6
11) Hypocrisy: Luke 18: 9-14
12) Discouragement: Luke 18: 1-8
13) Pride and arrogance in your prayer life/spiritual life:
Matthew 6:5

DAY FIVE ASSIGNMENT

ASSIGNMENT FOR TODAY:

In addition to any notes or thoughts that you had about today's lesson; I want you to do the following:

1) Continue to work on the letters that you need to write to God that we discussed yesterday. It is essential to work through all of these issues and prevent any unanswered prayers due to hard feelings, revenge, vengeance, bitterness, or hatred.

DAY SIX:

FAMILY DEVOTIONS AND PRAYER

You may be wondering why it is essential to have family devotions each day. Well, have you ever heard of the motto *"the family that prayers together stay together?"* Well, this motto is so true. If you want spiritual strength and unity within your marriage and home, you need to develop a relationship with each other and God. Daily prayer and Bible reading will put a bond between you and teaches you the basic principles of the word of God. The more you read and study God's word, the more your faith will grow. As your confidence and faith in God grows, you will find that your family can weather many trials and tribulations without showing any signs of wear and tear!

Family devotions are essential because you are training your children to have faith and trust in God. You are also teaching them what the Bible says, what to believe, and why. If you get a strong base in them, they will follow suit when they have children. It is essential to develop a personal relationship with Christ and nurture that relationship in front of them. They need to learn about the importance of a relationship with God at an early age.

There are other benefits to family devotions. Not only teaching your children the truth of God's word, but they will grow in the knowledge of the word of God and faith. The added benefit of the development of a family bond is unmeasurable. The power they will learn as they hear you pray a prayer covering protection and blessing each day will establish this practice in their lives forever. They will do the same with your grandchildren! The immeasurable benefit is the prayer covering (protection by the blood of Christ) that is placed over your family when you pray together. If you apply the blood of Jesus to your life and your children's lives, no matter what happens, Satan cannot cause them to turn away from God. If he does for a short time, you are guaranteed by an Old Testament promise that Satan cannot take your children out of the hands of a praying mother and father!

There are no Bible guidelines that state the time of day you should pray, how you should pray or what you should pray. Prayer is a time for you to communicate with God like you would with any other individual. Our attitude at the time that we are praying is an essential part of praying. We must come before God with a contrite/humble spirit.

What should devotional time include? It is a time to read at least one chapter in the Bible or one Bible story per devotion period. Devotional time should consist of reading and praying. We express our communication any prayer request that we have to God during our prayer time. This devotion time can consist of questions they have about the lesson, about God, what they are going through, or a time for sharing with you something God did for them that day at school, etc. Keep this devotional time as a "penalty-free" period of the day that they can share with you anything that was done without receiving punishment, even if they were wrong. Keeping this type of free-flowing communication with your children can keep the door open for you to help them have deliverances and blessings in their lives, instead of them learning to hide things from you deceitfully.

If you have children, there should be family devotions each day (preferably at night/bedtime) with your children. This allows you the opportunity to find out how their day went at school if there were problems, etc. Sometimes children will give a prayer request to God about something that they have not discussed with you. Do not use this as a time to violate their honesty, but encourage them to talk to God about it. You can then speak to them about it after devotion time.

The devotions that you have with your children should be in addition to your devotions each morning and evening. God will need time with you as parents to teach you things on a deeper level. God may want to give you instructions on dealing with your children's issues; they do not need to hear. Family devotions should occur at least once per day. Most people select nighttime before retiring to bed. Husbands and wives should do their nighttime devotions together for the same reason they have an evening devotion with their children; to discuss and pray over the day's events. I realize that some two-income households have parents working shift work. If this is the case, you may have to adjust the time of family devotions each day to a time that is best for both parents to be present. If you cannot work out a time where both are present, then let one parent continue with family devotions at bedtime. Consistency is the key to successful family devotions.

Husbands and wives need a separate time to read, pray, and discuss things that would not be appropriate in front of the children. This designated time helps you to draw closer together in your relationship. Your relationship with God will improve as you spend time together with God. God will give you answers on how to raise your children and be an example in front of them. You may be asking yourself why devotions should be done twice per day. The crucial reason is you need to start your day off with a good word or thoughts. You need prayer time with your children to pray over them a protection prayer and say a blessing. This will help them to learn in school, plus be protected from evil. A prayer covering over your children is a powerful tool against the attacks of Satan on their lives and minds. Remember, when you take the time to start your day with God, it always goes smoother for you and your children!

There will be days when Satan will try you. There will be days when everything goes wrong. If you started that day with a word, verse, thought, or devotional you read from a book, you will realize that word will keep you grounded and remind you to keep your attitude in check! There are numerous devotional books on the market that are three to five-minute devotions for starting your day. You will be surprised by what that good thought and scripture verse will do for you each day! Devotions can be short in the morning to get your day going. I take 15 minutes of my lunch break and spend it reading another devotion or a couple of chapters from the Bible if I feel my morning devotion was rushed due to time constraints or appointments. I listen to the Bible on CD in my car on the way and praise music on the way home. I spend that time thanking God for his blessing during the day and our safety. Praise is just as critical as reading God's word. We must remember to be grateful for his blessings on us!

There are days that the few minutes I spend with God at lunch is the only thing that keeps me sane. It is easy to lose your temper when working with people who do not possess a strong work ethic or who prefer to be lazy. Satan will send frustration to us in whatever fashion he can find that works on our nerves most. The only way to fight those battles is with the sword of God's word (part of our spiritual armor).

Ensure that when you establish family devotions, you set a time for devotions and bedtime prayers that are the same each night. For example, if bedtime during the week is 8:00 PM for your children, do your family devotions at 7:00 pm or 7:15 pm. Allow yourself 30-45 minutes for devotions and hear about their day. Then ask for prayer requests and pray with them in this time frame. You will save the last 15-minutes for final preps for bed. Ensure that you start each day with prayer and the word no matter what time you set for your devotions. It might be a short five minutes of reading a devotional from a book or a Christian calendar, but make sure that you put a scripture and a good thought into your mind to meditate upon all day.

You need a specific daily prayer time; if your schedule does not permit it, at least get started by praying in the shower or while in the bathroom getting dressed. Remember, you are God's bride. You would not like it if your spouse jumped out of bed, got dressed, grabbed some food, screamed and shouted at the kids, ran out the door, and never said a word to you in the mornings, so do not do this to God. Remember, **YOU ARE HIS BRIDE!** Communication is the key to marriage. Communication is the key to a relationship with God. Communication **BOTH** ways is essential for you to learn what God wants for you. So, talk to him, then sit down with his word (The Bible) and let him talk back to you!

DAY SIX ASSIGNMENT

ASSIGNMENT FOR TODAY:

In addition to any notes or thoughts that you had about today's lesson; I want you to do the following:

1) Take the time today for you and your spouse to establish devotion times for your family. Select a time of the day for your devotions and family devotions if you have children.

2) Meet with your children and explain to them tonight why you are starting this time of devotion. Do not be upset if there is resistance, to begin with, significantly if it cuts into their TV time. God will show you how to deal with this as you go. Just remember to keep a calm, non-argumentative attitude when implementing these changes.

DAY SEVEN:

UNDERSTANDING GOD'S PURPOSE AND PLAN FOR YOUR LIFE

Do you think that God has a plan and a purpose for your life? Do you believe that God individually designs a plan for each of us? Do you believe that God has enough time with all of the people in the world to take out time to create something just for me? YES!!! The Bible says that God has numbered the hairs on our heads. If your hair sheds as bad as mine, God has almost a full-time job, keeping a hair count on me. God is always present everywhere, knowing everything about everyone at all times. God is alive, not dead, always awake, never on vacation! He cares enough to design a plan for you and me and a purpose for our existence!

Remember, God has a purpose for you! God has already let us know that our divine purpose in life is to love him, serve him with our whole hearts, worship, praise, adore, and honor him in everything that we do. If we understand this purpose and fulfill it, we know our desired outcome will be answered prayers, blessings, and miracles! To do this successfully, we must possess the fruits of the spirit discussed in previous devotions. To refresh your memory, re-read each of the nine fruits of the spirit in the glossary. These fruits are essential characteristics that God expects to be present in our lives at all times. **Paul wrote these powerful words about our purpose:**

II Timothy 1:9: *"Who hath saved us and called us with a holy calling, not according to our works, but according to his own purpose and grace which was given us in Christ Jesus before the world began." Jesus knew before the worlds were formed that he would make us for the purpose of glorifying and honoring him. It is his divine purpose for us to evangelize the world and tell everyone that the end it coming, that the Rapture is near, that we must be ready to go!" (KJV, 2020).*

God has a plan for your life. A plan is a specific written plan, document, job description to be done, or a blueprint for a house. A plan can be a strategic plan or a job description designed with the organization's overall function in mind during its development stages. A plan gives you guidelines to follow. If each person follows through with his/her assigned duties on this plan, then he/she will reach a designated goal. If everyone meets their goals on time, then the product's delivery or service is successful.

There is a **divine plan** that includes God's plan, outline, job description, or blueprint for us to follow. If we complete our assignment in his plan, we will see God's divine plan's desired results. God's divine plan is: *"That all men should be saved."* Unlike most preachers tell you, God's divine plan is not your prosperity and increase in goods and assets. God's divine plan is for us to increase the family of God by evangelizing the world.

You are probably thinking, but I cannot do anything in this area; I cannot travel or go on mission assignments. That may be true. You can work and pay tithes into the church to support these missionaries who can be sent. You can read and pray every day and have the word alive in your life so that your life can be a witness to the people around you every day. Your mission fields may be your job or your family. We each have a part. Some work and send money so that others can be sent. At the same time, some individuals are capable of being the ones sent! Each of us has a small part to play in God's divine plan.

The Bible was also written with a purpose and a plan. The purpose was to provide us with the knowledge of God and what He expects of us. God's goal was to provide us with a copy of his plan (his blueprints) on how we should live. If we accept and plant his words into our hearts, we will see the fruits of the spirit grow in our lives. This enables us to reach out to others and share this knowledge with them.

I John 5:13: *"These things have I written unto you that believe on the name of the Son of God; that ye may know that ye have eternal life and that ye may believe on the name of the Son." (KJV, 2020).*

If we know or understand our purpose in life, we can succeed. Once you have completed this challenge, you need to immediately read the two books by Bruce Wilkerson that I mentioned in an early devotion. They are listed in the recommended books list. Once you have read these two small books, begin the ***Purpose Driven Life*** course by Rick Warren. This book and course will help you find out what God's plan is for your life and your family in more specific terms. Once you complete this in-depth study with Rick Warren, you will have more confidence in your relationship with God. You will understand what God expects of you and how to implement these changes. This book will help you to find that *Divine Purpose* in your life.

The more informed that we are of God's purpose and plan for our lives, the more productive we can be for Jesus. The more peace and contentment we will have in our lives. God wants us to study his word, to know and understand his divine purpose for us, the church, and planet earth. God appointed a universal purpose for every man, woman, and child; be saved and help get others saved! He created us to desire to love him, worship him, and give him honor and praise. Once we do, God will show us what part we play in his plan. He will lead us to the right job, the right house, the right spouse if you are not married, the perfect career, the excellent schools, etc., for YOUR life!

Jesus is concerned about every little detail of your life. If God knows the number of hairs on your head if he can take care of the lilies of the fields or feed the sparrows, then how much more does he care about you and me? He cares enough to design a plan just for you! Read his word and pray. He will show you the plan for your life and your home.

DAY SEVEN ASSIGNMENT

ASSIGNMENT FOR TODAY:

In addition to any notes or thoughts that you had about today's lesson, I want you to make a list of the following things in your notebook and pray this list to God:

1) Make a list of all the talents that you have that you could use for God.

2) Put an asterisk (*) beside the things that you love to do.

3) Put a circle around the asterisks to mark what you love to do that you are great at or possess expert skills performing.

4) Check with your local pastor to see if he needs anyone with your talents in the church or community. If he is not aware of a need, ask him to help you find a way to use these talents to help further God's divine plan.

DAY EIGHT:

INTEGRITY AND HONESTY:
The Gift of Love

Integrity is defined by Google.com (2020) as "the quality of being honest and having strong moral principles; the state of being whole and undivided. Synonyms are honesty, uprightness, honorable, upstanding, good character, principles and ethics, righteousness, virtue, decency, noble-mindedness, fairness, truthfulness, trustworthiness, and sincerity."

Today, I want us to study an incredible story of integrity and love found in the Old Testament. I will not quote the entire book of Ruth to you. However, this book has only four chapters. You can easily read them in one day. Try to find time today to read the entire story. I will give you the highlights of the story. Naomi was a Jewish woman from the area of Judah. Naomi is described as the lovable and faithful wife of a Jewish man named Elimelech. Naomi and her husband Elimelech decided that the famine was so bad in Judah that they would go to Moab. Friends and nomads had told them that Moab was not affected by this famine. So, they packed up their two sons and went to Moab.

Most theologians agree that Naomi was an obedient and devoted wife who delighted her husband and two sons. There was a drought in the land of Israel, making things hard for them. So, they decided to go to the land of Moab. (This was the country that had control over Israel at that time. So, travel to that country was easy). The fact that a happy little family wanted to move to another area to live and work seemed harmless enough. But was it? Is it essential for us to remain in God's will? Is it vital for us to follow God's commandments? Should we not move somewhere and participate in or take a job that might cause us to wander away from our faith in God? Let us take a look at this topic of following God, maintaining integrity, and giving the gift of love.

<u>Ruth 1:3-5</u> – *"And Elimelech Naomi's husband died, and she was left, and her two sons. And they took them wives of the women of Moab; the name of the one was Orpah, and the name of the other Ruth: and they dwelled there about ten years. And Mahlon and Chilion died also both of them, and the woman was left of her two sons and her husband."* (KJV, 2020).

According to Jewish history, it is believed that God shortened the lives of Mahlon and Chilion for their sins of transgressing the law and marrying foreign women. The Jews were not supposed to take wives of any other nationality. The Old Testament's first four books mention in several verses that the Jews were not to marry Moabite women. The reason for this law was that most heathen women worshipped idols. God did not want his chosen people tempted to walk away from him. We do not know if God killed these men because they disobeyed the Old Testament law. After all, it is not stated anywhere in the Bible. We know that God promises us a long life if we obey and serve him with our whole hearts.

Most theologians think that God allowed her husband to die because he was out of God's will and that her two sons died because they disobeyed God's commandment and married women from Moab. This possibly was true, considering they were under Moses's law and not under grace as we are today. However, it was Naomi that was left to suffer. She lost her husband and her sons. It did not seem fair that God was allowing all of these bad things to happen to her. However, if she had not lost her sons, she would have never returned to Judah. They would have stayed in Moab for as long as they were happy and being blessed. God had to allow her to suffer, to turn her eyes and mind back toward home. Once she thought about it, she decided she would be better off with her family and at home in Judah. So, she returned. Her daughter-in-law Ruth returned with her.

We may not know precisely why God took Naomi's husband and sons, but we can know one thing, God had a reason. Naomi was having trouble accepting God's reasoning. However, after Naomi returned to Bethlehem, she saw God's divine purpose and plan for her life and her daughter-in-law Ruth.

Ruth 1:7-14: *"Wherefore she went forth out of the place where she was, and her two daughters in law with her; and they went on the way to return unto the land of Judah. And Naomi said unto her two daughters in law, Go, return each to her mother's house: The Lord deal kindly with you, as ye have dealt with the dead, and with me. The Lord grants you that ye may find rest, each of you in the house of her husband. Then she kissed them, and they lifted up their voice and wept. And they said unto her, surely, we will return with thee unto thy people. And Naomi said, turn again, my daughters: why will ye go with me? Are there yet any more sons in my womb, that they may be your husbands? Turn again, my daughters, go your way; for I am too old to have a husband. If I should say, I have hope, if I should have a husband also tonight, and should also bear sons; Would ye tarry for them till they were grown? Would ye stay for them from having husbands? Nay, my daughters; for it grieves me much for your sakes that the hand of the Lord is gone out against me. And they lifted up their voice and wept again: and Orpah kissed her mother-*

in-law, but Ruth clave unto her." (KJV, 2020).

This is one of the most beautiful passages of scripture in the Bible; it shows us how much faith and love these two daughters-in-law had in Naomi. Can you imagine having daughters-in-law that would say good-bye to their families and move to a foreign country they have never visited with an older woman? Why would these ladies be willing to leave their families? Naomi was good to them and loved them as much as she loved her sons. They were daughters, not daughters-in-law to Naomi. They were attracted to this older woman that loved her God with all her heart. They saw her relationship with him and how it gave her peace and contentment, despite her losses. They were touched by her desire to return home to her family and serve this God of hers. I am sure that Naomi's faith and integrity caused her daughters-in-law to desire to know more about her God.

Ruth 1:15-17: *"And she said, Behold, thy sister in law is gone back unto her people, and unto her gods: return thou after thy sister in law. And Ruth said, Entreat me not to leave thee, or to return from following after thee: for whither thou goes, I will go; and where thou lodges, I will lodge: thy people shall be my people, and thy God my God: Where thou dies, will I die, and there will I be buried: the Lord do so to me, and more also, if ought but death part thee and me." (KJV, 2020).*

Orpah was finally convinced to go home, but there was something inside Ruth searching. It was a desire to know more about Naomi's God and to experience all that this God had to offer. Ruth not only committed herself to go with Naomi but to accept Naomi's family as her own. Ruth said, **"YOUR GOD will be MY GOD."** That day Ruth openly confessed to leave behind all of her idols and follow the Lord God Jehovah! It was probably hard for her to make a public commitment, but God rewarded Ruth. Let us take a look at the definition of obey and obedience to help us understand what Ruth was trying to accomplish.

After Naomi and Ruth returned to Judah, God blessed Ruth, and she met Boaz. (Boaz was the wealthiest man in the town). Boaz fell in love with Ruth and took her to be his wife. God blessed that union with a son, Obed, who was the grandfather of King David. What a blessing?

What looked bad for Naomi when she was in Moab was God redirecting her toward something good. Through her daughter-in-law, she was blessed with a new son through Boaz and with heirs. Sometimes we think that something is bad, and we do not deserve what is happening to us…. but sometimes, it is God just re-directing us. For some of us, it takes drastic measures for God to get us to listen to him. For the full story and all details, read the book of Ruth. It is only four chapters long. It is a beautiful love story of the love between a woman and her daughter-in-law, the magic of love between Boaz and Ruth, and how God gives beautiful endings to lives with rough beginnings!

Random House-Merriam Webster Dictionary (1995) defines **Obey** as the act of obeying; to obey is to follow, to do as instructed, or command with a positive attitude. To obey is to complete the task given entirely and thoroughly to the best of one's ability—this level of excellence is considered godly obedience. This dictionary defines **Obedience** as the act of obeying one's commands. This is something that God requires out of all Christians. No exceptions. Obedience is a requirement for eternal life with Jesus Christ.

When Ruth and Naomi reached Judah, Ruth went out into the field to gather grain. Even though she did not realize it at the time, God was leading her. I will not tell you the entire story because I want you to read all four chapters tonight. However, I will tell you that she obeyed Naomi's instructions with humility of heart. (God loves this in a man or woman). As a result, God allowed her to meet Boaz, the wealthiest man in the area. Boaz fell in love with Ruth. Ruth followed all of her mother-in-law's instructions, who played the matchmaker, and Boaz claimed Ruth as his wife. The story ends with God blessing them with a Son, whose name was Obed. Obed was the grandfather of King David. King David was in the direct lineage of the bloodline of Jesus through his mother, Mary. See how God works? Do you see the magnificence of his divine plan in this woman's life? Well, God has a plan just like this for you. If you trust God, obey his word, and serve him with all of your heart. You will see God's plan put into action for you, too.

The keys in this story are *obedience, faith, and integrity.* Please study the definition of these words because you will see them numerous times in the remaining lessons. Integrity is an essential character trait for every Christian. Both terms are in the glossary located at the back of this book.

DAY EIGHT ASSIGNMENT

ASSIGNMENT FOR TODAY:

In addition to any notes or thoughts that you had about today's lesson; I want you to do the following:

1) Do you have problems with your mother-in-law? If yes, then make a list of all of the things that she does that irritates you.

2) Make a list of all of the things that you like about her.

3) Make a suggestion list of the things that she could change regarding and what you will do to meet her half-way at least. Then pray over these three lists.

4) When the time is right…. you will know when…. you can discuss these lists with her. If an open discussion is not possible now, write a letter to her. Make sure you write with all of the love that you know-how.

5) If your mother-in-law is dead…. still, write the letter. You will be surprised how much better you will feel.

6) Make every effort to change how you handle your relationship with your mother-in-law. The same holds true for fathers-in-law.

Do not forget to read all four chapters of the

book of Ruth today!

DAY NINE:

COMMUNICATING WITH GOD YOUR WISHES AND DREAMS

We have already discussed reading God's word, praying, having personal devotions, family devotions, and devotions with your spouse. We have also discussed praising God, giving thanks, singing songs of praise, songs of worship, and meditating upon the word of God. All of these are ways to communicate with God. However, there is one more important method for communicating with God. You may not be a person who likes to write letters, so you may feel that this lesson does not apply to you. But hear me out on this topic…. you may change your mind.

With prayer being the primary key for communicating to God, we must get that prayer to him in the most effective way possible. If you have difficulty thinking of the words to say or are afraid for people around you to hear you, then voice those concerns or questions to God in writing. Once you write them out, it seems to help. No one will read your writings/notes. These are your thoughts and requests to God.

God wants to hear about our problems, desires, needs, dreams, and wishful thinking. He is our best friend. He wants us to talk to him and share everything with him. You do not have to worry about insulting God or causing him to turn away from you. When you share what you are thinking with God, he will communicate through the Bible what you need to do about that person or thing in your life. God cares about our desires and goals. Trust him and watch what happens in your life!

WHAT TO COMMUNICATE WITH GOD?

Here are some of the essential things for you to discuss with God. You may want to add to this list; however, this list should be a minimum of what you discuss with God for yourself:

1) All the dreams you have had from childhood to today that you got to live out or see granted. Thank God for allowing you the privilege of seeing these dreams and wishes come true.

2) All the dreams/wishes that you made from a child to today that **DID NOT** come true. Tell God why you think that they did not come true. If your dreams not coming true has caused anger, bitterness, or feelings of rejection, then you need to share these feelings with God in prayer. Let God know exactly how you feel about them. If you would still like to see these dreams or wishes come true, make sure you let him know.

3) If you have any other questions about these lost dreams/unfulfilled wishes, ask God about them. It is ok to question God. He will answer. You may not always like the answer, but if you sincerely ask, he will show you.

4) Daily pray over these letters you have written to the Lord. If you have very many lost or unfulfilled dreams, you may decide to write about them one at a time over several weeks. That will be ok too. Just do not forget to pray over the letters.

Once you tell God about those lost or shattered dreams, then pray over them. Get up and leave the shattered dreams in God's hands. He will begin to work things out for you or provide you with new dreams. God has a plan for each of our lives, including our happiness, blessings, prosperity, knowledge, and wisdom. He will provide them to us as we grow spiritually. As you go through this study, God will show you things; he may even communicate back to you through dreams or his word. Some of these questions you ask him may not even be answered for several months. God will give you an answer when he feels that you are ready to receive that answer. So do not grumble if you do not know the answer tomorrow!

You will also need to be prepared for God to change up some of those dreams. There is a possibility that you could have had a childhood dream to be a dancer or ballerina. Maybe the money was not there for the lessons. Now you are 32 years old, married with three children. Perhaps you desired to be an NFL Quarterback, but you are 45, got terrible knees, have an extra 50 pounds attached, plus a wife and four kids. To fulfill that dream today would not be possible. God may replace that dream with another dream, one that includes your children and family. See, even though you did not get your initial wish, God gave you something more valuable in your life…. a home…. a family……children!

If you have some dreams that are impossible for you to fulfill now at this stage in your life, pray and ask God to help you to look at your current circumstances and dream! Without dreams, we never succeed. Without dreams, we aimlessly drift through life. Without dreams, we never stick with anything until It is finished! You need dreams! You need plans. God will help you with new dreams to replace the older, impossible ones. Remember that prayer is the key to communicating with God. Reading his word is the key to him sharing with us. There is an answer in his word for everything and every situation in our lives. We only have to search to find that answer. God talks back to us sometimes in our dreams. Make sure that you take time each day to pray …. or write to God …. just communicate with him!

OTHER COMMUNICATION OPTIONS:

Another method of writing to God versus using letters is keeping a diary. I can already hear the men moaning over this suggestion. Do not feel pushed to do anything that makes you feel uncomfortable. A letter will do just fine. The issue is to put in writing your frustrations, questions, and request for God.

I like to keep a journal (diary) of my communications with God. Sometimes when I am writing, I remember things that I would probably forget to pray about otherwise. I also keep a prayer journal. As I think of something to pray about, I list them in my journal. (A notebook, notepad, legal pad, etc., will work fine). About once per month, I go back over the items on my list. I cross off all answered prayers. I put a date beside the number so I can remember when God answered that prayer. Any time I feel down or discouraged, I go to my prayer journal. I begin reading the answered prayers. It builds my faith and helps me to get control over my doubts.

DAY NINE ASSIGNMENT

ASSIGNMENT FOR TODAY:

In addition to any notes or thoughts that you had about today's lesson; I want you to do the following:

If you had a Fairy Godmother who offered you three wishes, what would your wishes include?

List them below:

1)

2)

3)

Keep your list in your notebook....do not discuss it with anyone. We will look back at this list later in the study. So be honest with yourself and list the top three things you desire TODAY. No matter how selfish these three things appear or if these three wishes include your family or not. It does not matter. List them here, and do not think about them anymore until we tell you to refer back to this list on a lesson later in this challenge.

<u>DAY TEN</u>:

FALLING IN LOVE WITH JESUS EACH DAY

Falling in love with Jesus every day is a MUST! This is not an option for our lives. Jesus has made it plain in the Bible that the church is the bride of Christ. We need to study what a *New Spiritual Bride* does in prep for her wedding and wedding night. We will have a wedding at the marriage supper of the lamb in heaven after the rapture of the church. This will be the ULTIMATE WEDDING. There has never been a wedding anywhere in the world that can compare with this wedding feast that we will be attending. To prepare for our wedding, we must learn a little more about the family. Let us start with the father of the groom. Then we will study about the groom. The Bible says that Jesus will be the groom and that we will be his bride. If we are going to go to a wedding in heaven, we need to get prepared and ready to go. Our preparations include having our hearts right, our language positive, our sins covered under the blood of Jesus, the fruits of the spirit active in our lives, and none of the works of the flesh present.

If we were preparing for an earthly wedding, we would send out wedding invitations to our friends and family. We would want everyone to join us in our celebration. About three years ago, I felt led to preach on *"The Wedding Invitation"* at a church one Sunday morning. The Lord gave me a dream and showed me an invitation. He gave me a list of names and said to take it to as many people on that list as I could reach that week. God said one person on that list was receiving their last invitation before death. He did not tell me who, but I knew it was serious, and I had to reach all of them.

I prepared the wedding invitations on wedding card stock, addressed the envelopes, and went to deliver them. I designed an invitation for every person that would be present at the Sunday service. My husband stood at the back door and gave out the invitations as everyone entered the service. On the envelope, it said do not open until instructed to by the preacher during her sermon. I got permission from the church leaders to come on Saturday and decorate the church. When you opened the door of the church, it was decorated like a wedding chapel. Bows were tied on the pews; the wedding arch was in place with white wedding flowers. Everyone entering was shocked. The decorations set the mood for something exciting, which was the effect that I wanted. I wanted everyone to understand this wedding!

When I began to preach, I told about the dream and how I had delivered the wedding invitations to specific individuals to come to the service because there would be a surprise wedding here today. No special attire or gifts needed, just their presence. As I looked across the congregation, I saw people I had invited present. My heart broke for the few that did not respond. I introduced my sermon title, *"The Wedding Invitation,"* and I read the scripture text of the parable Jesus told about the five wise virgins and the five foolish virgins waiting for the bridegroom to come.

At a specific point in my closing remarks, I had everyone open their wedding invitations. As I read the invitation out aloud, I asked them to write their name on the invitation's blank lines. (See the next page for this invitation; as you read it, write or say your name everywhere that a line is drawn). As I read the invitation out loud, I began to hear gasp and prayers start all over the church. I looked up and saw about half of the congregation crying. The Holy Spirit swept into that service. When I finished reading the invitation, I opened the altar for all who wanted to respond; Christians and non-Christians all fell on the altar crying and praying. You could feel such a strong presence of God. The crying from the people who responded at the altar still rings in my ears today. It was an incredible experience.

However, the individuals not coming to the service or not responding to the invitation were held responsible for that sermon. God sent that sermon to them and for them. Our God is a merciful God, who always deals with us to change. We can accept or deny it. The person who was going to die did not come to the service. The next week God gave me another dream and showed me this man dying in a car wreck. I sent him a message on Facebook to call me at his convenience. I shared with him the dream and told him that God said he was the one he had spoken about in the first dream. He promised me that he would come the next Sunday. He did not, so I text him again. We went through this several times over the next four weeks. In the fifth week, he told me he was coming to church that following Sunday. He promised he would be there. I asked him if my husband and I could come to pray with him. I felt it was so urgent, and I did not want him to wait too long. He said he had one more thing he needed to straighten out first.

I told him that he did not have to straighten things out before getting saved, "just come to Jesus as you are, and he will help you finish the rest." I felt the convicting power of the Holy Ghost accompanied with chest pains as I talked to him. I knew that he was running out of days. On the 40th day from my second dream, he was killed in a car wreck. He never made it to Sunday of week six! Within 45 days (six-weeks), we were burying this guy. We have no hope that he prayed or made it to heaven. Those are the worst funerals to attend! His sister told me he had a heart attack while driving his car (he was only 50 years old), left the road, hit a tree, and was instantly killed. This was his last invitation. God was merciful, giving him 40 more days (remember that probationary time frame I talked about in the introduction)? God always deals with us, but Satan's goal is to keep us from recognizing it!

A young lady with several children that was sent a special invitation to attend that Sunday made fun of my invitation. She posted hateful and disrespectful comments on Facebook that week and the Sunday after the service. She said it was just a gimmick to get people to come to church! Within months she was divorced and homeless. She moved her two daughters into a man's house that she was not married to and did not know well. A year later, crying and upset, she called for prayer. She was so heartbroken. Her daughter had been molested. Instead of repenting, her anger toward me became more intense as she told me of her troubles. Then she verbally flew into me, getting me told off! She blamed me for her crisis and wrecked life. She hung up, angry. However, I still kept praying for her. I knew it was the spirits attached to her life that were talking, not her! I begged God for mercy for her! Her anger at me was her anger at herself.

On that call, I took every opportunity possible to witness, reminding her that God was at the altar, where she left him. That she was the "runaway bride" that he still loved. Thankfully the seeds of that call took root. Several months later, she gave her heart to the Lord. He put her marriage and home back together. But nothing will ever remove the scars from her daughter's life. Do not wait too long to respond to God. Do not push God away. That nagging feeling inside you that you need to change is the Holy Spirit dealing with you. You may not be guaranteed another chance like this mother; you may have a 40-day expiration date! As you read the invitation below, do not let this opportunity pass you by; do not turn God away! Give your heart to God today, accepting his wedding invitation to the event of a lifetime!

A Special Wedding Invitation for:

_____

God, the Father, and the Holy Ghost would like to request your presence at a wedding to join the Son of God, Jesus Christ, with _____ at the wedding ceremony of a lifetime.

This incredible event will take place in Heaven on a day to be announced by the Father. You must be prepared and ready to leave for this wedding at a moment's notice, in the twinkling of an eye. Once the Father calls for the bride to come, there will not be any time to get ready. You must decide today and be ready!

To RSVP for this wedding and accept Jesus' proposal to be his bride, you need to run right now to the mercy seat (the alter) and enter your request by accepting the Lord Jesus Christ as your personal Lord and Savior. It is urgent, do not wait!

This Wedding will be a lengthy event in Heaven, with a supper to die for (the marriage supper of the Lamb). If you accept, your honeymoon will follow back on earth for a thousand years of peace, love, happiness, and unity (the Millennial Reign), whereas the Bride of Christ, you will rule with Jesus for 1000 years!

Your reservation is urgently needed today. This invitation is for you, _____, and it expires today at 12 Midnight.

With all my love and prayers that you will accept,

Your Heavenly Father, God

I hope and pray that you responded to the invitation on the previous pages. I welcome you as a brother or sister in Christ! Please write to me and let me know of your decision to accept Christ. If you are on death row, in solitary confinement, or the SHU (Special Housing Unit), and not allowed mail privileges, ask to speak with a Chaplain. Share with them that you have accepted Christ so that they can get you support and study materials. Ask them to contact us. We will help you too! Welcome to our family!

Now that you are part of the family of God let us learn more about our Heavenly Father, our Lord and Savior, Jesus Christ, and the Holy Spirit! These are your three new best friends!

OUR HEAVENLY FATHER:

The Bible says that God is our Father, the head of the church. We are his children, and he loves us like we love our children. We are the bride of Christ. If we are the bride of Jesus, then we are to love God like we would love our father-in-law here on earth. We are to love Jesus like we would our spouse. Once we become the bride of Christ, we become an heir with Jesus to heaven. This indicates that we have been grafted in the family through "marriage." We are one of God's heirs—one of his children. What a tremendous promise! Let us look at some of God's character traits to understand better what God expects of us.

GOD IS THE FATHER OF THE FATHERLESS:

Psalms 68:5: *"A Father of the fatherless and a judge of the widows is God in his holy habitation." (KJV, 2020).*

If you let Jesus mold you, he will make you into his bride. Jesus desires each of us to accept this invitation to be in heaven with Him for eternity. If you accept God into your heart, he will help you to become a witness for him to your family and friends. God needs you to help him get more people ready for this wedding, for the rapture of the church!

Isaiah 64:8— *"But now Lord, thou art our Father; we are the clay and thou our potter. And we all are the works of thy hands." (KJV, 2020).*

The Bible says that we are born with an evil heart as earthly human beings until God gives us our new hearts. If our children were born evil, we would do everything in our power to help them change. God has this same love for us. He loves us more than we love our children. God knows how to take care of us better than we know how to take care of our children. Considering that most of us would give our lives for our children, you can imagine how God feels about us. He gave his only son to die in our place.

Matthew 7:11— *"If ye then, being evil, know how to give good gifts unto your children, how much more shall your Father which is in heaven give good things to them that asks him?" (KJV, 2020).*

This description sounds to me like a description of the world's most wonderful father! I am proud to be his child. I am grateful to be the bride of Christ, being adopted into the family by grace. Now, do you understand why I say that it is so crucial for you to fall in love with Jesus more and more each day? Why is it so essential to desire to be with him and to be his bride? Why is it so important to be in preparation for that ultimate wedding day and feast? This is an event that we do not want to miss under any circumstances. We want to make it in the rapture; we want to be with the one who loves us so much that he would give his life for us. We want to be with Jesus forever!

Each day as we learn to communicate with Jesus and read the word, we fall in love with him. As we grow in our reading and praying, we grow spiritually. As we teach our family devotions and share Christ's good news with our family and friends, we feel a bond develop between God and us. That feeling is fantastic. I cannot describe this to you, but I can say it is something you have to experience first-hand. There are no words to describe the feeling that you feel when you know that Jesus loves you!

Do not let a day go by without reading and praying. Do not let a day go by that you are not talking to the greatest love of your life. During a trial that seemed like one of those that would not end between 2001 and 2002, the Lord gave me the song "Jesus, I love you" in this book's appendix. This song was my way of telling Jesus how much I loved him. Every time in my life that I have gone through a trial, I have kept singing this song.

During the years 2004-2006, I had days I could not sing. I had days that were so hard that I could not find my song. I felt like the children of Israel in captivity when the prophet asked them, "Why are you not singing and praising God?" My response was the same as theirs, "How can I sing in a strange land? How can I sing in prison?" I would remember that Paul and Silas, around midnight one night, with their feet in stocks and bonds (the modern-day equivalent would be handcuff and shackles), they begin to sing. Guess what, a miracle happened! You must read this story!

Acts 16:25-40: *"And at midnight, Paul and Silas prayed, and sang praises unto God: and the prisoners heard them. And suddenly there was a great earthquake so that the foundations of the prison were shaken: and immediately all the doors were opened, and every one's bands were loosed. And the keeper of the prison awaking out of his sleep, and seeing the prison doors open, he drew out his sword and would have killed himself, supposing that the prisoners had been fled. But Paul cried with a loud voice, saying, do thyself no harm: for we are all here. Then he called for a light, and sprang in, and came trembling, and fell before Paul and Silas, and brought them out, and said, Sirs, what must I do to be saved? And they said, believe on the Lord Jesus Christ, and thou shalt be saved, and thy house. And they spoke unto him the word of the Lord, and to all that were in his house. And he took them the same hour of the night, washed their stripes; and was baptized, he and all his, straightway. And when he had brought them into his house, he set meat before them and rejoiced, believing in God with his entire house. And when it was day, the magistrates sent the sergeants, saying, let those men go. And the keeper of the prison told this saying to Paul; the magistrates have sent to let you go: now therefore depart, and go in peace. But Paul said unto them, they have beaten us openly un-condemned, being Romans, and have cast us into prison; and now do they thrust us out privately? Nay verily; but let them come themselves and fetch us out. And the sergeants told these words unto the* *magistrates: and they feared when they heard that they were Romans. And they came and besought them, and brought them out, and desired them to depart out of the city. And they went out of the prison and entered into the house of Lydia, and when they had seen the brethren, they comforted them and departed." (KJV, 2020).*

So, after I would remember this story, I would start to sing. Sometimes, the tears were flowing so fast and strong that absolutely no sound would come out of my mouth, no matter how hard I tried, but my spirit would cry and sing this song:

"Jesus, I love you; Master, I adore you; Savior, you are all that I need. Father, you are awesome. You gave your only Son, and you did that just for me. Jesus, I love you; Master, I adore you; Savior, you are worthy of all the honor and the praise. Father, you are my greatest love, so I pledge to serve you for the rest of my life."

I made my mind up while I was in County Jail, before going to prison, I would not let anything destroy my relationship with my Jesus. It did not matter what had happened to me. It did not matter how many people had lied on me and took bribes under the table to testify against me. I knew the truth. I knew that God knew the truth. Numerous people's comments and statements told in the courtroom by the FBI agent on the stand were fabricated. The people whom the FBI and prosecutor said made these sworn statements came to me after I got out of prison, telling me that they had never even had conversations with them, might less given them those testimonies. It was hard to accept that I had lost 25 months of my life because a jury had been lied to, and the jury foreman had been paid under the table to swing the vote against me. It is hard to believe that such corruption could happen in an American courtroom. What I had to learn was to forgive them. I am not angry with them anymore. I know that they were only pawns in the hands of Satan, who was trying to stop my mission work. I knew what my relationship was with my Lord, and I knew that nothing was going to stop me. If Paul and Silas could sing in prison, I could too. I knew that I could fall more in love with my Jesus in prison! So, I kept singing, reading, and praying. Guess what! That is what happened. My relationship with Jesus grew in prison!

I came out of prison more in love with Jesus than I had ever been in my life. I thought I had a relationship with God that was wonderful. I thought I had found the ultimate place to be with him. However, in prison, I discovered that there were about ten more levels higher than I could go than I had ever thought possible. I now enjoy a relationship with him that I cannot find words to describe, but I invite you today to join me. Come on up…. higher and higher to be with Jesus! Come on up and step into this new realm of joy. Even in the trials, you can still sing how much you love him and promise to serve him for the rest of your life, regardless of what happens! Allow yourself to grow closer to God each day. Learn to love his word and to pray. There are so many rewards that come from a close intimate relationship with our Lord and Savior. Do not worry about what people will say. You do not have to tell them. This is just between you and God. They will see a difference in you and wonder what it is all about; just let them look and wonder. When they ask, then you can share Jesus with them! The more we love him, the more time we want to spend with him. For your assignment today, look in the appendix for the song, *"Jesus, I Love you."* Read this song to the Lord in its entirety. Make it your pledge to him today!

DAY TEN ASSIGNMENT

ASSIGNMENT FOR TODAY:

In addition to any notes or thoughts you had about today's lesson and reading of the Song, *"Jesus, I love you."* I also want you to make a list of the following things in your notebook and pray this list to God. **Write today's date in your notebook and then write this statement out and sign it:**

"Jesus, I come to you today to make my pledge of love to you. You loved me so much that you gave your only son for me. You took my place on Calvary; you died in my place so that I could go free. That is the most awesome love I have ever seen in my life. I do not feel worthy to accept that kind of love. You are royalty, the son of God, the Son of the King of Kings. I have nothing to bring and lay before a King that would be gracious enough or good enough for what you did for me. The only thing that I have that I can give to you is ME. So today, with all the humility that I know how, I am bringing me and laying me before you as my gift. It is not much, but I DO PROMISE TO LOVE YOU AND TO SERVE YOU FOR THE REST OF MY LIFE!"

Make sure each day that you re-read this pledge and promise to the Lord. Renew your commitment to God as often as you feel necessary. You will never be sorry for pledging to give him the rest of your life!

Please write to us and let us know that you have accepted Christ as your personal Lord and Savior! We will add you to our prayer list and pray over your request daily. There is power in prayer, especially corporate prayer! God will help you to serve your time and leave a changed man or woman for him. God will help you turn your life around permanently!

DAY ELEVEN:

GOOD MORNING, HOLY SPIRIT!

When you get up each morning, the first thing you should do is greet your Lord and Savior, just like you do your spouse. "***Good Morning, Holy Spirit***!" Greet him with lots of humility and thanksgiving in your heart. You want him to know that you are proud to be in the family of God. Act like it!

I do not want to re-teach the facts that Benny Hinn has covered in his book, "Good Morning, Holy Spirit." But note that this is the fourth book you want to read after completing this challenge. You want to understand the spirit of God more clearly and get a grip on this wonderful gift that he has for you called the Holy Ghost/Holy Spirit! However, for the purpose of this challenge, I want to introduce you to the wonderful benefits of having God first in your life, having a relationship with Jesus Christ, and allowing the Holy Spirit into your life. To help you understand the Holy Spirit's functions, we need to review a few scriptures informing us of his benefits and blessings. Yes, the Holy Spirit does live in us if we desire to let him in:

Ezekiel 36:27: *"And I will put my spirit within you and cause you to walk in my statues and ye shall keep my judgments and do them."* *(KJV, 2020).*

John 14:17: *"Even the Spirit of truth; whom the world cannot receive, because it sees him not, neither knows him; but ye how him, for he dwells with you and will be in you."* *(KJV, 2020).*

I Corinthians 3:16: *"Know ye not that ye are the temple of God and that the Spirit of God dwells in you?"* *(KJV, 2020).*

Joel 2:28: *"And it shall come to pass afterward, that I will pour out my spirit upon all flesh; and your sons and your daughters shall prophesy your old men shall dream dreams, your young men shall see visions."* *(KJV, 2020).*

Acts 2:38: *"Then Peter said unto them, Repent and be baptized every one of you in the name of Jesus Christ for the remissions of your sins and that ye shall receive the gift of the*

Holy Ghost." (KJV, 2020).

Acts 4:33: *"and with great power gave the apostles witness of the resurrection of the Lord Jesus, and great grace was upon them all." (KJV, 2020).*

Acts 19:11: *"and God wrought special miracles by the hands of Paul so that from his body were brought unto the sick handkerchiefs or aprons and the disease departed from them, and the evil spirits went out of them." (KJV, 2020).*

Will there be an outpouring of the Holy Spirit in the last days? Will more people come to know this wonderful gift of God? Yes! Does the Holy Spirit have power? Can he lead me and teach me so that I can live without sin in my life? *Yes, the Holy Spirit is powerful!* If I want this wonderful gift, how do I get it? You can receive the Holy Spirit by simply praying and asking God to give you this wonderful gift. Make sure that you go before him humbly and with a contrite spirit. If there is any sin in your life, then he will not give you this gift. So, you need to know that you pray and cleanse yourself of any sins. Ask the Lord to forgive you and make you righteous through Jesus Christ's blood. If you are sincere in your prayers, you are saved, and you long for a closer walk with Christ, then he will give you the Holy Spirit to be your leader, guide, and teacher. He is the best prayer partner you can have in your life.

REMEMBER: Greet him each day, "Good Morning, Holy Spirit!"

DAY ELEVEN ASSIGNMENT

ASSIGNMENT FOR TODAY:

In addition to any notes or thoughts that you had about today's lesson, I want you to make a list of the following things in your notebook and pray this list to God:

1) Spend your time in prayer this morning for this wonderful gift.
2) Spend time thanking God for all that he has done for you and your family.
3) Do not forget to pray over your prayer list and lists in your notebook that you have completed so far.

DAY TWELVE:

READING THE BIBLE

God wants us to read and study his word. It is through his word that we get to know him better. It is through his word that we learn his commandments, and he talks back to us. It is not a complicated process. It is just a process that requires discipline to have a lifestyle change that includes adding Bible studies and prayer to your daily routine.

There are a few points about the Bible that we need to learn today. We read God's word so that we can grow spiritually. The Bible is to our "souls" like food is to our bodies. The Lord wants us to develop a love for reading his word. He wants us to want to spend time with him each day. This is an area where we have to have discipline, and usually, it is difficult at first. However, once you get accustomed to adding daily reading and prayer plus family devotions to your life, you find that it becomes easier. The word of God is powerful. We can acquire that power in our lives if we study this word. There are many examples of studying the word of God. Let us take a look at some of the scriptures that inspire us to this knowledge.

THE BIBLE IS FOOD FOR OUR SOUL:

Deuteronomy 8:3: *"And he humbled thee and suffered thee to hunger and fed thee with manna which thou knew not, neither did thy fathers know; that he might make thee know that man doth not live by bread only, but by every word that proceeds out the mouth of the Lord doth man live." (KJV, 2020).*

Job 23:12: *"Neither have I gone back from the commandment of his lips; I have esteemed the words of his mouth more than my necessary food." (KJV, 2020).*

Psalms 119:103: *"How sweet are thy words unto my taste; yea, sweeter than honey to my mouth." (KJV, 2020).*

I Peter 2:2: *"As newborn babes, desire the sincere milk of the word that ye may grow thereby:" (KJV, 2020).*

God will plant a love for the Bible inside of you. If you ask God each day to help you to love his word, he will grant it. Ask God to give you understanding and knowledge about the Bible. You will be surprised by what God will show you, and the Holy Spirit will teach you! What we receive from the Bible is spiritual food. The meat (protein) of our spiritual diets is the words and instructions found in the Bible. God's words are life to us, helping us grow spiritually, develop faith, build character, produce fruit, and experience miracles.

Psalms 119:47: *"I will delight myself in thy commandments, which I have loved;" (KJV, 2020).*

Psalms 119:72: *"The law of thy mouth is better unto me than thousands of gold and silver." (KJV, 2020).*

The Bible, the word of God, has power. You can quote the Bible to Satan, and he will have to leave your presence. You can quote scriptures to support the prayers you are praying, and they will be answered. God's word heals, mends, and helps us to forgive those who hurt us! The word of God is like a defensive weapon. The apostle Paul called it our sword. Knowledge of God's word is better to have than fortunes and fame. With an understanding of God's word, we possess the power to do all things with God's help!

Ephesians 6:17: *"And take the helmet of salvation and the sword of the spirit which is the word of God." (KJV, 2020).*

The word of God is like a probing instrument. It looks inside us, finds the areas we need to change, and brings it to our attention. It is almost like a secret agent! You need to study about putting on the whole armor of God, especially the helmet of salvation in Ephesians the 6th chapter.

Hebrew 4:12: *"For the word of God is quick and powerful and sharper than any two-edged sword, piercing even to the dividing asunder of soul and spirit and the joints and the marrow and is a discerner of the thought and the intents of the heart." (KJV, 2020).*

REASONS WHY WE NEED TO STUDY THE BIBLE:

John 5:29: *"Search the scriptures; for in them ye think ye have eternal life and they are they which testify of me." (KJV, 2020).*

Acts 17:11: *"These were those who were nobler than them in Thessalonica, in that they received the word with all readiness of mind and searched the scriptures daily, there to those things were so."* (KJV, 2020).

Romans 15:4: *"For whatsoever things were written aforetime was written for our learning that we through patience and comfort of the scriptures might have hope."* (KJV, 2020).

I cannot stress how important it is to have a scheduled time of Bible reading and prayer each day. I have placed in the appendix of this book several "Read through the Bible Guides." Select one that will fit your schedule, and then make a copy of that page, so you can fold it and place it in your Bible. You can then place a checkmark by the day after you complete your Bible reading. You may want to read Christian books that I have recommended, complete Bible studies, and watch Christian TV. However, **DO NOT** avoid reading the scripture passages that are listed on the schedule that you select. You need to make sure that you read through the Bible at least once per year. The only way you will know if your Pastor is preaching is biblical or whether to watch some of the TV preachers or not is to read the word of God for yourself. If they begin to teach or preach something that contradicts what you have read in the Bible, change the channel. Do not let others deceive you or confuse you. Remember, there are rewards for studying God's word. Those rewards include inner peace, hope, forgiveness, and eternal life.

DAY TWELVE ASSIGNMENT

ASSIGNMENT FOR TODAY:

In addition to any notes or thoughts that you had about today's lesson, I want you to make a list of the following things in your notebook and pray this list to God:

1) Select the read through the Bible study guide that will work best for you.

2) If you are unsure which one to select, start reading through the New Testament in 90 days. That one will not overwhelm you but will help you have a relatively strong base at the end of 90 days.

DAY THIRTEEN:

STUDYING THE BIBLE

I recommend setting aside a specific time each day in the morning and at night before retiring to bed to read and pray. You need a designated time and place to study the Bible. It is imperative to read and re-read it multiple times a year. You need to establish a specific time each day to study the word. This can be a joint effort with the family or done individually. This study or devotion time is when you read a chapter(s), making sure to complete the story or thought you are reading—lookup any words you do not understand with a dictionary or Bible concordance. As you grow in the knowledge of God's word, you will need to invest in a useful reference Bible and commentary to help you gain more understanding.

One of the easiest ways to start Bible studies in your home is to write to one of the companies that I have listed in the appendix under the section "Recommended Bible Studies." These companies furnish Bible study booklets and courses to all prisoners and inmates in jails free of charge. Some even provide copies for their families for free. A couple of these companies furnish these courses for free to anyone. Others charge non-incarcerated individuals a small fee to cover copy costs or postage. At any rate, they are very inexpensive. You simply read the materials they send you to look up the scriptures and complete the worksheets enclosed. Then you mail them back to the company for grading. Once you have completed all sections of a course, they will send you a certificate. This is a great way to get started studying God's word. After you have completed a number of these courses and you have managed to add to your library a good Study/Reference Bible, Concordance, Commentary, and Dictionary, you will be able to take a chapter at a time and conduct your detailed studies.

If you have children, you need to incorporate them into your Bible Study time. One of the best tools is to go to www.biblestorybooks.org and click on *The Bible Story* icon. They have a 10-volume hardback set that takes you through the Bible with the main stories. It is in a simple, easy to understand format. I love to read through them myself from time to time, even though I had these books as a child growing up, and I have taught most of these lessons many times. For New Christians, it is a great way to get a basic understanding of the various concepts of the Bible in a format that is easy to understand and is biblically correct.

You can also order the books online or by writing to Biblestorybooks.org, P. O. Box 754, Seaside, OR 97138. These are the best books that I have found for children. If you do not know much about the Bible, these will be great for you too. A daily Bible study includes the daily reading of the word or listening to the word. Refer to the appendix section for reading guides and how you can get the Bible apps, audio Bibles, and CDs.

Remember, read, re-read, and then re-read again. Go through the Bible at least once per year working up to four times per year. The word is key to answered prayer, promises, miracles, etc.

DAY THIRTEEN ASSIGNMENT

ASSIGNMENT FOR TODAY:

I want you to continue to work on writing your letters to God. Write about each incident that affected you or the individuals that hurt you. Refer back to the Day-4 assignment. Continue working on this point until you have completed all of these letters and prayers to God. He will help you find the information you need in his word with your daily reading and praying. This will help you pray for the answer as you address each of these areas of concern in your prayers.

DAY FOURTEEN:

STANDARDS AND CONVICTIONS

I am sure that you wonder what standards and convictions are and why they are significant in this challenge. I have already mentioned these terms a couple of times in other devotions. I have given you a formal definition of convictions below. However, the simple explanation is a list of the do(s) and do not(s) you want to follow and teach your children.

CONVICTIONS:

These are your standards or guidelines that you have determined that God wants/desires of your life. When you pray and establish your standards and convictions, please note that the minimum must include having the "fruits of the spirit" present in your life and NONE of the "works of the flesh" present. Look up the definition of each of these. Why must we have standards and convictions? If we do not have established standards and convictions, then we will change our minds about what God wants out of us and what God wants us to do or not to do every time we talk with someone. If we do not have standards and convictions, we lose our focus. We quickly lose sight of the prize, waiting for us on the other side.

How can I know what my standards and convictions should be? We are going to go over the minimums, the things that the Bible requires. There are things listed in the Bible as "MUST" for you to enter heaven and the things that it says that MUST NOT be present in our lives because they are an abomination to God, and he will not let them enter.

MINIMUM STANDARDS AND CONVICTIONS:

Your minimum convictions should include you having the fruits of the spirit and none of the works of the flesh present in your life. We should not be involved with people, events, or activities that promote the works of the flesh. We should not attend a church that does not preach that the works of the flesh are a sin. This should be the first item on our minimum list of convictions.

The "**works of the flesh**" are defined as the 17 things listed in Galatians 5:19-21. They are *adultery, fornication, uncleanness, lasciviousness, idolatry, witchcraft, hatred, variance, emulations, wrath, strife, seditions, heresies, envying, murders, drunkenness, and revellings.* Each one of these is defined in this glossary. These attitudes and actions SHOULD NOT be present in a Christian's life. *(The Bible says that these are an abomination and will not be allowed to enter into heaven.)*

We should be promoting the fruits of the spirit in our lives. We should be reading and studying God's word, having Christian fellowship, reading books, and watching movies that promote these characteristics' growth in our lives and our families. The "**fruits of the spirit**" are defined as the nine characteristics listed in **Galatians 5:22**. These are the attitudes and behaviors that God desires out of all of us daily. The nine fruits of the spirit are *love, joy, peace, longsuffering, gentleness, goodness, faith, meekness, and temperance.*

MAXIMUM STANDARDS:

This should be anything else that God has shown you personally that you should not do to prevent yourself from inviting one of the works of the flesh into your life. These personal convictions could also be something that God has shown you or lead you to do or not do to be rapture ready. Do not judge others by your PERSONAL standards and convictions…your maximums. Those are for you only, your maximum convictions, which are necessary for you to make it in the rapture. Do not take this lightly.

You will want to spend time going over each of the works of the flesh, as defined in the Glossary or the Day-19 devotion. Read the glossary definitions today and familiarize yourself with them. Begin praying and start making your conviction list.

DAY FOURTEEN ASSIGNMENT

ASSIGNMENT FOR TODAY:

In addition to any notes or thoughts that you had about today's lesson, I want you to make a list of the following things in your notebook and pray this list to God sincerely:

1) Start a list of the things you feel that God does not want you to do, and beside it, write why. List a scripture or a work of the flesh in parenthesis beside each item. This will help you to determine what activities to not participate in or which clothes not to wear. Add to it as you go through this challenge. God will lead you as to what he wants for you and your family.

2) Once you have completed this challenge or have been released to go home, you will need to establish house rules with your spouse. This list will help you accomplish that task.

3) This list will also provide your children, why not. It is not enough to tell children, especially teenagers, no because the Bible says so. They need to know why! If they understand why it is easier for them to make the right judgment call when placed in a situation that would cause them to want to participate in something wrong.

DAY FIFTEEN:

PRAISE WITHOUT CEASING

We talk a lot about praying without ceasing; (which means to pray continually or to go with a prayer in your heart.) Why not praise God without stopping? He inhabits the praise of his people. He loves to hear us praise him. He loves to be reminded of the wonderful things that he has done for us...., so it makes me want to "Praise him without ceasing."

Hebrews 13:15: *"Let us offer the sacrifice of praise to God continually, that is, the fruit of our lips giving thanks to his name." (KJV, 2020).*

Once you have given your heart entirely to the Lord and accepted that new heart that he has for you, you become grateful for the things he has done for you. You begin to see things through God's eye, not yours. People will sometimes think you are crazy because this will make you an optimist versus a pessimist. They will not always like the new you, but keep it up. God inhabits (he enjoys and delights in) the praises of his people. When you begin to praise him for what he has done, you will find that he is delighted that you are giving him the honor and glory for things in your life that he will begin to bless and move for you even more.

Part of praising God is having trust in God and obeying his commandments continually. One way we can prove to him that we love him, that we trust him with our lives, and that we are committed to our pledge to serve him for the rest of our lives is to praise him. Praise God even when things are difficult for us to deal with or to understand, praise him anyway. Praise him even when things look bad or wrong. Show God that you trust him, and he can trust you. God will; he will not leave you or forsake you. He has a plan for your life, a plan to prosper you, not destroy you. Do not question God about the why's! Just praise him!

We must remember that sometimes God takes us and transplant us into a group, a job, or a situation just like someone would move a plant or a bush in their yards, for a specific purpose. Sometimes God does not warn us of the reason for that assignment. It would be our human nature to tell God, "No, I do not think I want that assignment," or "God, I think you can find someone else," or we might just say, "NO! I'm not going." So, God transplants us so smoothly that we do not even realize what he has done till we arrive. It is those times of testing that are the hardest. It is those times when we say, God, please get me out of here. That is not what he wants. He wants us to "bloom where we are planted." Regardless of how ugly the place or how unpleasant the circumstances, God has a plan. He has a mission for you. Do not miss the blessing that is waiting for you at the end of the trial. Do not miss the blessing there for you for blooming.

I know that most of you have heard the wise old tale that goes, "When life gives you lemons, do not get mad, just make lemonade!" There is so much truth in that comment. If we can learn to be as Paul said, "I am content in whatsoever state I am in," while walking in perfect peace! When you reach this level, you have now stepped into God's realm of real peace. Make up your mind today to praise God no matter what; to praise God regardless of the circumstances or the trial; to glorify God in every way that you know how and praise him continually. Below are some of the scriptural ways to praise God and the reasons why.

WAYS TO PRAISE GOD

The Bible gives us a list of reasons why we should praise God and how to praise him. We can praise him in song, with musical instruments, with dance, and silently. We can praise him publicly or in private. We can praise him in our thoughts and the meditations of our hearts.

PRAISE GOD IN SONG:

Psalms 9:11: *"Sing praises to the Lord, which dwells in Zion; declare among the people his doings."* (KJV, 2020).

PRAISE GOD WITH MUSICAL INSTRUMENTS:

Psalms 33:2: *"Praise the Lord with the harp; sing unto him with the psaltery and an instrument of ten strings."* (KJV, 2020).

PUBLICLY PRAISE GOD:

Psalms 67:3: *"Let the people praise thee, O God; let all the people praise thee."* (KJV, 2020).

We can also share God's love, mercy, & grace by sharing his blessings and praises with everyone we meet. When we testify of God's goodness, our faith is built, and others are drawn to God.

Isaiah 42: 12: *"Let them give glory unto the Lord and declare his praise in the islands"* (KJV, 2020).

CONTINUAL PRAISE TO GOD IN OUR HEARTS:

Hebrews 13:15: *"By him, therefore let us offer the sacrifice of praise to God continually that is, the fruit of our lips giving thanks to his name." (KJV, 2020).*

THE REASON THAT WE ARE TO PRAISE GOD IS:

I Peter 2:9: *"But ye are a chosen generation, a royal priesthood, a holy nation a peculiar people, that ye should show forth the praises of him who hath called you out of darkness into his marvelous light." (KJV, 2020).*

Examples in the Bible of unceasing praise to God can be found in these scriptures. Take the time to look at each one of them up and read them. Psalms 35:28; 71:6; 104:33; and 145:1; and Revelations 4:8 and 5:13.

DAY FIFTEEN ASSIGNMENT

ASSIGNMENT FOR TODAY:

In addition to any notes or thoughts that you had about today's lesson; I want you to do the following:

1) Make a list of all the things in your life that you want to praise God for doing or giving to you.

2) Make a list of all of the people you want to praise God for in your life.

DAY SIXTEEN:

PLEASE GOD OR MAN

Are you living each day studying the word of God and trying to find out what God wants in your life? Or are you living your life based upon what your colleagues and friends are telling you that you should be doing? Are you frantically trying to please your parents, in-laws, children, boss, and best friends all at the same time? Do you feel some days like you are on a roller coaster, and you would pay someone to make it stop? Or you would give years off your life if someone would wave a magic wand over your life and make your problems go away? This is a common problem with the modern family in America today. The need to have everything that everyone else has, the need to be the best and have the most is driving people away from God, destroying their families, decreasing the communication and love between family members, and causing teens to commit suicide. Is there hope for this situation? Yes! Let us talk about this today. We need to decide if we are going to please God or man with our lives.

Remember the story I mentioned last week about Moses leading the children of Israel out of Egypt's bondage and taking them to Canaan. Still, Moses did not lead them across the Jordan River into Canaan? Joshua took Moses' place as their leader and helped them conqueror, the land, and settle down in the "promised land." Joshua was a young man when they left Egypt. He was at an impressionable age. However, early in his life, he decided that he wanted to be like Moses. He decided that he wanted a relationship with God like Moses had at that time. He wanted to know more about this God and how to communicate with him. Joshua's zeal caused him to listen to Moses and learn everything that he could about God. This was important! It molded the rest of his life and brought him success. Let us take a look at the character of Joshua:

a) He was a Christian—He believed in God the Father.
b) He was a devoted warrior—He learned the skills to fight and help defend the Children of Israel when they went through lands and areas where they had to fight. (See Exodus 17).
c) He was an optimist—He was one of the spies that went into Canaan for Moses. He looked at the giants in the land and all of the problems. But he also knew the power of his God, and his faith gave him an "optimist's" viewpoint instead of a pessimist. Joshua saw the glass half full, not half empty!
d) His relationship with God was solid. His faith was firm. His mind was made up.

e) He possessed leadership skills. He would lead others, but he did not let others change him.
f) He had a teachable spirit, one that God could lead.
g) He was steadfast in his purpose. He did not let anything or anyone turn him from God's divine plan for his life.
h) His victories were always won because of his unchanging, unwavering faith in God.
i) As he was dying, Joshua gave a farewell address to the children of Israel. Joshua challenged them to continue to live according to the laws God had given to Moses, to be faithful to their worship, and to stay away from the forces of evil and idolatry. Joshua summed his challenge up with the following comment:

Joshua's motto in life was one of sincere faith, unchangeable under all circumstances. Joshua had experienced this relationship with God at a level that the children of Israel had not experienced. Joshua knew that he knew that he knew what he wanted from his God.

Joshua 24:15: *"And if it seems evil unto you to serve the Lord, choose you this day whom ye will serve; whether the gods which your fathers served that were on the other side of the flood or the gods of the Amorites, in whose land ye dwell: but as for me and my house, we will serve the Lord." (KJV, 2020).*

What are you going to do? Choose today to serve God and to follow his commandments regardless of what your family, friends, or colleagues decide. Serve God with all of your hearts! There are so many great points in Joshua's character that serves as positive examples for us today. However, there is another man in the Bible that we need to discuss today. He may not have been the warrior that Joshua was or the leader, but he was obedient to the Lord. His name is Naaman.

Naaman was the chief captain of Benhadad. He reported directly to the King of Syria. Naaman was a great man in a high position in the Government in Syria. His wife had a little Jewish maid as her personal servant. This little girl was not ashamed to share with her mistress about the God of Israel. Naaman was healed of leprosy after he went to see the prophet, Elisha. Let us look at this story in the scriptures:

II Kings 5:1-15: *Now Naaman, captain of the host of the king of Syria, was a great man with his master, and honorable because by him the Lord had given deliverance unto Syria: he was also a mighty man in valor, but he was a leper. And the Syrians had gone out by companies and had brought away captive out of the land of Israel a little maid, and* *she waited on Naaman's wife. And she said unto her mistress, Would God my lord was with the prophet that is in Samaria, for he would recover him of his leprosy. And one went in, and told his lord, saying, Thus and thus said the maid that is of the land of Israel. And the king of Syria said, go to, go, and I will send a letter unto the king of Israel. And he departed and took with him ten talents of silver, and six thousand pieces of gold, and ten changes of raiment. And he brought the letter to the king of Israel, saying, now when this letter is come unto thee, behold; I have therewith sent Naaman my servant to thee, that thou may recover him of his leprosy. And it came to pass, when the king of Israel had read the letter, that he rent his clothes, and said, Am I God, to kill and to make alive, that this man doth send unto me to recover a man of his leprosy? Wherefore consider, I pray you and see how he seeks a quarrel against me. And it was so when Elisha the man of God had heard that the king of Israel had rent his clothes, that he sent to the king, saying, wherefore hast thou rent thy clothes? Let him come now to me, and he shall know that there is a prophet in Israel. So Naaman came with his horses and with his chariot and stood at the door of the house of Elisha. And Elisha sent a messenger unto him, saying, Go and wash in the Jordan seven times, and thy flesh shall come again to thee, and thou shalt be clean. But Naaman was wroth, and went away, and said, Behold, I thought, He will surely come out to me, and stand, and call on the name of the Lord his God, and strike his hand over the place, and recover the leper. Are not Abana and Pharpar, rivers of Damascus, better than all the waters of Israel? May I not wash in them and be clean? So, he turned and went away in a rage. And his servants came near, and spoke unto him, and said, my father if the prophet had bid thee do some great thing, would thou not have done it? How much rather then, when he saith to thee, Wash, and be clean? Then went he down, and dipped himself seven times in Jordan, according to the saying of the man of God: and his flesh came again like unto the flesh of a little child, and he was clean. And he returned to the man of God, he and all his company, and came, and stood before him: and he said, Behold, now I know that there is no God in all earth, but in Israel: now, therefore, I pray thee, take a blessing."* (KJV, 2020).

As this story unfolds in the end, you can see that Naaman wanted his miracle, but he had his own ideas about how that miracle would be delivered. He was a man of great honor and standing. He would have done anything that the prophet had asked if it would have required him to be elaborate or flashy. Sometimes, it is easy for us to get caught up in this arena of life. With all of the influence of Hollywood and TV Evangelism on our churches and our lives, it is easy for us to desire to be flashy with what we do for God. That is not necessary.

We need to learn to listen to God, not to man when working for God. God has a way that sometimes seems foolish to us. God has a way that sometimes seems almost degrading to us. But it is just a simple test of our faith in him. He wants us to be obedient to his commandments. He gave Naaman a simple task of just going down to Jordan River and dipping seven times. It was a harmless task. Naaman **ALMOST missed his miracle** because he **ALMOST let his pride stop him** from obeying God. Sometimes fear grips us and almost chokes us. We are disobedient to God because we are SO AFRAID of what other people will say or do if we follow God's commandments. We have to remember that we will be obedient in all things, no matter how simple or stupid, just like Naaman. He had to get to the point that he did not care what his soldiers thought when they saw him dipping in the Jordan River. He had to decide whether he would obey God or do what he thought other people would do in that situation!

Decide today that you are going to obey the Lord for the rest of your life. Decide today that you will be obedient to the Lord in all things, regardless of what people do or say to you. You will be surprised at how God helps you and how he works miracles for you when you obey him!

DAY SIXTEEN ASSIGNMENT

ASSIGNMENT FOR TODAY:

In addition to any notes or thoughts that you had about today's lesson; I want you to do the following:

1) Make a list of all the things that you want God to fix in your life.

2) Keep this list in your notebook and handy, so you can add to this list as we go through this study and even after the challenge is complete.

3) As God answers these prayers and moves…. make sure you mark the date on your list. So, you can refer to these lists later and use them to remind you of the things you need to praise the Lord for doing for you.

DAY SEVENTEEN:

DO NOT JUDGE OTHERS, BUT JUDGE YOURSELF

You are probably asking, "What is wrong with judging or condemning others if they are doing wrong?" We are not to judge others because we do not know what God is working on or doing with them. We do not know where they are at this point in their relationship with God. We can look at a person's life to see if the "**works of the flesh**" are present or not. If you see the works of the flesh present, RUN from that person. If you work with them, Ok, but do not get involved with them on a social level. Birds of a feather flock together. Evil will always pull good down. A rotten potato left in the bag will cause the whole bag to rot. You can be nice and work with a positive "team attitude" without letting them change you.

If the people you are hanging around have the "works of the flesh" present in their lives, separate yourself from them, even if it is family. They will pull you down before you can become established with God. All of the works of the flesh are defined in the glossary and the Day-19 lesson. Review the definitions. It would help if you judged yourself, not others. You need to judge yourself not by what other people think, say or tell you, but by the word of God. If you listen to people, you will become discouraged. It does not matter what other people think about you or what they tell on you. They cannot add one day to your life or take away the rewards that God has for you. They cannot keep you out of heaven; only you make that determination.

Look for the **fruits of the spirit** in others. If they do not possess them, then stay away from them. You do not want to become like them. If they have the fruits of the spirit present in their lives, it is ok to join them. You will find the positive Christian influence encouraging, and it will help you to grow spiritually. Commit today to stay away from the works of the flesh. It may be challenging at first, but as you commit to this separation and you refuse to judge and criticize people, you will begin to grow in Christ

As you grow in your spiritual walk with Christ, you may even find people in the churches you attend that may not be where they need to be with the Lord. They may be committing acts that you know are a sin or abomination to God. Do not judge them. Pray for them, separate yourself from them. If they ask you why you can, with love, show them why you feel that they are involved in things or a lifestyle you cannot associate. Use the time to witness to them without criticizing them, judging them, or degrading them. Remember, Jesus came that they might NOT be lost.... not to murder them with your tongue! Do not judge them!

DAY SEVENTEEN ASSIGNMENT

ASSIGNMENT FOR TODAY:

In addition to any notes or thoughts that you had about today's lesson; I want you to do the following:

1) Make a list of all the people who have "controls" in your life.

2) Assess each person on your list. See if the works of the flesh or the fruits of the spirit are active in their lives.

3) Now, pray for these people in your life daily. If you have the option to move people with the works of the flesh in their lives out of your life, do so. If not, pray that God helps you deal with them at work, etc., without them influencing you negatively.

DAY EIGHTEEN:

CHURCH ATTENDANCE

You may be asking yourself why you should go to church. If you ask this question to 100 people, you will get many different answers on this topic. However, it can be summed up into a straightforward reply: "It is essential for you to have friends and to be around other people who believe as you do. These need to be friends that have the same Christian standards and goals in their lives. This allows them to be able to encourage you, pray for you, and provide you with spiritual support as needed, but most of all, keep you accountable for your Christian walk." If you do not ever go to church, you will not develop these types of relationships.

Is it essential to have these friends and relationships? If you do not have Christian friends to hang around with or consult when you have questions, Satan will always make sure that there is always a non-Christian person around who will lead or advise you wrong. They will tempt you to walk away from the truth, forget the Bible, and do what feels good. Is it essential during this challenge to attend church? Yes, if you have not already started attending church, then you need to immediately. It may take you several weeks to find a church that you feel comfortable attending, so you need to start looking now.

You may be confused about what type of church you need to attend when you get out of prison or what kind of services in the prison chapel to attend. Not all religions that come to the prison are of God. You need to look for a church that believes in at least the following points. You do not want to overlook not even one of these points. If they do not have all of these points listed on their "We Believe" cards or bulletins ask the pastor, chaplain, or guest speaker about what they believe if they do not have a card or pamphlet to share with you. If the preacher tells you that one of these is not important, run from that church!

1) The Bible is the Word of God. Holy men wrote it of old as they were inspired by the Holy Ghost/Holy Spirit.

2) Jesus Christ is the Son of God, born of the Virgin Mary.

3) God, the Father, in Heaven, is the only God. We believe in the Trinity God-head. The father, the Son, and the Holy Ghost.

4) As a man, Jesus Christ came to earth, lived here, and was crucified on a cross between two thieves for crimes he did not commit. He was a perfect sacrifice for our sins.

5) Jesus died in our place so that we could have eternal life. Jesus' blood covers all of our sins if we ask him.

6) There is no other way to go to the Father, God, or heaven except through Jesus. We must have his blood applied to our lives. We cannot go to heaven without accepting Jesus Christ as our personal Lord and Savior.

7) There is God the Father, Jesus, the Son of God, and the Holy Spirit. A Trinity, all God.

8) Jesus died on the cross and rose again after three days. He is alive today in heaven sitting at the right hand of the Father making intercession for you and me.

9) Jesus is coming back again to this earth to take his bride with him. This is called the rapture of the Church. It could be any day, any time, therefore, we must be ready.

10) There will be a great tribulation period of seven years after the rapture of the church. Some Christians left behind when the rapture takes place will make it to heaven through the tribulation period. After the tribulation period with Christ, we will return to earth to reign here for 1000 years with perfect peace, no wars, and no hunger for a period where Satan will be bound and not allowed to be loose.

These points listed above are the ten fundamental beliefs. These should be minimal criteria. There are other components that you should look for also. You need to be in a church where the pastor preaches on sin, stands for the truth taught in the Bible, and does not compromise to have a broader membership and more money. You need to know that the people teaching the Sunday school classes that your children are attending are qualified and have a relationship with Christ.

Make sure that the pastor preaches against ALL of the seventeen (17) of the works of the flesh. He needs to preach that the works of the flesh WILL NOT enter into heaven. You do not want to get into a church without standards or convictions. You do not want to waste your time. Make sure that the pastor does not believe in or teach situational ethics. This is where the pastor determines what is right or wrong based on the circumstances surrounding the situation. He or she should be making choices based on what the Bible says.

CAN I JUST WATCH CHURCH ON THE TV?

Refer back to my first comments about Christian fellowship and accountability. It is easier for us to follow a pattern or guideline if we know that others are looking to see if we are following. The same concept carries forward in an AA/NA meeting (Alcoholics Anonymous or Narcotics Anonymous). This is an excellent concept of accountability. So, adapt it to your personal spiritual life. It is not a technique to make you miserable; It is just a technique to help you remain accountable to the Bible's teachings. If there is someone around you can discuss a topic with, debate a point, pray over it, and make a decision based on what the Bible says, then that is better for you than just ignoring it. These guidelines are not to cramp our lifestyles or to make us miserable.

These guidelines help us prevent planting bad seeds that we will one day have to reap in this life. If you plant roses in your yard, you cannot get angry when they begin to grow with their thorns versus the carnations that you wanted. You must remember that all life concepts can be summed up into one physical law of "planting and reaping." Everything in life that happens to us results from an action taken by us or by someone else that affected us. Everything is the result of a seed that was planted. If we know and understand this concept, why would we plant seeds that we do not want to reap in our lives? We do not, it is sometimes Satan that makes us think that we do, or it looks easier to make the other choice. So, decide today that you will choose friends who will help you make the right choices. Select a church that will teach the truths you need to hear and preach against the sins you need to avoid living this life so you can be blessed. Church attendance is discussed in several places in the New Testament, contrary to popular beliefs and teaching that church attendance is unnecessary. Look at what the Bible has to say on this subject:

<u>**Matthew 12:9:**</u> *"And when he was departed thence, he went into their synagogues."* (KJV, 2020).

A synagogue was the temple or church of that day. Jesus set the example for us by going to the Synagogue himself. He went to church at the appropriate, appointed times and worshipped with the people as the custom was in that day. Here is another scripture that shows not only his attendance at church but his teaching at church also.

Mark 1:21: *"And they went into Capernaum, and straightway on the Sabbath day he entered into the synagogue and taught."* *(KJV, 2020).*

Luke 4:16: *"And he came to Nazareth where he had been brought up and as his custom was, he went into the synagogue on the Sabbath day and stood up for to read."* *(KJV, 2020).*

Acts 13:14*: "But when they departed from Perga, and they came to Antioch in Pisidia, then they went into the synagogue on the Sabbath day and sat down." (KJV, 2020).*

Paul gives us another reminder under grace to continue with church attendance. As we see the end of time approaching, he tells us to be even more zealous about church attendance and fellowship with other Christians.

Hebrews 10:25: *"Not forsaking the assembling of ourselves together, as the manner of some is, but exhorting one another and so much the more as ye see the day approaching."* *(KJV, 2020).*

DAY EIGHTEEN ASSIGNMENT

ASSIGNMENT FOR TODAY:

In addition to any notes or thoughts that you had about today's lesson; I want you to do the following:

1) Make a list of the convictions that you think you should look for in a church. Put the items that you have learned so far in this study and continue to add to this list each day as you feel led.

2) Keep this list handy so that you can refer to it as you read through the Bible. You will find over the next year that you may add things to this list.

3) The right church for you and your family is extremely important. So do not skip this list!

DAY NINETEEN:

GARBAGE IN…. GARBAGE OUT!

There are a few simple rules for controlling the things that are feed to your mind. There are some basic rules to follow. Pray before you speak. Think about what you are going to do before you do it and consider the consequences of the actions you are about to make. If your actions result from revenge or a desire to see the other person suffer because you are bitter and cannot forgive them, then pray and re-think your plan! Remember…garbage in---garbage out. If you are constantly feeding your mind TV programs where people are taking care of business and dealing with others in less than courteous ways…. controlling, manipulating, and even engaging in deceitful behaviors to acquire what they want…then, after a while, you will begin to feel that it is ok; everyone is doing it! *Remember, you are what you watch, and you are what you listen to each day.*

As a simple guide or rule to help us decide what we should put into our minds and hearts, Paul gave us some simple guidelines. He gave us Galatians 5th chapter, the list of the *WORKS OF THE FLESH*, and the fruits of the spirit. The first list is the things that God *DOES NOT WANT IN OUR LIVES*. These are the things that God says are an <u>abomination</u> unto him and that he cannot and will not tolerate. He even says that you cannot go to heaven with any of these spirits active in your life. So, this list is SERIOUS. Then Paul discusses the desired personality traits that we should have in our lives. He calls these the fruits of the spirit.

I am not going to discuss the fruits of the spirit today. These are part of a devotion lesson later in this study. However, I feel that we need to look at the definition of each work of the flesh so that you will understand why I am stressing so strongly that we must control the garbage going into our minds and why. To help you know and understand the definition of each of the 17 works of the flesh, I have included detailed definitions in the glossary. I feel that I need to take time today to discuss each of these briefly. You will hear more about these works of the flesh in the next few weeks. This brief discussion will help you understand why you are what you watch and what you listen to; look at the brief definitions of these words.

THE WORKS OF THE FLESH
A CONDENSED VERSION

ADULTERY AND FORNICATION:
A sexual relationship with a person other than the person's spouse is called adultery. Fornication is a sexual act between two people not married to each other or anyone else. The act of violating one's marriage vows by engaging in pornography, prostitution, internet sex, petting, fondling, or sexually inappropriate talk, communications, or behavior with a person other than the individual married. Both words are used interchangeably by most people, even though the popular definition of fornication is sexual relations between two non-married individuals. Most TV programs promote adultery. Almost all secular songs encourage either adultery or fornication. Whichever word choice you make, both are a work of the flesh and not acceptable.

UNCLEANNESS:
Uncleanness is a condition of impurity. This category includes but is not limited to Paul's day's prevalent acts under the Roman rule. The common types of uncleanness that Paul preached against were: sodomy, homosexuality/lesbianism, pederasty, bestiality, and all types of sexual perversion, especially those resulting in harm to the human body or abnormal use/abuse of the human body. This also included molestation, incest, and sexual abuse of minors. A lot of rap music promotes all of these areas. It is incredible how TV programs have begun to promote as "NORMAL LIFE" the homosexual/lesbian lifestyle or the Free-sex, open relationship affairs. Just use a condom, and it is OK!

LASCIVIOUSNESS:
This is behavior that is lustful, unchaste, and lewd. Lasciviousness is also considered the promotion of or the partaking in actions, events, etc., which tend to produce lewd emotions (like heavy petting between non-married individuals) or viewing things that make one desire or lust after sex or lewd things. This is the major reason most Christians have to avoid so many worldly pleasures; just so he/she will not commit lasciviousness.

IDOLATRY:
The act of image worship. In the Bible times, they worshipped idols made of wood, stone, gold, silver, bronze, and other precious stones. Today, people worship possessions and things that they hold to be dear to their hearts. An idol to a Christian is anything that takes first place in our hearts. God is to have first place, family second, and all others last. You can make

an idol out of a car, boat, or even money. If your job and desire to make money keep you out of church or reading and praying, then it is your idol.

WITCHCRAFT:

This is the practice of sorcery, dealing with evil spirits, magic, magical incantations, enchantments, séances, casting of spells, and charms by casting evil spirits or using mind-altering drugs or potions. These are all evil, regardless of the desired outcome. In other words, it does not justify the use of these methods if one is seeking love, good, health, or blessings for themselves or others. There are several programs now on prime-time TV that is promoting communications with the dead, using witches to solve crimes, using numerology, signs, stars, etc. Some programs promote "good-white witches" in their fight against evil and powers of darkness, right down to the harmless Disney ghost movies. No matter how clean and simple they are promoting a movie, turning to a source other than God for your knowledge and power is idolatry. If you encourage this type of TV programming to your children, do not get upset when they turn to drugs and the occult instead of God in their times of need. You will have planted the seed of witchcraft in their lives.

HATRED:

A state of mind or attitude whereby one is not forgiving or refuses to let go of ought, grudge, or desire revenge against an individual. This attitude is also characterized by bitterness, malice, ill-will, anger, abhorrence, or dislike toward another person. So much violence is seen on TV. This includes the video games that you let your children play with each day to "babysit" them. Choose other activities for them that are Bible-related.

VARIANCE:

A person with a personality trait or character trait loves dissension, discords quarreling, arguing, fighting, debating, and disputes. This also describes a person who thrives on chaos and confusion in groups or churches. They are categorized as a person who gets his/her way by stirring-up things. Many TV programs promote people using whatever methods necessary to get what they want in life regardless of who they have to hurt. This is planting a seed subconsciously in our children that violence is ok!

EMULATIONS:

This is a personality trait or character trait that is demonstrated by extreme displays of envying, jealousy, and deviant behavior to put down another person for the sake of lifting one to the top. In other words, a person who is always stepping on others, hurting them to get the promotion, the publicity or the reward/raise, etc. Some people call these individuals "zealous." However, their zeal goes above the bounds of motivation.

WRATH:

This personality trait or character trait is very noticeable due to the person's anger, indignation, resentment, and fierceness. They seek revenge or the public destruction of another individual. Violence on TV promotes not only hatred, variance, emulations, but also wrath and strife.

STRIFE:

A person who loves to create strife and conflict has a personality trait or character traits that love to see contention, disputing, and strife. It is usually a person who loves to publicly display angry words or start arguments and sit back and watch them mushroom. A person who loves strife also loves revenge and will show bitterness and hatred in their lives. Spend 15 minutes talking to them, and you will see their love for chaos if this work of the flesh is present in their lives.

SEDITIONS:

This is characterized by "divisions" or cliques in a group or church. A person with a sedition spirit loves to cause divisions and strife in a group or church to control the situation or outcomes. A popular definition for a person with a spirit of seditions is an individual who loves to cause disorder, disarray, and strife in religious groups, government, or the home.

HERESIES:

Heresies include false witnesses and accusations made against someone that are not true. Heresies' spread gossip and rumors as facts, thereby defaming another person's character, integrity, or honesty. See devotion on Gossip, busy-bodies, and look up bearing false witness.

ENVYING:

Envying is a character trait or emotion displayed by an individual that causes pain or ill will to others. It is an emotion that is jealous of the good or blessings that others are enjoying. It is the inability to show joy or thankfulness when others win or get what they desire or deserve. Envy is the base of all degrading and disgraceful passions in a person's life.

MURDERS:

A murder spirit is a person with an attitude or personality trait that desires to mar or destroy others' happiness and peace. A murderous attitude is an attitude of hate, an attitude that desires to "kill" good things for others. This also means to be a person who kills (murders) other human beings physically. See the violence on TV and in Rap music. Some rock and roll music is about cop killings, etc. too.

DRUNKENNESS:

Drunkenness is a state of being drunk or out of control of your everyday functions due to alcohol or mind-altering drugs that have caused a total loss of inhibitions. Many TV programs and secular music promotes drugs, alcohol, and smoking—all of these things harm the body.

REVELLINGS:

Revellings include rioting, lascivious and boisterous feastings with obscene music and their sinful activities like orgies. This was a widespread display of lewd behavior during the Roman rule over Israel, during Paul's days. How many times have you listened to secular music and heard at least five or six of these seventeen works of the flesh mentioned or promoted in a song? Almost every song! If you feed your mind, the very things that God says are an abomination and will not enter into heaven, then how are you going to be spiritually ready for the rapture? Why would you want to put things into your mind that God disapproves of…when you are trying to keep praise on your lips and in your heart for him? One of these will occupy your mind; most of the time, with gloomy, sinful thoughts, whereby Christian songs will feed good, peaceful, and positive thoughts to you all day.

How many times have you sat down and watched a movie or TV program and seen all of the seventeen works of the flesh demonstrated before your eyes? Plenty! Most "R" rated movies will include all of the works of the flesh. Even some PG-13 movies will show the majority of the works of the flesh. We should be on guard as to what we allow our minds to be fed. We need to know that if we watch it enough, listen to it enough, or discuss/talk about it enough, we will convince ourselves that It is ok. This is one of the "cunning tricks" of Satan to deceive us. He knows that we will eventually give in to our flesh's desires if we are slowly "desensitized" to it being a sin or something terrible. A person does not wake up today and say, "I am going to be an adulteress today. I am going to through away my marriage and children and walk away." No, it comes gradually over time. The simple jokes and sharing sessions can lead to something more. Then one day, you wake up and realize, "Oh no, I did not mean to get that involved! What happened to me?" You became desensitized to what was wrong with that situation. That is why the Bible says to shun the appearance of evil or evil communication. If we "hang around" with it…. after a while, it will not seem so bad!

DAY NINETEEN ASSIGNMENT

ASSIGNMENT FOR TODAY:

In addition to any notes or thoughts that you had about today's lesson; I want you to do the following:

1) Make a list of all the things you have been doing or listen to that violate God's commandment. You will notice how many of them have the works of the flesh in their lives.

2) Sit down with your spouse and your children and establish some guidelines for what will be watched, listened to, play, or games utilized in your home. Explain to your children why. Teach them this lesson. If you will take time to answer their questions so that there will not be any resentment to the new rule; It is a proven fact that if your children know and understand why they will come closer to complying without slipping around doing these things behind your back.

DAY TWENTY:

WHEN BAD THINGS HAPPEN TO GOOD PEOPLE

Hannah was the Jewish wife of Elkanah. Most of us recognize her name as the mother of the prophet Samuel. But in the beginning, Hannah was just a barren woman who could not give her husband any children. She was accused and made fun of by her husband's other wife because she could not provide Elkanah with sons, too. In her desperation, one day, Hannah cried out to the Lord to remove her reproach. She wanted a son so bad that she was willing to even bargain with God. Sometimes, God has a plan for us, yet he knows that we are not quite ready to listen or obey, so he has to resort to drastic measures to get our attention.

Under normal circumstances, Hannah would have never promised to give her son to the Lord as soon as he was weaned. But God knew that he wanted to provide Hannah with a son and that he had a divine plan for that Son. For that plan to be implemented fully, Samuel should be raised in the temple and groomed to take the prophet's place and position to Israel. So, God left Hannah barren until she cried out to him, sincerely. It started as a bad situation; I am confident her circumstances caused people to look at her and say, "poor Hannah." However, Hannah's faith never wavered. God heard her prayer, and her situation ended joyously with Hannah having a son, Samuel. Then Hannah gave Samuel to the Lord. Samuel became one of the greatest Old Testament prophets. Hannah was blessed with other children too! What looked terrible was just God working on his divine plan! Read the following verses about her prayerfulness.

I Samuel 1:10-11: *"And she was in bitterness of soul, and prayed unto the Lord, and wept sore. And she vowed a vow, and said, O Lord of hosts, if thou wilt indeed look on the affliction of thine handmaid, and remember me, and not forget thine handmaid, but wilt gives unto thine handmaid a man child, then I will give him unto the Lord all the days of his life, and there shall no razor come upon his head."* **Verses 27-28**: *"For this child, I prayed, and the Lord hath given me my petition which I asked of him: Therefore, also I have lent him to the Lord; as long as he lives, he shall be lent to the Lord. And he worshipped the Lord there."* *(KJV, 2020).*

This is a beautiful story of a mother's love and devotion to her Lord and Savior, to her first-born son, and her thankfulness for God's blessings on her life. When things looked terrible, God turned it around for good in her life! The hardest thing that we have to do is keep a positive attitude and stand in faith, claiming God's word over our lives' incidences. It is challenging for us to praise God when things are going wrong. It is even harder to praise God when you lose everything and do not see any hope in sight.

As I am revising this second edition, we are in the middle of the COVID-19 pandemic in America. Over 200,000 people have lost their lives, and millions are sick. This pandemic has affected millions around the world too. In the area where I live, we have buried 13 family members and close friends in the past six months. This is so hard to accept. We are seeing more people under 60 than over 60 dying from this horrible disease. Several family members have ruled this pandemic a "blessing" because this illness allowed their sons and daughters to get things right with God.

It would be better to have your health fail you and spend time preparing to die (including getting things right with God) than to live and miss the rapture! The destruction of the flesh for saving the soul is scriptural (we will discuss in a later chapter). Our ultimate goal in life should be to be ready to go in the rapture, no matter what happens!

Sometimes, we face trials, not because there is sin in our lives or things we need to change. Occasionally, we face difficulties because God is re-routing our direction to keep us from evil. Numerous times in my life, I have had something happen that would delay me from leaving on time. I would be upset that I was running late. Then I would almost get to my destination and see a horrible wreck that I would have been in if I had not been delayed.

We should never get angry or upset when God re-routes us, slows us, or changes our schedule for the day. Each time this happens, it is God protecting us. I pray every night about my schedule for the next day. I ask God to re-direct me as he desires, and I promise that I will not grumble. I ask him to keep me from evil and evil from me. This is a promise that I can stand on each day. God cares about everything in our lives, including our schedule! It is hard to give him control, but once you learn to let go, you can realize how much God really answers your prayers.

GOOD LUCK, BAD LUCK STORY, WHO CAN SAY?

One day I was at a church, and I heard a pastor tell a story about a Chinese man and his son. That story and its message were so powerful. I thought I would never forget the story. I am not sure where this pastor heard this story or if it is published anywhere else. I have searched for the story in its entirety and original form to share with you, but I have not been able to find it. I will share with you the parts that I can remember.

One day there was this Chinese man who owned a lot of land. He employed people to help him and his son with working in these rice fields. He had been blessed, and his crops always seemed to produce. He employed several people from his village. Then one day, war broke out in their country. All of the young men were being drafted. All of the sons in this village, including his son, received orders to report for training. They were all going to be sent to war in a couple of weeks. The son tries to help his Father get everything prepared and ready before he left for the war. He was up on a ladder repairing the roof when a rung (step) on the ladder broke, and he fell. As a result of that fall, he broke his leg. This seemed horrible because his son would not be able to go off to war. As the boys were leaving for war, people looked at the old Chinese man and said, "Oh my, what bad luck for his son?"

As time passed, the son's leg was not healing as fast as he desired. The son was not able to get around might less help his Father with his duties. So, the people still kept saying, "Oh my, what bad luck for the Father!" Then week by week, the boys all began coming home in body bags to be buried. The war was not going in favor of the people in this village. Each week there were more boys to bury for the people who worked for this little Chinese man. Each time they buried his village's son, this Chinese man would say a prayer for the family and thank God that his son was safe.

Then one day, the war was over, and the last body bag came home. The Chinese man realized that all of the boys that had left that village had died in that war. As he looked over the incident that happened to his son and all that it had cost him in medical bills, he looked up and said, "Good Luck, bad luck, who can say?"

Sometimes we look at a situation and think that it is bad luck, what is happening to us. There are times we even get angry at God and accuse him of being unfair. However, it is not him being unfair; it is God turning the bad into something good for us if we can only have the faith to believe in him and the patience to wait!

At times, people ask me if God allows bad things to happen to good people. I always say yes, and share this story with them. What you and I think is bad, maybe a miracle or blessing in disguise. Others have asked me if God allows us to suffer to get ready for his work or spread the gospel message. I always respond yes, and tell them the Story of Paul and his missionary journeys. As you read the book of Acts in your Bible studies, your faith will be built as you learn from Paul; a man who suffered much for the sake of spreading the gospel of Jesus Christ to the Gentiles.

Why does God allow this to happen? We may not always know the answer to this question. Sometimes, we do not understand why. At times, God tells us the why before we even face the trial, as he did with me when he prophesied that I was going to prison for a crime that I did not commit because he had a mission that he needed to send me on for him. He also wanted this book. If I had never gone to prison, I would have never had the motivation to put in writing this challenge. I would have never had the opportunity to use this challenge and witness to people who would not have ever gone to church.

If I had not gone to prison, I would not have written the book "*Living a Christian Life in Prison.*" A book that I hope and pray helps many men and women find their way to Jesus and helps them continue in that walk by faith with him. I am sure now of my standing with God. I have no questions in my mind or heart that I am ready for the Rapture. I am prepared to go if I should die tomorrow. What a small price, 25 ½ months in prison, were for the results that were obtained. **It would have been worth it for JUST ONE SOUL!**

One thing we all learn when we are in the period of "bad luck," we need Jesus more now than ever! We learn to lean on God, trust him, and pray more sometimes during the bad luck phases of our life. Praying more with a thankful heart is all that God wants from us…. our total commitment and total dedication to his purpose and plan for our lives.

Do not let bad luck turn you away. Good luck, bad luck, who can say?

DAY TWENTY ASSIGNMENT

ASSIGNMENT FOR TODAY:

In addition to any notes or thoughts that you had about today's lesson, I want you to make a list of the following things in your notebook and pray this list to God:

1) Take time today to thank the Lord for all of the things that he has done for you.

2) Make a list if you need to remind you what to thank the Lord for when you pray. Spend plenty of time praising him for all the times that he took something bad and turned it for good in your life.

DAY TWENTY-ONE:

WHY IS GOD SO CONFUSING?

Have you often wondered why so many religious things seemed confusing? Have you wondered why at times, it seems that even God conflicts himself? Do you find the topic of God confusing? Or have you wondered why life has to be complicated? I may not have the answer to all of these questions, but let me share something with you about God and his plans for man. I will even share a couple of examples in the Bible that appeared confusing initially, but there was a purpose in the end. Hopefully, after reading this lesson, you will understand God better, and the Bible will not be as confusing for you to read.

Job was a man that had served God all of his life. He had raised his family to love the lord also and to keep all of God's commandments. The Bible says that Job was **PERFECT and UPRIGHT** before the Lord. That is a very high commendation. Let me summarize what happened in Job's life and then look at the scriptures to support these findings. It appears that Job was a godly man, a loving father, and even though he was extremely wealthy, he had not been spoiled by his prosperity. He was not arrogant or deceitful in his dealings with others. Job was just and honest with the people who worked for him. Job dealt honestly in all business deals. He was the spiritual leader of his family and extended family.

One day, Satan entered into God's divine presence, asking why God showed special favor to Job. Satan told God that the only reason that Job served him was because of all of the gifts and blessings that he kept giving to Job. Satan challenged the Lord. "Let me tempt him, and you will see that he will curse you!" But God had faith in Job. God told Satan to do anything he wanted to Job, except take his life. God knew that Job's faith was genuine. So, God allowed Job to be tried to test that faith. How unfair does that seem?

If you have ever watched an exquisite jewelry maker of the purer gold (18-24Kt) prepare his gold for the making of necklaces or rings, you will be amazed by the process whereby he gets the gold to that 18 or 24 karat gold stage. First, the jeweler takes the gold bar and places it in a special-type pot placed over an open fire. Usually, it is a unique gadget that he has designed that will allow him to hang that pot on poles over the fire where he can pull up a chair or stool close by and watch the gold melt and become a liquid. Once the gold bar is liquid, he will begin to stir in that hot liquid with a special rod or stick that will not burn. He has to stir the liquid to release the impurities in the gold. Once the trash and impurities are loosened, they will float to the top. Then the jeweler takes a particular scooper and scoops up the trash, and discards it. He must continue to stir and pick out the trash until he has it all out of the pot.

The next step requires him to heat the gold to a temperature hot enough to burn out any other ores present. When I asked how long he had to continue to heat the gold after all of the trash was out, he responded to me, "It varies with each bar of gold. Some have more iron ore than others. Some gold chunks or bars are purer. However, the more ores present, the hotter I must get the mixture, and the longer it must cook." I asked if he had a special thermometer to use. He said no. It was my time to be puzzled. "Then how do you know when it is hot enough and when it has boiled long enough?" His answer shocked me!

"The gold is to a pure state (24kt) when the liquid is clear enough that I can see my reflection in the pot!"

Oh, how like our Savior! We are his gold. He must put us in the pot and bring us to a liquid state and get all of the trash out of us before he can craft us into designer jewelry for him. He must allow trials to test us and hardships to come our way, until when in the middle of the trial, when Satan has cranked the heat high…. Jesus looks over and sees his reflection in us!" We have to be pure gold for Jesus to use us. We cannot have any trash in our lives. We want more than anything else to be ready. So, what is a little testing if it will ensure that we are rapture ready?

Let us take a look at the scriptures about Job's character. You will notice he possessed the character traits of patience, longsuffering, complete trust in God, unwavering faith, and compassion. Job believed God knew what he was doing when he lost everything, and his children died. Job even remained true to his wholehearted commitment to God when his health failed him. The scriptures below support each of these character traits.

James 5:11: *"Behold, we count them happy which endure. Ye have heard of the patience of Job, and have seen the end of the Lord; that the Lord is very pitiful, and of tender mercy."* *(KJV, 2020).*

Job 1: 13-19: *"And there was a day when his sons and his daughters were eating and drinking wine in their eldest brother's house: And there came a messenger unto Job, and said, The oxen were plowing, and the asses feeding beside them: And the Sabeans fell upon them, and took them away; yea, they have slain the servants with the edge of the sword; and I only am escaped alone to tell thee. While he was yet speaking, there came also another, and said, the fire of God is fallen from heaven, and hath burned up the sheep, and the servants, and consumed them, and I only am escaped alone to tell thee. While he was yet speaking, there came also another, and said, The Chaldeans made out three bands, and fell upon the camels, and have carried them away, yea, and slain the servants with the edge of the sword; and I only am escaped alone to tell thee. While he was yet speaking, there came also another, and said, Thy sons and thy daughters were eating and drinking wine in their eldest brother's house: And, behold, there came a great wind from the wilderness and smote the four corners of the house, and it fell upon the young men, and they are dead, and I only am escaped alone to tell thee."*

Job 2:7-9: *"So went Satan forth from the presence of the Lord, and smote Job with sore boils from the sole of his foot unto his crown. And he took him a potsherd to scrape himself withal, and he sat down among the ashes. Then said his wife unto him, dost thou still retain thine integrity? Curse God, and die."*

Job's character and faith in God remained true when his friends no longer had sympathy for him. When his friends blamed him for what was happening and what had happened, Job still refused to curse God. In the end, Job's faith brought the victory he needed. In the scriptures below, read Job's answer to his friends.

Job 16:1-3: *"Then Job answered and said I have heard many such things: miserable comforters are ye all. Shall vain words have an end? Or what emboldened thee that thou answer?"* *(KJV, 2020).*

Job 19:1-27: *"Then Job answered and said, how long will you vex my soul? And break me in pieces with your words? These ten times have ye reproached me: ye are not ashamed that ye make yourselves strange to me? And be it indeed that I have erred, mine error remained with me. If indeed ye will magnify yourselves against me, and plead against me my reproach: Know now that God hath overthrown me, and hath compassed me with his* net. Behold, I cry out of wrong, but I am not heard: I cry aloud, but there is no judgment. He hath fenced up my way that I cannot pass, and he hath set darkness in my paths. He hath stripped me of my glory and taken the crown from my head. He hath destroyed me on every side, and I am gone: and mine hope hath he removed like a tree. He hath also kindled his wrath against me, and he counts me unto him as one of his enemies. His troops come together, and rise up against me, and encamp round about my tabernacle. He hath put my brethren far from me, and mine acquaintances are verily estranged from me. My kinsfolk has failed, and my familiar friends have forgotten me. They that dwell in mine house, and my maids, count me for a stranger: I am an alien in their sight. I called my servant, and he gave me no answer; I entreated him with my mouth. My breath is strange to my wife, though I entreated for the children's sake of mine own body. Yea, young children despised me; I arose, and they spoke against me. All my inward friends abhorred me: and they whom I loved are turned against me. My bone cleaves to my skin and to my flesh, and I am escaped with the skin of my teeth. Have pity upon me, have pity upon me, O ye my friends; for the hand of God hath touched me. Why do ye persecute me as God, and are not satisfied with my flesh? Oh, that my words were now written! Oh, that they were printed in a book! That they were graven with an iron pen and lead in the rock forever! For I know that my redeemer lives and that he shall stand at the latter day upon the earth: and though after my skin worms destroy this body, yet in my flesh shall I see God: Whom I shall see for myself, and mine eyes shall behold, and not another; though my reins be consumed within me." (KJV, 2020).

Job 30:1-10: "But now they that are younger than I have me in derision, whose fathers I would have disdained to have set with the dogs of my flock. Yea, whereto might the strength of their hands profit me, in whom old age was perished? For want and famine, they were solitary; fleeing into the wilderness in former time desolate and waste. Who cut up mallows by the bushes and juniper roots for their meat? They were driven forth from among men (they cried after them as after a thief;) To dwell in the cliffs of the valleys, in caves of the earth, and in the rocks. Among the bushes they brayed; under the nettles, they were gathered together. They were children of fools, yea, and children of base men: they were viler than the earth. And now am I their song, yea, I am their byword. They abhor me; they flee far from me, and spare not to spit in my face." (KJV, 2020).

When Job opened his heart back to the Lord, and God began to deal with him, instead of staying in his depressed state, he decided to pray for his deliverance and pray for his friends. Victory is always won when we turn to help others and stop worrying about our issues, needs, or problems. God does not tolerate selfishness in our lives. See how God responded to Job!

Job 42:10: *"And the Lord turned the captivity of Job when he prayed for his friends…. the Lord gave Job twice as much as he had before." (KJV, 2020).*

Job's victory was remarkable. God restored to Job everything that he had lost, double-fold. He restored to him seven more children too. Job's second phase of his life was more blessed than the first phase. All because Job refused to give up. He held onto his faith in God even when things looked bad!

Job 42:11-13: *"Then came there unto him all his brethren, and all his sisters, and all they that had been of his acquaintance before, and did eat bread with him in his house: and they bemoaned him, and comforted him over all the evil that the Lord had brought upon him: every man also gave him a piece of money, and every one an earring of gold. So, the Lord blessed the latter end of Job more than his beginning: for he had fourteen thousand sheep, and six thousand camels, and a thousand yoke of oxen, and a thousand she asses. He had also seven sons and three daughters." (KJV, 2020).*

Job stood steadfast to his faith in God. Even when he thought God was confusing, even when he believed God had been unfair to him, Job still said, "I will serve him!" Job knew that he served the one true God. He knew what his God had done for him in the past. If his God never worked another miracle for him, he knew he would still serve him for all the past blessings. This was an honorable trait in Job. One that God rewarded. **Job had NEVER-THE-LESS-FAITH.** It did not matter what came or went in his life. He knew his God would move again. Job had his mind made up that regardless of what happened to him, he would always serve God, and he would forever praise God in every circumstance. It is like the song that Karen Wheaton (1989) sings, "I may not know how, I may not know when, but I know he will do it again!" This song was written by Dawn Thomas (UKN), now known as *Constant Change*. I looked for the original copyrighted sheet music for this song but could not find it. However, the way Karen Wheaton sings this song, you walk away understanding that even though we may not know when or how we can be guaranteed one thing, we are God's children, and he will move for us, no matter what we are facing. Does who we are, where we live, or what we are suffering impact God's response? No, we are his children, and God will not leave us! God will always be there with us through everything if we ask him.

Do not let the test of your faith in God cause you to walk away. Do not let Satan make you think God is confusing. It may appear so on the surface, but he is not. He is the Lord God Jehovah. He is the Alpha and the Omega, the beginning and the end; he is the victor! We must be like the words of the Song, "Shackled" recorded by "Mary, Mary," (2007), "I have been down for so long, it seems that all hope is going, but as I raise my hands, I seem to understand that all I have to do is praise him through my circumstance....so take these shackles off my feet so I can dance....cause I want to praise, yes, I want to praise him!" This is all that he wants out of us...our praise...even through the rough times!

DAY TWENTY-ONE ASSIGNMENT

ASSIGNMENT FOR TODAY:

In addition to any notes or thoughts that you had about today's lesson, I want you to make a list of the following things in your notebook and pray this list to God:

1) Make a list of the things about God that you do not understand.

2) Use this list as a guide for your Bible Studies. Start Searching God's word for the answer to these things about God that puzzles you.

3) Make a list of questions you would like to ask God if you were the person that the news media asked to be the person to conduct the live TV Interview of God or Jesus.

4) Make sure you list everything you could think about to ask God.

DAY TWENTY-TWO:

WHY IS LIFE SO UNFAIR?

Sometimes we feel like life is so unfair to us. We feel like everyone is against us and that nothing is going to work out for us. Do you have days that you feel like for every step forward you take that you take five steps backward? We all do! But even though we feel that life is unfair, we must remember a few basic principles.

1) God has a divine plan and purpose for our lives.

2) If we live right and obey his commandments, he will not allow anything to harm us or destroy us, no matter what we go through.

3) God will never leave us or forsake us. He will always be with us in our trials.

4) Sometimes God lets bad then happen or what we say is bad luck, keeping us from an even greater danger or mistake.

5) What evil men and women do to us to harm us; God will utilize for our benefit.

6) There are times that God is only testing our faith in Him and our patience. So do not fail the test. Do not become discouraged because life seems unfair. Just ask him what he wants you to do for him in this trial or learn through it. There is ALWAYS a purpose for everything that we go through.

Many times, I have heard people ask why God didn't stop evil from happening to them. God is a longsuffering and merciful God. He does not **MAKE** anyone follow his commandments. Because God has placed in each of us a "will" and given us the right to choose good or evil, God will never force a man or woman to be good. It is our choice. Because God does not enforce it 100% of the time that "good rules" or "good wins over evil," people think that God is unfair. However, God is not unjust; he is merely allowing us the right to choose. It is up to us. So, make the choice today that it will always be "good or the right path" for you; always strive to be right through Jesus; always be what God wants in your life!

DAY TWENTY-TWO ASSIGNMENT

ASSIGNMENT FOR TODAY:

In addition to any notes or thoughts that you had about today's lesson, I want you to make a list of the following things in your notebook and pray this list to God:

1) Pray over all prayer lists and to-do lists from this challenge so far.

2) Ask God to show you someone that you can go to and encourage that is feeling down. Let God use you to help someone who feels like life is so unfair right now, to realize that God is there for them!

DAY TWENTY-THREE:

THE JONES TRAP

Are you the type of person that has to have everything you see? Do you go shopping with no intention of maxing out the credit cards but come home with loads of bags of things that you got on sale that were good buys, but not necessarily NEEDS? Every time you see one of your friends with a new electronic gadget or a new dress or the latest designer shoes and purse, do you start scheming to figure out a way to squeeze that into your budget or charge it to your credit card? Do you feel that you must have a luxury car on the latest model every couple of years?

Have you noticed that the more you get, the more you think that you need, or the more you desire? Each time you go into debt for a new vehicle, as soon as the new wears off or one of your friends buy something bigger, better, or more unique. Then you start "shopping" again to trade your last purchase off? You are never content with anything that you purchase. I heard one lady describe herself in one of my study groups one day. She said, "Well, I have swapped and traded everything in my life at some point except my kids!" Are you this type? Are you unhappy and never satisfied? There is a solution!

Let us define discontentment and dissatisfaction. We will take a look at what the Bible says about both of these conditions. Then we will look at covetousness. This is the condition that results from discontentment and dissatisfaction. **Discontentment** is mentioned in the Bible, where men have become so disappointed with God that they complained to him. If you would like to read those stories, read the following chapters in the Bible: **Job 10; Job 23; Psalms 55; Psalms 77 and Psalms 142**. I find that no one could say it better than King David in Psalms. It seems that when I am feeling down that, I can go to the book of Psalms. King David always seems to write psalms that precisely describe how I feel or the questions I have of God.

Dissatisfaction is an emotional condition that has been around for a long time. In all his riches and glory, King Solomon reigned over Israel, was discontented and dissatisfied with his life. (Bible History tells us that King Solomon was the richest man to have lived at that time). King Solomon had everything, yet, nothing satisfied him.

Ecclesiastes 2:11: *"Then I looked on all the works that my hands had wrought and on the labor that I had labored to do and behold all was vanity and vexation of spirit, and there was no profit under the sun."* (KJV, 2020).

Oh my, what a powerful statement from the Richest man on earth! Money could not buy him happiness, nor satisfy that longing in his soul for his creator. King Solomon's problem was that his heart longed for a relationship with God. That is the only thing that brings complete satisfaction to our lives and homes.

Once you allow discontentment and dissatisfaction to take over, a few more of their friends move in. These friends are known as envy, jealousy, greed, covetousness, and finally, discouragement arrives. Once Discouragement moves in, we begin looking for reasons to miss church and ways to avoid our "church family & friends." Let us take a look at the main one in this group. **Covetousness** is a feeling or emotion that is a cousin to jealousy. It is a feeling of envy of the personal possession or prosperity or relationships of another person. To covet another person's possession is not only a sin but leads to the implementation of other spirits into your life.

Exodus 20:17: *"Thou shalt not covet thy neighbor's house; thou shall not covet thy neighbors' wife, nor his manservant, nor his maidservant, nor his ox, nor his ass, nor anything that is thy neighbors." (KJV, 2020).*

Jeremiah 6:13: *"For from the least of them even unto the greatest of them every one is given to covetousness; and from the prophet, even unto the priest every one dealt falsely." (KJV, 2020).*

Luke 12:15: *"And he said unto them take heed, and beware of covetousness; for a man's life consisteth not in the abundance of the things which he possesseth." (KJV, 2020).*

The spirit of discontentment is one of the snares or traps used by Satan to keep us occupied with other things. If you are continually looking for something, searching, planning, conniving, and scheming to try to get something, then you do not have time to read, pray, and study God's word. That is all Satan wants…. keep you from God's word. Satan hates the Bible more than anything else on earth. If he can keep you from reading and praying, then he can attach spirits to your life that will keep you from growing spiritually. Which makes us unhappy, discontent, and dissatisfied. Eventually, Satan will be able to drive you away from God.

This condition, I call the "Jones Trap" (*a cousin to the spirit of greed*), is a condition or spirit that Satan uses to destroy you, your home, and your children. It will take you to a place in your life where you do not want to be; it will cost you more than you are willing to pay, and it will usually bring you down in life and keep you a lot longer than you thought ever possible.

Most of the ladies I talked with in prison admitted that they would not have been caught with their crimes if it had not been for greed. They had to make one more dope run, steal one more person's ID, make one more fake bank loan, just one more, that is all they needed, and they would quit! Well, that last, "one more" got them caught! This is Satan's best quality, deception! He convinces you, just one more night of fun, one more illegal event, then you can stop or just one more affair or one more thing you need. You must remember that anything Satan uses on you or causes to happen in your life is for one reason; it is to draw you away from the cross, to put a barrier between you and God, and to destroy your relationship with Jesus Christ. So, do not let him win! Decide today that you will not fall into the "Jones' Trap." You can learn to be content as Paul said he was "in whatsoever state he was in."

LEARN TO SACRIFICE:

It is ok to do without something sometimes, just to prove to yourself that you can. If you feel that there is something in your life that you must have every week or a luxury that you feel that you cannot do without each day, prove to yourself that you can by "fasting or sacrificing" that luxury for a week. If you cannot go for a week without it, you are addicted, and it has become an idol.

Avoid the snares that Satan sets financially for people. The majority of people who will read this book are from middle-class families. You have to live on a budget to make all of the payments you have and keep food on the table. If Satan can get you borrowing all the money, you can get, mortgaging everything, and maxing out all of the credit cards, and then he is on his way to destroying your home. The number one cause for divorce in American families is financial difficulties that result in discontentment, dissatisfaction, and usually, one or both having an affair. Do not set yourself up. Do not let Satan snare you in the oldest trap in the world…. the money traps! Be a good steward of your money. For women, read the **31st Proverb.** It tells you the duties of the wife/mother.

For men, your instructions for being the head of the house and your family's spiritual and financial leader are scattered in every book in the New Testament. Study it, learn it, and let God show you what to do as a husband to direct your family and keep you out of financial trouble. Is it so bad to not have something? Is it so bad to wait a month or two to get something and pay for it, versus charging it and paying interest now?

DAY TWENTY-THREE ASSIGNMENT

ASSIGNMENT FOR TODAY:

In addition to any notes or thoughts that you had about today's lesson, I want you to make a list of the following things in your notebook and pray this list to God:

1) Sit down with your spouse and commit to each other that you will consult with the other before making significant purchases.

2) Agree with your spouse not to charge anything else unless it is a bare essential that is needed or parts for the car or garage bill, etc., that is necessary so that you can go to work.

3) When you see something you want, make a list. Then discuss with your spouse before purchasing. Use each other as "double checks" to prevent yourself from becoming involved in "impulse buying." This will also keep you from walking into the "Jones' Trap" with buying everything because your neighbor or friend has it.

DAY TWENTY-FOUR:

MATERIALISM AND IDOLS

Are you a workaholic who is obsessed with everything being organized and perfect? Are you sure, or are you just an entrepreneur American caught in the trap of Materialism? The side effects are the same. At times we classify our problems as workaholics when we are just addicted to materialism or have acquired idols in our lives that need to be torn down.

MATERIALISM:

There are many examples of materialism; and the nasty attitudes and deceit that it brings to a person's life in the Bible. In the New Testament, you will note that the Sadducees made decisions about the synagogue based on materialism. Some decisions were made based on the Roman government's promises to them. The synagogue leaders made selfish political choices at times. Their hearts were not always searching for what was best for the synagogues. I want to look at a scripture that addresses materialism from the church leader's perspective.

The Sadducees were concerned about two things. 1) Tricking Jesus into discrediting himself, and 2) Controlling Jesus' popularity. They feared Jesus' fame was growing, and they were losing control. The leaders did not want anything hindering them from collecting money. They felt the need to protect their temple's revenue streams by discredit Jesus' words.

Matthew 22:23: *"The same day came to him the Sadducees, which say that there is no resurrection, and asked him, saying, Master, Moses said, if a man dies, having no children, his brother shall marry his wife, and raise up seed unto his brother. Now there were with us seven brethren: and the first when he had married a wife, deceased, and, having no issue, left his wife unto his brother: Likewise, the second also, and the third, unto the seventh. And then, at last, the woman died also. Therefore, in the resurrection, whose wife shall she be of the seven? For they all had her. Jesus answered and said unto them; Ye do err, not knowing the scriptures or the power of God …. have ye not read that which was spoken unto you by God, saying, I am the God of Abraham, and the God of Isaac, and the God of Jacob? God is not the God of the dead but of the living." (KJV, 2020).*

These Sadducees were so afraid of losing their control over the people and the financial impact that it would have on the money coming into the synagogue that they willed harm toward Jesus versus lose anything themselves. This was a sad state for them to be spiritually. However, if we are not careful, Satan will lead us into this same trap, making us lust after and covet what everyone else has in their lives and homes. Our desires should be toward spiritual things, ministry, and seeing souls saved. These things should be more important to us than personal financial wealth and earthly possessions. It is ok to have the things you need. It is ok to enjoy something that God blesses you with in your life. However, you should not "desire" them more than God or allow those things to keep you from God's purpose and plan for your life. The scriptures below explain to us what our spiritual desires should be and what to expect them.

SPIRITUAL DESIRES:

II Chronicles 15:15: *"And all Judah rejoiced at the oath; for they had sworn with all their hearts and sought him with their whole desire, and he was found of them, and the Lord gave them rest round about." (KJV, 2020).*

Isaiah 26:9: *"With my soul have I desired thee in the night; yea, with my spirit within me, will I see thee early; for when thy judgments are in the earth, the inhabitants of the world will learn righteousness." (KJV, 2020).*

Luke 6:21: *"Blessed are ye that hunger now, for ye shall be filled. Blessed are ye that weep now, for ye shall laugh." (KJV, 2020).*

Psalms 42:2: *"My soul thirsts for God for the living God; when shall I come and appear before God?" (KJV, 2020).*

Psalms 63:1: *"O God, thou are my God, early will I seek thee, my soul thirsts for thee my flesh longs for thee in a dry and thirsty land, where no water is." (KJV, 2020).*

Have you found that you are too busy to enjoy life? Are your finding your home and life a constant whirlwind of chaos and confusion? Do you feel or does your family tell you that you only survive on adrenaline or in crisis management mode? You need to stop and ask yourself one question today. Has materialism mastered me, or am I the master of my life?

We must learn to put God first. We must slow down and take time to focus. We must not lose sight of God's purpose and plan for our lives. Listed below are some scriptures on spiritual bondage for you to think about today. You do not want to be in this condition. You do not want "things" controlling you. You do not want "idols" in your life, pulling you from God.

SPIRITUAL BONDAGE:

John 8:34: *"Jesus answered them, Verily, Verily, I say unto you, whosoever committed sin is the servant of sin."* *(KJV, 2020).*

Acts 8:23: *"For I perceive that thou art in the fall of bitterness and in the bond of iniquity."* *(KJV, 2020).*

Romans 6:16: *"Know ye, not that unto who ye yield yourselves servants to obey, his servants ye are to whom ye obey; whether of sin unto death or of obedience unto righteousness?"* *(KJV, 2020).*

Romans 7:23: *"But I see another law in my members, warring against the law of my mind and bringing them into captivity to the law of sin which in my members."* *(KJV, 2020).*

II Timothy 2:23: *"and that they may recover themselves out of the snare of the devil that is taken captive by him at his will."* *(KJV, 2020).*

II Peter 2:19: *"While they promise them liberty, they themselves are the servants of corruption; for of whom a man is overcome of the same is he brought into bondage."* *(KJV, 2020).*

COMMANDMENTS TO PUT AWAY YOUR IDOLS:

Here is a list of scriptures that you can read on your own time that deals with God's commandments to put anything away from us that could be considered an idol.   Read these when you have a chance.

Genesis 35:2   Joshua 24:14   I Samuel 7:3

I Kings 15:12   II Kings 3:2   II Kings 23:24   II Chronicles 15:8

There is nothing wrong with being blessed with material things; having a home, a career, or unique things in life for your family. Where the sin comes in is when you allow these things or jobs to pull you away from God when they take first place in your life, and your focus on your purpose becomes clouded. We should not allow Satan to snare us in his trap of materialism. If you have been caught in this trap, pray and ask God to help you get out of the situation you are in and promise him that you will not allow yourself to get back into that position again.   Once you are free from the "spirit of materialism," you will find that you can grow spiritually and be blessed beyond your wildest dreams. God only wants you to desire the spiritual gifts he gives more than the gifts of this world. There is no reason to be in spiritual bondage or bond to your "idols." You can enjoy a relationship with God, spiritual blessing, and materialism when they come in this order and through God. God desires that we should prosper, even as our soul prospers.

DAY TWENTY-FOUR ASSIGNMENT

ASSIGNMENT FOR TODAY:

In addition to any notes or thoughts that you had about today's lesson, I want you to make a list of the following things in your notebook and pray this list to God:

1) Make a list of the things that have kept you out of church for the past six months. This is true even for the inmates reading this book. Why have you not gone to the chapel services?

2) Analyze each one and determine whether it was an emergency, a necessity, or materialism pulling you away.

3) If you found "things" that were pulling you away, pray over them, and ask God to show you what he wants you to do about them so that they will not control your life.

DAY TWENTY-FIVE:

TOO BUSY FOR GOD

Gideon was a judge in Israel. He was called a mighty man of valor. He was the son of Joash, of the tribe of Manasseh. In Gideon's day, the children of Israel were being terrorized by Midianite robbers throughout the country. Gideon was a prophet sent to the children of Israel to rebuke their sinful lifestyles and turn their hearts back to the one true God of Heaven!

Gideon had not planned to lead the children of Israel until the Lord sent an angel to him in the 6th chapter of Judges in the Old Testament. Gideon made every excuse that he could to try to get out of this assignment. He told the Lord that Israel had forsaken him and that he was unfit to take the message to them that God wanted Gideon to take.

If Gideon had been here today, he would have been telling God that he was busy with his business and farm. It was already too much on him; besides, the people would not listen anyway! I can hear him telling God, "You see, they have all of the money they need, Lord, good jobs, nice vehicles to drive, and money to spend. They would rather be at the beach this weekend or on the river. What makes you think that they want to hear anything that I have to say about you?" We tell God every time he leads us to do something special for him, and we make excuses for why we cannot. We think of all the excuses we can. Our three most favorite ones are:

1) God, I am too busy; plus, you have made my load too heavy. I do not have time.

2) God, these people are too busy to participate. They will not listen.

3) It would be a waste of my time even to try to start this project!

4) We act like God has never done anything before on earth. We then start with all of the other reasons why. Usually, the prime one is, I do not have the money, or I am not educated enough to do that, Lord!

THE CHARACTER OF GIDEON

Let us take a look at the character of Gideon. Why did God choose him? What was there about Gideon that made God insist that Gideon was the right man for this job? God had his reasons; they were Gideon's humility, caution, obedience, and love for God.

1) The first characteristic mentioned was **Humility**: (Judges 6:15) Gideon went humbly before the Lord. He did not feel worthy of being the one selected for this position of Leadership.

2) The second was **Caution**: (Judges 6:1). Gideon made sure that he understood what God wanted him to do. He did not take counsel with others. He sought God's will and made sure that he understood what God wanted.

3) The third was Gideon's desire and love for God or his **Spirituality**: (Judges 6:24) Gideon shows his steadfast faith in God.

4) The fourth characteristic of Gideon's personality that impressed God was his **Obedience:** (Judges 6:27) Gideon obeyed the Lord in every situation, even if he did not understand what God was doing. He did not question God; he just obeyed. God cannot use a man or woman that will not listen to him and obey his commandments.

There were other characteristics in Gideon's behavior that were considered outstanding. These included divine inspiration, divine fellowship, strategic planning, tactfulness, loyalty to God, and trust in God. Let us look at each of these characteristics.

DIVINE INSPIRATION:

Judges 6:34: There is no question that the Lord was leading Gideon.

DIVINE FELLOWSHIP:

(Judges 6:36, 7:4; 7:7; 7:9): With the fleeces Gideon placed before the Lord, it is obvious that Gideon shared a unique relationship with God. He was not ashamed to go to his master, talk to him, or even question him with humility.

STRATEGY:

Judges 7:16-18: Gideon was a man with a strategy…. the man with the plan.

TACTFULNESS:

<u>Judges 8:1-3:</u> Gideon knew how to handle touchy situations effectively.

LOYALTY TO GOD:

<u>Judges 8:22-23</u>: There was no question of Gideon's loyalty to God and his total commitment to God's purpose and plan.

WEAKENED BY PROSPERITY:

<u>Judges 8:24-31:</u> God showed Gideon that sometimes he has to weaken us, bring us down, or cut down our size to use us. If we have excess baggage in our lives, we cannot be effective. In Gideon's case, he had too many men. These men did not have faith. They were dragging the others down.

We need to have the character of Gideon. He was a man that was not too busy to listen to God. Gideon was never too busy to pray and seek God's will on issues. You cannot be too busy to have a relationship with God if you want his peace, help, and blessings. These things cannot be accomplished in our lives if we are utilizing "little white lies," deceitfulness, and promises that we never intended on fulfilling when we made them manipulate people to do what we want. We must have honesty and integrity in our lives. We must spend time with God to have a relationship with him, grow spiritually, and be blessed.

There are two traits/actions that God will not accept in our lives. If you have a problem with either of these, pray and ask him to help you. He will lead you and guide you daily. God is longsuffering; however, after a while, he will not continue to overlook these two traits and will draw you aside to be tested and tried to see if, after you walk through the refiner's fire, whether or not you can lay these down.

The first one is lying. Lying is the act of telling something or making a statement that is not true, or it can be a false statement that is said as a statement of fact. Even leading someone to believe something other than the truth is considered lying.

The second one is deceitfulness. Deceitfulness is the act or attitude whereby a person plans to deceive another individual or group. Deception is created when we say something that causes another person to believe something other than the truth. Deceitfulness can also mean the twisting of facts in a fashion whereby it "deceives" them into making the wrong conclusions or assumptions.

Do not allow yourself to be so "busy" with what you want, your ways, and personality traits that you do not have time for God to lead and guide you each day. You want to make time to pray and talk with God each day, then time to read his word and hear what he has to say back to you. You cannot afford to be too busy not to read and pray. There are also many things that Satan wants to involve you in. Satan's goal is to trap you. Sometimes Satan uses our closest friends and family. We tend to overlook them and not even pray and ask God if we should get involved or not. Do not let your schedule get so full…. that there is no place for God!

DAY TWENTY-FIVE ASSIGNMENT

ASSIGNMENT FOR TODAY:

In addition to any notes or thoughts that you had about today's lesson; I want you to do the following:

1) Take time to meditate upon God's word today.

2) Take time to analyze your schedule and see what is important

3) Make a list or notes of areas that you feel you may need to make some changes in or adjustments in schedules. It may take you a few weeks to clear some things out of your life. So, make a list and start tackling them one by one.

DAY TWENTY-SIX:

WHEN TO TALK, WHEN TO LISTEN

One of the hardest things for us to do in life is to "shut up and listen." We all have problems in this area. It is human nature to give your opinion about whatever topic is being discussed. It is hard to realize that sometimes we are more effective witnesses if we stop talking and just listen to what is being said around us. We don't need to explain ourselves to everyone or explain every situation to the people around us, even though we feel that we needed to make sure that everyone knows the "truth!"

Sometimes, our arrogant attitudes drive us to the point of making sure that everyone knows our points. Everyone knows what we know or how great we are…. this is the opposite of what God wants for us. He wants humility and the fruits of the spirit in our lives, not arrogance, not pride, not conceit or haughtiness.

HUMILITY

Let us take a look at what the scriptures say about humility. The Bible is full of scriptures that continuously remind us of our need to have humility in our lives in all aspects.

Proverbs 16:19: *"Better it is to be of a humble spirit with the lowly Than to divide the spoil with the proud."* (KJV, 2020).

Proverbs 22:4: *"By humility and the fear of the Lord are riches and honor and life."* (KJV, 2020).

Proverbs 29:23: *"A man's pride shall bring him low, but honor shall uphold the humble in spirit."* (KJV, 2020).

Isaiah 57:15: *"For thus saith, the high and lofty one that inhabited eternity, who name is Holy; I dwell in the high and holy place with him also that is of a contrite and humble spirit to revive the spirit of the humble…. revive the heart of the contrite."* (KJV, 2020).

Matthew 18:4: *"Whosoever, therefore, shall humble himself as this little child, the same is greatest in the kingdom of heaven." (KJV, 2020).*

The Bible is also full of **examples of humble people:** There are numerous examples of people in the Bible that, with the help of the Holy Spirit, mastered the trait of humility in their lives. Some of them suffered a lot before they got to this place of humility. However, they are examples for us. We can do this! We can change! The Holy Spirit is there to help us through each step of this process.

JACOB:

Genesis 32:10: *"I am not worthy of the least of all of the mercies and of all the truth which thou hast shown unto thy servant for with my staff I passed over this Jordan, and now I am become, two bands." (KJV, 2020).*

KING SAUL:

I Samuel 9:21: *"And Saul answered and said, am not I a Benjamite of the smallest of the tribes of Israel, and my family the least of all the families of the tribe of Benjamin? Wherefore then speaketh thou so to me?" (KJV, 2020).*

KING DAVID:

II Samuel 7:18: *"Then went King David in and sat before the Lord and he said who am I Oh Lord God? And what is my house that thou hast brought me hitherto?" (KJV, 2020).*

KING SOLOMON:

I King 3:7: *"and now O lord my God thou hast made thy servant king instead of my father David, and I am but a little child. I know not how to go out or to come in." (KJV, 2020).*

JOHN THE BAPTIST:

Matthew 3:14: *"But John forbade him, saying I have need to be baptized of thee and comes thou to me?" (KJV, 2020).*

THE CENTURION:

Matthew 8:8: *"The centurion answered and said, Lord, I am not worthy that they should come under my roof, but speak the word only, and my servant shall be healed."* *(KJV, 2020).*

SPIRITUAL BONDAGE:

Spiritual Bondage is not one of the character traits that God wants in our lives. He wants us to be humble and obedient, but not under spiritual bondage of fear. The Bible lists several scriptures that explain the types of spiritual bondage and what to look for to prevent becoming one of its victims.

John 8:34: *"Jesus answered them, Verily, Verily, I say unto you, whosoever committed sin is the servant of sin."* *(KJV, 2020).*

Acts 8:23: *"For I perceive that thou art in the fall of bitterness and in the bond of iniquity."* *(KJV, 2020).*

Romans 6:16: *"Know ye, not that into who ye yield yourselves servants to obey, his servants ye are to whom ye obey; whether of sin unto death or of obedience unto righteousness?"* *(KJV, 2020).*

Romans 7:23: *"But I see another law in my members, warring against the law of my mind and bringing them into captivity to the law of sin which in my members."* *(KJV, 2020).*

II Timothy 2:23: *"and that they may recover themselves out of the snare of the devil that is taken captive by him at his will."* *(KJV, 2020).*

II Peter 2:19: *"While they promise them liberty, they themselves are the servants of corruption; for of whom a man is overcome of the same is he brought into bondage."* *(KJV, 2020).*

If you allow the Holy Spirit to lead and direct you, you will know when to talk and listen. You will know when to present with a meek and humble spirit. There are times and situations when it is best to listen and not speak…. especially those situations that tempt us to argue with the other person. This does not mean to sulk or pout. Those two traits are not acceptable either. But there are times just to nod and walk away with the right attitude.

I found that when I want to rip someone's head off or throw something at them, if I can find the strength to smile, say OK, and walk away, I can remain humble. Even when I was not OK with the outcome, I found that it was easier for me to go to my special place and do some serious praying over the issue once I left. Serving God is not always easy. We cannot always get other people to change their minds. I have found that if I pray over it, sometimes these individuals will change their minds. They do not always know what happened to cause them to change! But God does! It is always best when God does the persuading and not us! So yes, there are times that it is best to listen. Then there are times when we must speak up and stand up for what is right. The Holy Spirit will guide you if you allow him to talk to you each day. God is concerned about our daily schedule and duties. He wants to lead us in all aspects of our lives. But we must submit to God's will.

DAY TWENTY-SIX ASSIGNMENT

ASSIGNMENT FOR TODAY:

In addition to any notes or thoughts that you had about today's lesson, I want you to make a list of the following things in your notebook and pray this list to God:

1) Pray over the list of the people that have hurt you and make sure that you do not have any un-forgiveness in your heart. Ask God to give you a heart of humility.

2) Review your list and determine if you need to get a release from anger from anyone on this list. If you do, then write them a letter. Ask their forgiveness and tell them you have become a Christian. Do not let anything or anyone hinder you from God's blessings on your life.

DAY TWENTY-SEVEN:

FASTING

According to Dictionary.com (2020), fasting is "an abstinence from food, or a limiting of one's food, especially when voluntary and as a religious observance." There are numerous references to fasting in the Bible. Several types of fasting can be done. We will discuss the purpose of fasting, the benefits, and the types of fasting in this lesson.

Why is fasting necessary? Fasting is a specific sacrifice that one makes to prove to God that nothing in life is more important than him. Usually, we fast food because it seems to be a significant factor in most Americans' lives. However, you can fast TV or radio for a week. You can fast getting massages, spa treatments, manicures, etc., for a week or a month. If you can prove to God that you can live without something for a week or two, then you have proved to him that it is not an IDOL in your life. This is the most crucial concept of fasting. Proving to you, Satan, and God that you do not have any other Gods before God Almighty!

Is fasting scriptural? Yes. There are numerous times that fasting is mentioned in the Bible and many different types of fast performed in the Bible. On one day, King David wanted a drink of water from the well of a particular city so badly. When one of his men brought him that water, he sacrificed the water to the Lord by pouring it out onto the ground as he prayed and made his request to the Lord.

If you want to do more research on fasting, then you can read the following scriptures and look at the commentary notes in the back of your Bible for these verses and the topic of *"fasting."*

Isaiah 58:6-14   Mark 2:18-20   II Corinthians 12:9-10

Growing in faith through fasting: Matthew 17:14-21

Early church practice of fasting: Acts 13:1-3, and Acts 14:21-23.

The Daniel Fast: Daniel 10:2-3: (we are going to discuss this type of fast in detail).

WHAT IS THE PURPOSE OF THE FAST?

Fasting is an act of sacrifice to show our humility, our ability to sacrifice and prove that we do not have any idols in our lives, taking 1st place instead of God. The purpose of the fast is to prove that you do not have any idols in your life and nothing in your life has more control over you than God. When we sacrifice or fast, we show God that we want what we are praying over or requesting from him **VERY MUCH**. We get God's attention with our fast. It also humbles us! Yes, it is essential to fast for this reason. We gain control over our own life, our eating habits, and desires. We prove to ourselves, Satan and God, that we do not have any other idols before him, not even the idol of "selfishness," because fasting is the ultimate demonstration of self-sacrifice.

<u>Types</u>: **There are numerous types of fast. The most popular five types are listed below.**

1) **<u>Total Fast</u>**- no water and no food. The hardest of all types of fast. This is usually only selected for a meal and no more than for a day.

2) **<u>Food Fast</u>**—Liquids Only. No solid foods. This can include all liquids, milkshake (no more than 1 per day), and juices, but no solid foods or soups. This fast can be done for more extended periods but not recommended for longer than seven days.

3) **<u>Partial or Juice Fast</u>**: A fast where solid foods are decreased to soups and salads only with liquids and juices. This type of fast can be done for more extended periods, even up to 30-40-Days, provided you ensure that you get your essential vitamins and minerals to prevent dehydration.

4) **<u>Daniel Fast</u>**: This fast allows fruit and vegetables with liquids. No meats and no American bread. Arabic bread with hummus or tahini is used with this fast in the Middle East or Arabic/Jewish families. No sweets. One milkshake per day or a glass of milk is allowed.

5) **<u>Addictive items Sacrifice Fast</u>**: You may fast a luxury that you have, an event you feel that you cannot live without attending, TV or radio, or anything else that you find you just think you must have every day or every week. I have seen people "sacrifice" their manicure, massage, and spa treatment for a week and take the money that they would have spent on those items and donate them to a local mission, outreach program, or missionaries at their church. I have also seen people addicted to Diet Coke decide that they would not drink diet coke for two to three weeks. They were going to prove to themselves that they could live without the cokes and lay their sacrifice before the Lord with their petitions/requests.

Why is it important to fast? What will I gain from fasting? Does the Bible even mention fasting as a requirement of Christianity? The Bible lists several scriptures on fasting.

Joel 1:14: "*Sanctify ye a fast, call a solemn assembly, gather the elders and all of the inhabitants of the land into the house of the Lord your God and cry out unto the Lord.*" *(KJV, 2020).*

Joel 2:12: "*Therefore also now, saith the Lord, turn you even to me with all of your heart and with fasting and with weeping and with mourning.*" *(KJV, 2020).*

Matthew 6:17: "*But thou, when thou fast, anoint thine head and wash thy face that thou appear not unto men to be fasting, but unto God which is in secret.*" *(KJV, 2020).*

There are also examples of people who fasted in the Bible. The scriptures also tell us what the purpose of the fast was or what was achieved by fasting. Here are these *examples of people who fasted.*

MOSES:

Exodus 34:28: "*And he was there with the Lord forty days and forty nights; he did not neither eat bread nor drink water. And he wrote upon the tables the words of the covenant, the Ten Commandments.*" *(KJV, 2020).*

ISRAEL:

I Samuel 7:6: "*And they gathered together to Mizpeh and drew water and poured it out before the Lord and fasted on that day and said there, we have sinned against the Lord. And Samuel judges the children of Israel in Mizpeh.*" *(KJV, 2020).*

ELIJAH:

I Kings 19:8: "*And he arose and did eat and drink and went in the strength of that meat forty days and forty nights unto Horeb the mount of God.*" *(KJV, 2020).*

EZRA:

Ezra 10:6: "*Then Ezra rose up from before the house of God and went into the chamber of Johanan the son of Eliashib, and when he came thither, he did eat no bread, nor drink water; for he mourned because of the transgression of them that had been carried away into* *captivity." (KJV, 2020).*

DANIEL:

Daniel 10:3: *"I ate no pleasant bread, neither ate flesh nor drink wine, neither did I anoint myself at all till three whole weeks were fulfilled." (KJV, 2020).*

JESUS:

Luke 4:1: *"Then was Jesus led up of the spirit into the wilderness to be tempted of the devil, and he had fasted forty days, and forty nights, he was afterward an hungered." (KJV, 2020).*

PAUL:

Acts 9:9: *"And he was three days without sight, and neither did eat nor drink." (KJV, 2020).*

THE DANIEL FAST

One of the five major types of fasting and one of the most popular types is the Daniel Fast. The reason for its popularity is that you can fast for an extended period and still function in your everyday duties or work without collapsing or becoming ill. To learn more about this type of fasting, read the entire book of Daniel. Concentrate on Daniel chapter 10 to see the sacrifice that Daniel and his buddies made for the glory of God.

Steps:

1) A few days before you start the fast, make your meals lighter, and eat less meat so that your body will not go into shock when you cut those foods out of your diet.

2) Set a date and time for when the fast will start and when it will end. Make your commitment firm. If not, you will not stick with the fast.

3) Start each day off with prayer. Find another time during the day to pray and end each day with prayer. Daniel prayed three times each day.

4) To remain focused on your fast, make out a prayer list before starting the fast so that you can remember what to pray over. You can add to the list as you go through the fast and mark off items as they are answered.

5) Read your Bible daily while fasting. Spend more time in Bible study than you usually do.

Tips

1) The fast can last as long as you want.

2) Do not eat meat or consume alcohol during this fast. This is a fast of fruits and vegetables.

3) Stay away from sugars, sodas, cake, ice cream, and other products with sugar. Honey is good, but make sure it is pure natural honey.

4) Make your meals, vegetables, salads, fruit, and water.

5) Drink at least 6-8 glasses of water each day. Drink even more water when you are experiencing weakness or headaches.

6) When you stop the fast, gradually go back to normal food to help your system become accustomed to digesting complex carbohydrates and proteins again.

DAY TWENTY-SEVEN ASSIGNMENT

ASSIGNMENT FOR TODAY:

In addition to any notes or thoughts that you had about today's lesson; I want you to do the following:

1) Make a prayer list of the things that you need to fast and pray over.

2) Decide something that you can fast for one day and give it up

3) Then later this week, I want you to select a day that you can fast all foods and drink only liquids that day and pray over the remaining items on your list that have not been answered.

4) Keep a record of the prayers answered, the day, and how answered. This will build your faith later when you feel discouraged.

DAY TWENTY-EIGHT:

FAITH: BY FAITH ABRAHAM….

Faith is one of the greatest assets or gifts that can be given to a Christian. However, it seems that it is the easiest gift for Satan to keep away from Christians. It seems almost beyond our grasp to obtain faith. However, the process is so simple. But the only way to obtain faith is to **READ THE WORD OF GOD DAILY!!**

You cannot obtain faith without feeding yourself faith in a daily dose. Today, let us read the entire **11th chapter of Hebrews**. It is a chapter devoted to faith. As we go through this chapter in this study today, you will see why it is essential to study faith and strive to obtain it.

Hebrews 11:1-40: *"Now faith is the substance of things hoped for, the evidence of things not seen. For by it, the elders obtained a good report.* **Through faith,** *we understand that the worlds were framed by the word of God so that things which are seen were not made of things which do appear.* **By faith Abel** *offered unto God a more excellent sacrifice than Cain, by which he obtained witness that he was righteous, God testifying of his gifts: and by it, he being dead yet speaketh.* **By faith, Enoch** *was translated that he should not see death; and was not found, because God had translated him: for before his translation, he had this testimony, that he pleased God. But without faith, it is impossible to please him: for him that cometh to God must believe that he is and that he is a rewarder of them that diligently seek him.* **By faith Noah**, *being warned of God of things not seen as yet moved with fear, prepared an ark to the saving of his house; by which he condemned the world, and became heir of the righteousness which is by faith.* **By faith Abraham**, *when he was called to go out into a place which he should after receive for an inheritance, obeyed; and he went out, not knowing whither he went.* **By faith**, *he sojourned in the land of promise, as in a strange country, dwelling in tabernacles with Isaac and Jacob, the heirs with him of the same promise: For he looked for a city which hath foundations, whose builder and maker is God.* **Through faith, Sara** *herself received strength to conceive seed and was delivered of a child when she was past age because she judged him faithful who had promised. Therefore, sprang there even of one, and him as good as dead, so many as the stars of the sky in multitude, and as the sand which is by the sea shore innumerable. These all died in faith, not having received the promises, but having seen them afar off, and were persuaded of them, and embraced them, and confessed that they were strangers and pilgrims on the earth. For they that say such things declare plainly that they seek a country.*

And truly, if they had been mindful of that country from whence they came out, they might have had the opportunity to have returned. But now they desire a better country, that is, a heavenly: wherefore God is not ashamed to be called their God: for he hath prepared for them a city. **By faith Abraham**, *when he was tried, offered up Isaac: and he that had received the promises offered up his only begotten son, Of whom it was said, That in Isaac shall thy seed be called: Accounting that God was able to raise him up, even from the dead; from whence also he received him in a figure.* **By faith, Isaac** *blessed Jacob and Esau concerning things to come.* **By faith Jacob**, *when he was a dying, blessed both the sons of Joseph; and worshipped, leaning upon the top of his staff.* **By faith Joseph**, *when he died, made mention of the departing of the children of Israel; and gave commandment concerning his bones.* **By faith Moses**, *when he was born, was hid three months of his parents because they saw he was a proper child; and they were not afraid of the king's commandment.* **By faith Moses**, *when he was come to years, refused to be called the son of Pharaoh's daughter; Choosing rather to suffer affliction with the people of God, than to enjoy the pleasures of sin for a season; Esteeming the reproach of Christ greater riches than the treasures in Egypt: for he had respect unto the recompense of the reward.* **By faith**, *he forsook Egypt, not fearing the wrath of the king: for he endured, as seeing him who is invisible.* **Through faith**, *he kept the Passover, and the sprinkling of blood, lest he that destroyed the firstborn should touch them. By* **faith**, *they passed through the Red sea as by dry land: which the Egyptians assaying to do were drowned.* **By faith, the walls of Jericho fell** *down after they were compassed about seven days.* **By faith, the harlot Rahab** *perished not with them that believed not, when she had received the spies with peace. And what shall I more say? For the time would fail me to tell of Gideon, and of Barak, and of Samson, and of Jephthah; of David also, and Samuel, and of the prophets: Who* **through faith** *subdued kingdoms, wrought righteousness, obtained promises, stopped the mouths of lions, Quenched the violence of fire, escaped the edge of the sword, out of weakness were made strong, waxed valiant in fight, turned to fight the armies of the aliens.....And others had trial of cruel mocking and scourging....bonds and imprisonment; were stoned....were slain with the sword, being destitute, afflicted, tormented.... all, having obtained a good report through faith." (KJV, 2020).*

As you will notice, *faith is the substance of things hoped for, evidence of things* **NOT** *seen.* Faith is a belief in something or someone you cannot see, but you know it is present because of divine power or works. Take, for example, the wind. You may hear the wind blowing outside. You may even go to the window and look out and see the trees blowing in the wind. The wind may even be so strong that it is blowing and bending the trees over. You may see the effects of the wind.... but you do not see the wind. Yet you know that the wind is what causes the blowing and the trees to bend. That is a simple way to explain faith. Faith knows that something or someone is there even if it cannot be seen or touched; faith in God. This passage of scripture also tells us that **FAITH** is the basis of pleasing God. If we do not have faith in him, we do not trust him. If we do not trust him, we will not obey him. Obedience is not an exception for the Christian.

If you were married to someone who refused to listen to you, refused to talk to you, and would not have anything to do with you, and when they did stop, it was only to tell you that you were crazy and did not know what you were doing; would you continue to live with that person? No! So why do you think God would want to continue to have a relationship with us and continue to bless us when we treat him that way? If you do not read his word and pray, you are disobedient to his commandments to commune with him daily. If you do not praise and honor God or have faith enough in him to trust him, you are treating God the same way!

We must be continuously reassured of God's love for us and his assurance that he will be faithful in all that he plans to do for us. This is accomplished by reading and praying. If we read and pray and trust him, we can learn to have confidence in what he says will happy or come to pass. We can have faith to believe and accept eternal life; accept that he guarantees us answered prayer and eternal life. Faith gives us hope to believe in and accept the things that we cannot see.

There are numerous things that we accept by faith in the Christian walk. Salvation, righteousness, forgiveness, a future, the resurrection of Christ, the resurrection of the dead, the promise of his soon return to take us to heaven, the promise of our reward in heaven, God's grace and mercy, God's forgiveness of our sins, our righteous through Christ Jesus, God's help to be more Christ-like each day, relief from all sorrows, pain, and tears, and that we will one day be rejoined with our family and loved ones. These are all things that we must accept by faith!

Faith helps us launch out and embrace this wonderful gift he has given us to help us accept this challenge and accept the new heart God will provide us. We can learn to have faith like Abraham had, and by faith, Abraham trusted God! This is a precious gift he has promised each one of us. It is ours for the asking. We only have to reach out and accept it. Do not let Satan cheat you out of this beautiful gift. But it can only be obtained through reading God's word and praising him continually for the things that He has done for you and the miracles that he has provided to you.

DAY TWENTY-EIGHT ASSIGNMENT

ASSIGNMENT FOR TODAY:

In addition to any notes or thoughts that you had about today's lesson, I want you to make a list of the following things in your notebook and pray this list to God:

1) Write down the things that you want faith enough to believe God to do in your life.

2) Sincerely, pray today, asking God to help you trust him completely and have faith in his word.

3) Make a list of the things you need to praise the Lord for doing for you. The times he spared your life, the times something terrible could have happened, but somehow you were rescued...... give God the praise for each event.

4) Thank God each day for your health, family, job, and possessions that you have that he is allowing you to enjoy and use. All that you have and all that you are is because God gave it to you! Thank him for it.

DAY TWENTY-NINE:

FAITH AND PRAYER: THE JABEZ PRAYER

Today's devotion will talk about how to "walk by faith" and how to "pray to be blessed." We have discussed prayer on several days already in this challenge. I am sure by now that you see the importance of daily prayer. We have discussed all the ways to pray and to take our petitions to the Lord. The devotion today is not another technique to use. It is just the story of a man who, by faith, prayed, and God answered his prayers.

Jabez did not lead the children of Israel out of Egypt, win battles for them, serve as their king, or lead them across the Jordan River or the Red Sea. Jabez did not conquer Canaan's Land, evangelize the world, or die a martyr. He did not have any of the miracles of the apostles and Paul in his life. But God still determined that he needed honorable mention in the Bible. Read the following verses:

I Chronicles 4:9-10: *"And Jabez was more honorable than his brethren: and his mother called his name Jabez, saying because I bare him with sorrow. And Jabez called on the God of Israel, saying, 'Oh that thou would bless me indeed, and enlarge my coast, and that thine hand might be with me, and that thou would keep me from evil, that it may not grieve me!' And God granted him that which he requested."* (KJV, 2020).

There is a book that has been written by Bruce Wilkerson called *"The Vine."* This is a dynamic book and one that I strongly recommend that you read after completing this study. I recommend that you read *"The Vine"* first, then his book on the Jabez prayer second. Follow these two books by reading Rick Warren's book, *"The Purpose Driven Life."*

In the meantime, while you are waiting to finish this challenge, I want to talk with you briefly about the Jabez Prayer. I do not want to tell you all the "keys" you will find in Mr. Wilkerson's' book, but I want to introduce you to the Jabez Prayer. I want to introduce you to build your faith and help you with five basic things that you can pray for if you are struggling with developing a prayer life. Once you study Mr. Wilkerson's book in detail, your prayer life will be changed as you learn to pray as Jabez did with faith!

Now when Jabez was born, his mother gave him a name that meant "sorrow" for some unusual reason, why we do not know…but what a way to start one's life! Jabez was of the tribe of Judah. There is one thing that is unique about how Jabez is mentioned in the scriptures. It is the simplicity and almost "oh by the way" attitude of his listing here. However, one can recognize when hundreds of others are just listed here in standard genealogy format that something special is to be noted by the fact that Jabez has more than only a listing. He has a full paragraph that has been contributed to him in this chapter.

In Jabez's short prayer, he asked for five things:

1. Lord, bless me indeed (blessing request)
2. Enlarge my coast (asset blessing request)
3. Let your hand be with me (Protection request)
4. Keep me from evil (Protection from evil and sin request)
5. Keep me from grief (Protection from sorrow and bitterness request)

Oh, how wonderful that a simple prayer could be so thorough and cover so many claims. It does not take long speeches or eloquent words to impress God. Simple and straight to the point will do just fine! I want you to read one more chapter (Hebrews 10th chapter). In Hebrews 10:22, the author discusses that an acceptable prayer to God must be sincere and offered with complete reverence and with godly fear in a humble attitude. This chapter also suggests that an individual should come with a contrite, apologetic, and remorseful attitude for their sins. He talks about bringing an offering of praise to the Lord. He wants to hear from us and commune with us, but he does not want the entire conversation to be "give me this Lord; oh, please give me that!" He wants our praise and honor.

I want you to remember a straightforward situation. You are going to meet the Queen of England or the King of Saudi Arabia. Would you approach their throne with a whining attitude, annoying tone of voice, demanding that the king or the queen give you what you desire right now? NO! If you did, you would no longer be able to come before them or serve them! So, what on earth makes you think you can approach God this way?

THE PROTOCOL FOR MEETING A KING OR QUEEN

1) One approaches with dignity, respect, and humility. Bowing or curtseying, whichever is the custom for that country.
2) Upon introduction to the king or the queen, one would express why he/she feels so honored to be in their presence.
3) Then you would thank the king or queen for all that they have done for you.
4) Last you would ask your petition and only after permitted to do so would you communicate with dignity, integrity, honesty, and humility to the king or queen.

This is the same protocol that we should meet God with when we pray. Our God is more deserving of our respect and humility than even an earthly king or queen. Let us approach God with all the glory, honor, and praise that he is worthy of…. then watch him move for us! Our heavenly Father desires to grant all of our requests. He wants us to prosper and to be in good health, even as our souls prosper.

MEDITATE UPON THESE THREE SCRIPTURES. THEY ARE GOD'S PROMISES

<u>I Kings 2:3</u>: *"And keep the charge of the Lord thy God, to walk in his ways, to keep his statutes, and his commandments, and his judgments, and his testimonies, as it is written in the law of Moses, that thou may prosper in all that thou doest, and whithersoever thou turn thyself." (KJV, 2020).*

<u>Isaiah 54:17</u>: *"No weapon that is formed against thee shall prosper, and every tongue that shall rise against thee in judgment thou shalt condemn. This is the heritage of the servants of the Lord, and their righteousness is of me, saith the Lord." (KJV, 2020).*

<u>II John 1:2</u>: *"Beloved, I wish above all things that thou may prosper and be in health, even as thy soul prospereth." (KJV, 2020).*

DAY TWENTY-NINE ASSIGNMENT

ASSIGNMENT FOR TODAY:

In addition to any notes or thoughts that you had about today's lesson, I want you to add the Jabez Prayer to your prayer list for each day. Quote it word for word and watch God start moving in your life.

DAY THIRTY:

DEALING WITH LOSS AND THE PAST

It is so hard for us to deal with the loss of a loved one, especially the death of a child, divorce, abandonment, or rejection, regardless of the reason. It is hard for us to let go of the past and to move forward. That is one reason why the Devil uses this to harass most Christians. He knows that this is a weakness in the Adam Nature of man, that unless we are completely sold out to the Lord, we will not be able to control. Suppose he can always "remind us of our sinful pasts" or remind us "of the past" in general or continually "remind us of hurts." In that case, he can keep us depressed, lonely, in self-pity mode, angry, bitter, and generally miserable with our lives.

If Satan can add anger at God to the above list, he knows he will eventually get us to walk away from God. That is Satan's goal. God wants us to serve him with our whole hearts and willingly serve him for the rest of our lives! Satan desires for our lives the opposite of what God wants.

I am not an expert on dealing with death and dying. Even as a nurse, I struggle from time to time to help families deal with these issues. Yes, I lost a spouse in our marriage annulment, and I have lost grandparents, uncles, and aunts to death. But I have never lost a child or spouse to death. I cannot even begin to imagine what that would be like to give up a child. However, if you have experienced the loss of a child to death, I want to recommend you go to the "*Focus on the Family*" website. It can be found at this URL. (www.focusonthefamily.org). It is the official website for James Dobson's ministries. He is a Christian psychologist and has written many books regarding dealing with loss and healing.

I feel that you can obtain something from him that will help you in this area. As for dealing with the loss of a spouse and children in a horrible accident, the best book that I have found that I can recommend to you is "*Into the Deep.*" It was written by Robert Rogers, who lost his wife and four children in the flood of 2003 that hit Kansas. He is now in full-time ministry internationally. He has written a book about this experience and how God restored him. This book will encourage you and help you learn how he dealt with his losses, anger, and emptiness.

"*When I lay my Isaac Down,*" written by Carol Kent, deals with losing an only child to prison. Life without the possibility of parole for murder is the most dreaded sentence a mother can hear. This is a wonderful book. It will build your faith and teach you how to stand firm amid a trial. God completely redirected their lives and ministry. They went from a comfort zone as ministers to a prison ministry. They had to learn how to deal with this change and the anger/frustration it generated for them. These books will build your faith even if you have not suffered a loss in your life.

I am not considered an expert in death and dying and hate to advise people on these subjects. However, I still want to share some scriptures with you to give you essential points for addressing some of your feelings on this topic or helping others get the appropriate help.

THESE SCRIPTURES HELP US TO UNDERSTAND WHY WE SHOULD BE READY FOR DEATH

LIFE IS BRIEF:

<u>I Chronicles 29:15</u>: *"For we are strangers before thee and sojourners as were all our fathers; our days on the earth are as a shadow and there is no abiding." (KJV, 2020).*

LIFE IS SHORT: LIKE A VAPOR, VANISHES BEFORE US:

<u>James 4:14</u>: *"Whereas ye know not what shall be on the morrow. For what is your life? It is even a vapor that appeared for a little time and then vanished away." (KJV, 2020).*

LIFE IS PRECIOUS:

<u>Matthew 6:25</u>: *"Therefore I say unto you, Take no thought for your life, what ye shall eat or what ye shall drink; not yet for your body, what ye shall put on. Is not the life more than meat and the day more than raiment? (KJV, 2020).*

<u>Matthew 10:31</u>: *"Fear ye not, therefore, ye are of more value than many sparrows." (KJV, 2020).*

<u>Matthew 16:26</u>: *"For what shall a man be profited, if he shall gain the whole world and forfeit his life? Or what shall a man give in exchange for his life?" (KJV, 2020).*

It is so important that we do not take life for granted. That we make memories with our family members and that we bless our children often. We do not know when we will lose someone dear to us. We need to accept the facts that life is brief, sometimes concise. But life is exceptionally precious, that God cares about us more than the birds, and he wants us to enjoy life

148

while we have it. He wants us to prosper as our souls prosper. He wants us to value nothing higher than him and nothing else more elevated than our lives. If we can remember those points, we can make it through these struggles.

Then we have the promises that the Lord has given to us that he will not put more upon us than we can bear; he will never leave us nor forsake us. He will always be there for us and with us. God has a plan for our lives. He will not leave us out in the cold. God wants to see that plan fully developed in us. He wants us to know that he will always be there with us. And finally, but not least of all, promises are found in **Jeremiah 29:11-13.**

Jeremiah 29:11-13*: "For I know the thoughts that I think toward you, saith the Lord, thoughts of peace, and not of evil, to give you an expected end. Then shall ye call upon me, and ye shall go and pray unto me, and I will hearken unto you. And ye shall seek me, and find me when ye shall search for me with all your heart." (KJV, 2020).*

Do not ever give up on life. Do not ever end your life; you are precious to God because you are his. God created you for his glory and honor, so taking your life would tell God that he is not worthy of you. We are the ones not worthy of this wonderful gift of eternal life that he has given to each one of us that accepts him as our Lord and Savior. We must trust him that he knows what he is doing, even if it seems wrong. Do not let discouragement overtake you or feelings of helplessness. Find someone to talk to that can pray with you and help you to find answers. There **IS A REASON** for everything in life.... we only have to seek God for that reason.

DAY THIRTY ASSIGNMENT

ASSIGNMENT FOR TODAY:

In addition to any notes or thoughts that you had about today's lesson, make a list of all the questions you need God to answer for you. This list should include questions about any losses you have had to deal with in your life. Pray daily over this list and continue to read and pray. Be patient. In time, God will give you an answer to each of these questions.

DAY THIRTY-ONE:

FORGIVENESS

Forgiveness is the character trait or ability not to hold a grudge, seek revenge, or teach someone else a lesson or the desire to ensure that others learn the lessons that you think they deserve. Forgiveness is a trait whereby you can genuinely forget the pain someone else has caused you and not seek revenge. Jesus taught us that we must forgive those that hurt us as many times as seventy (70) times seven (7) times in a day. That is 490 times a day! That is a lot! If you forgive someone that many times in a day. There is no time for anything else! God wants us to FORGIVE in ALL situations, ALL the time. When someone does something to us or takes something away from us, the laws of the land demand punishment to be given to that individual. If you have been raped and the courts press charges against the rapist and subpoena you to testify against him, then you do not have a choice. That is the result of him reaping the seeds that he has sown. It has nothing to do with you seeking revenge on that person.

Vengeance is mine saith the Lord. I will repay; it is not for us to seek vengeance or revenge. Although you may feel that you deserve the right because of things that have been done to you, to crank up the fire and throw people in or stand there as the Grand Master giving the orders for the types of punishment and torture that an individual deserves, but this is not God's way. He does not want us to have the works of the flesh in our lives but to be fruitful witnesses, not seeking revenge or having hate, bitterness, and malice in our lives.

If we burn all of our energy trying to find a way to get even with others, we will not have any energy left to love….We will not have any energy left to praise God and glorify him….we will not have any energy left to work for God, benefit the community, and love our families and spouses….no time left for anyone but ourselves and our desire to get even. If we spend our time, energy, and money trying to avoid someone we do not want to forgive, we waste valuable talents, assets, and money that God has given us to work for him, glorify him, win the lost and help others.

We do not have time for "un-forgiveness." There are reasons why we must forgive our fellow neighbors and friends. The primary reason is we want to have God forgive us. The second reason is we do not want spirits of bitterness or hate growing in our lives. So, we must forgive. If we allow unforgiveness to grow into bitterness, anger, resentment, and hate, then we lose the blessing of the Lord for our lives and our families. Plus, Galatians 5:19-21 says that hatred is one of the works of the flesh; it is an abomination unto God and cannot enter into heaven. So how do you think you are going to heaven with un-forgiveness in your hearts?

Matthew 6:14: *"For if ye forgive men their trespasses, your heavenly Father will also forgive you."* (KJV, 2020).

Mark 11:25: *"And when ye stand praying, forgive, if you have aught against any that your Father also which is in heaven may forgive you of your trespasses and sins."* (KJV, 2020).

Jesus also gave specific instructions about how often to forgive in **Luke 17:4**: *"And if he trespasses against thee sent times in a day and seven times in a day turn again to thee saying, I repent; thou shalt forgive him."* (KJV, 2020).

Ephesians 4:32: *"And be ye kind one to another, tenderhearted, forgiving one another, even as God for Christ's sake hath forgiven you."* (KJV, 2020).

Colossians 3:13: *"Forbearing one another and forgiving one another, if any man have a quarrel against any; even as Christ forgave you, so also do ye."* (KJV, 2020).

I desire forgiveness from God. I do not know about you, but for me, that is reason enough for me to forgive the people who lied on me and hurt me. The book of Mark's writer gives us instructions. God was specific in his word about forgiving and forgetting the faults of our neighbors. We want God's mercy and forgiveness; we must provide the same to our family, friends, colleagues, and everyone we meet. Forgiveness is the key that unlocks the door to happiness in your life and the door to God's blessing on you and your family! Do not miss this opportunity.

DAY THIRTY-ONE ASSIGNMENT

ASSIGNMENT FOR TODAY:

In addition to any notes or thoughts that you had about today's lesson, I want you to make a list of the following things in your notebook and pray this list to God:

1) Review the list that you made earlier in this challenge of the people who have hurt you.

2) Review the letters that you have written. If you have received responses and the situation is resolved, mark that one off your list. If not, keep praying over it.

3) If you have not written the letters or talked with those individuals to resolve these issues, you need to pray today sincerely over this and ask God to show you how to move forward. It is never easy, but you must resolve the past hurts in your life and learn to forgive.

LAWANDA NALL

DAY THIRTY-TWO:

ENVY, COVETOUSNESS, & SELF-CENTEREDNESS

What is envy, covetousness, and self-centeredness? Let us take a look at the definition of these words before we start today's devotional. All of these definitions were taken from the Random House Webster's Dictionary, (c) 1993.

Envy/Envying: A character trait or emotion displayed by an individual that causes pain or ill will to others. It is an emotion that is jealous of the good or blessings that others are enjoying. It is the inability to show joy or thankfulness when others win or get what they desire or deserve. Envy is the base of all degrading and disgraceful passions in a person's life. *(This is one of the works of the flesh that should NOT be present in our lives. The Bible says that these are an abomination and will not be allowed to enter into heaven.)*

Covetousness: A feeling or emotion that is a cousin to jealousy. It is a feeling of envy of the personal possession or prosperity or relationships of another person. To covet another person's possession is not only a sin but leads to the implementation of other spirits into your life, like envy.

Self-Centeredness: Self-centeredness is a character trait of a selfish or self-centered person. A self-centered person is an entirely selfish individual. He/she is incapable of denying themselves anything for the benefit of another.

Selfish: A person with an attitude that only allows them to strive for, achieve, or pursue things that benefit them or provides for them what they feel that they need or want. It is all about them, and no one else. They do not take into consideration the feelings of others or the consequences of their actions. Several spirits accompany **envy and covetousness**. They are bitterness, hatred, and malice. Let us look at the definition of those words:

Bitterness: Bitterness is an attitude or personality trait whereby an individual harbors negative feelings toward someone else who has inflicted pain in their life. Bitterness is the root of hatred, which is one of the works of the flesh.

Hatred: Hatred is a state of mind or attitude whereby one is not of a forgiving nature or refuses to let go of ought, grudge, or desire for revenge against an individual. This attitude is also characterized by bitterness, malice, ill will, anger, abhorrence, or dislike toward another person. *(This is one of the works of the flesh that should NOT be present in our lives. The Bible says that these are an abomination and will not be allowed to enter into heaven.)*

Malice: Malice is a deliberate act to induce harm or discomfort to another individual. You may have revengeful thoughts that lead to you taking malicious actions against another person. It usually involves lying, deceit, and inflicting harm on another. There are a few spirits that accompany **self-centeredness:** They are discontentment, dissatisfaction, and resentment.

Discontentment: A state of not-being satisfied or content. An emotional state where one is not satisfied with their life, home, job, church, etc.

Dissatisfaction: The opposite of satisfaction. If someone is dissatisfied with a product, spouse, or home, they will not be happy. This is an unhappy, miserable person.

Resentment: An attitude whereby one person hates or despises another person. You can resent another individual. This means that you openly criticize, degrade, or manipulate that person for your good. Do not let discontentment cause a root of bitterness to grow in your life or resentment toward others. You must learn that all of us will be blessed when it is time for us. Our friends may all receive their blessings and miracles before we do. It is ok. Do not let resentment and envy take over. You must be a giver, not a taker in all situations. See the definition below for these two words. Then decide which one you are, a giver or a taker.

Giver: A person who loves to do nice things for others. This describes someone who obtains pleasure for helping others, giving, sharing, loving, and showing compassion to those in need. They are always seeking something to do for someone else, not looking to see who can do something for them.

Taker: A taker is a person opposite of a giver. They do not understand the joy of giving, sharing, and compassion. A taker is an incredibly selfish, self-centered individual. Most of the time, these people are unhappy and discontent with everything they get in life, including their marriages and homes. God desires for us to be loving and kind. He wants us to have Jesus Christ at the center of our lives at all times. He wants us to seek ways to fulfill his plan for our lives and not spend time in our "pity parlors" feeling sorry for ourselves because we do not have what others have or spend time coveting what the sinners around us have been enjoying. To understand what God wants out of us, we must first understand the meaning of a Christ-Centered Life, the character traits of a kind/loving person, and the true meaning of love, not the lust the world describes to us as love.

1) **Christ-Centered:** A lifestyle choice whereby one has Christ at the center of their life, home, and career. It is a choice because he/she loves their Lord and Savior.

2) **A loving person**: one capable of love.

3) **Love:** a feeling or emotion that expresses how one feels about another person. It is a feeling that shows kindness, patience, and long-suffering to and for another individual. Here are many types of love; the kind of love a parent has for a child, the love between a husband and wife, the love between two friends or colleagues. There is divine love also. It is a strong, tender, compassionate type of love where someone is willing to give EVERYTHING, including his/her life, for the person that he/she loves. This is what Jesus did for us…he gave his life for us. *(Love is one of the fruits of the spirit that we should have active in our lives at all times).* Another Character trait that God wants in our lives is the ability to be **a forgiving person**: a person capable of forgiveness…one who understands forgiveness.

4) **Forgiveness:** The character trait or ability to not hold a grudge, seek revenge, or teach someone else a lesson or the desire to ensure that others learn the lessons that you think they deserve. Forgiveness is a trait whereby you can genuinely forget the pain someone else has caused you and not seek revenge.

SCRIPTURES, WE MUST REMEMBER

Psalms 37:1: Fret not thyself because of evildoers, neither be thou envious again the workers of iniquity.

Proverbs 3:31: Envy thou not the oppressor and choose none of his ways.

Proverbs 14:30: A sound heart is the life of the flesh, but envy the rottenness of the bones.

Proverbs 23:17: Let not thine heart envy sinners but be thou in the fear of the Lord all the day long.

I Corinthians 13:4: Charity suffered long and is kind; charity envies not, charity vaunted not itself and is not puffed up.

Galatians 5:26: Let us not be desirous of vainglory, provoking one another envying one another.

Do not forget that we cannot afford to allow covetousness or self-centeredness to take over our lives. We want to experience everything that God has for us...therefore, we must try to avoid the things that will prevent us from enjoying a true relationship with Christ.

DAY THIRTY-TWO ASSIGNMENT

ASSIGNMENT FOR TODAY:

In addition to any notes or thoughts that you had about today's lesson, I want you to make a list of the following things in your notebook and pray this list to God:

1) Add to your prayer list anyone that you find yourself envying or coveting things that they have.... Ask God to help you to do something good for that person. This may be tough, but you will have victory over this spirit if you reach out to that person with love and give something to them.

DAY THIRTY-THREE:

TEMPER, TONGUE & TAMING YOUR DESIRES

The topic of taming our tempers is so hard for most of us to imagine, might less grasp the concept of controlling our tempers. We are so accustomed to getting our way in every aspect of life that we lash out in anger when someone else dares to stop us or make us wait. I was in a store when a lady approached the sales counter. It was evident that she was in a hurry. She was yelling at someone on her cell phone. She stopped her talking on the phone and said to the cashier, "How long will it be before someone can handle my return? The lady said, "as soon as I get through checking these people out, I will help you."

There were three (3) people in line behind me. This lady looked at the sales clerk and said, " I am sorry I cannot wait that long. Can someone else come out from the back and help me? The clerk replied, "No, I'm the only salesperson here." The lady rudely turned and asked if she could be next in line. All of the people waiting behind me looked at each other, shrugged their shoulders, and said, "Sure, go ahead." This lady did not even bother to say, Thank you. It was evident that she was in a hurry and had something significant to do. I do not think anyone had a problem letting her go first; it was the display of arrogance that was frustrating. Her attitude demonstrated, "You owed me this favor!" Sometimes, it is not the temper tantrum we pitch like a 2-year-old; it is the reaction style that is as bad as the lash out!

I have been in stores when angry customers would come in and make scenes, also. I think a cell phone store is probably the worst store to be in when an angry customer arrives. It is incredibly aggravating when your cell phone does not work. I also understand when someone loses a client or a sale because of a dropped called. However, I do not understand taking it out on the salesperson at the cell store. They have no control over the towers, the computers, or the operations of the phone. They can only sell you a phone, answer questions about your account or take your phone to give to the repair technician when he comes in; they cannot work magic.

But it is so amazing to me the anger that these people have and the demands that they make as a result. One day a man demanded a Singular Wireless salesperson to pay him for the Sale he lost because of his dropped call. He had a copy of the contract and the price quote with him. The bid was more than $ 500 because the sales clerk's remark was, "Sir, I can take your complaint in writing if you want to sit down over there and write it out.

I will attach this bid and quote to the complaint. It will have to go to our regional office for approval."

"I am not waiting for the regional office to approve; you need to credit my account for this amount while I wait, or I am taking my business across the street to Verizon. The sales clerk responded, "Well, I guess you will have to go to Verizon. I cannot give credits and make adjustments on accounts or refund merchandise exceeding $500.00, including taxes. So, I cannot approve this credit you are requesting."

This man looked at everyone in the line and told them that they were crazy if they were in there to get a Singular wireless phone. He said that they would have billing errors, be charged too much, and not have adequate service. He went on a rampage in the store. Everyone looked at him like he had lost his mind or he was on drugs. What did this profit this man? Nothing! It just made him look like a fool.

As adults, we may not lie down on the floor, kick our feet up in the air and scream at the top of our lungs, but some adults do pitch temper tantrums like this guy in the Cell Phone Store. That fit did not hurt anyone, just him. It did not cost anyone else in that store a cent. I am sure Cingular did not honor his claim. So, he did not profit anything either! However, if he had a blessing from the Lord waiting to be delivered to him, delivery was stopped. God does not reward immature, childish behavior that demonstrates direct disobedience of his commandments or behavior that gives spirits control in our lives. So, this man only hurt himself that day. Do not let Satan steal your blessing that the Lord has planned for you because you cannot control your temper or your tongue.

Tomorrow's devotion will be on *"Gossip and Busy-Bodies"* and how to tame your tongue in that aspect. Today we will talk about taming your tongue by controlling your "lash backs" and temper tantrums. Most temper tantrums are accompanied by verbal outbursts also. Once you control your temper, your tongue usually comes under control in these types of situations. The other kind of tongue taming that we need to talk about will be discussed tomorrow.

Most anger outbursts that adults experience is for the same reason that most children have temper tantrums, we do not get what we want, or we are afraid we are losing, so we lash out! But we must learn to tame our desires as well as our tongues. We do not need to get everything that we desire!

The apostle James's entire book (named after him) is full of excellent advice for controlling our tempers, desires, and tongues. Tomorrow's devotion will cover James 3rd chapter, which deals with the tongue, gossip, busy-bodies, and the consequences. If you can learn to be content in whatsoever state you are in and praise God regardless of the circumstances, you will acquire patience. The frequency of emotional outbursts decreases with patience, and the need or desire to tell people off goes away. It is incredible what a change of heart and attitude occurs when Jesus takes control of our lives!

What happens when you choose NOT to control your tongue, temper, and anger:

Matthew 5:22: *"But I say unto you that whosoever is angry with this brother without a cause shall be in danger of the judgment and whosoever shall say to his brother, Raca, shall be in danger of the council, but whosoever shall say, 'Thou fool shall be in danger of hell fire."* (KJV, 2020).

James 1:19: *"Wherefore, my beloved brethren, let every man be swift to hear, slow to speak and slow to wrath."* (KJV, 2020).

Make your choice to let Jesus have control of your life. Decide that you will praise God, regardless; be content and avoid things, activities, and individuals that will cause you to want to lust after or covet what others have that you do not. Do not allow Satan to put the works of the flesh in your life. You cannot control your desires or emotions. But you can keep those desires from renting out a room in your mind and staying for a while. When this occurs, you will convenience yourself that it is not a sin to commit that sinful act for you.

After making this choice, Satan will see to it that your lust or covetousness consumes you. If you choose to kick out the voice of Satan and not dwell on those evil thoughts, God will move, and you will see things begin to turn around for you.

DAY THIRTY-THREE ASSIGNMENT

ASSIGNMENT FOR TODAY:

I want you to pray that God will help you control your temper, tongue and tame the desires in your life that cause your tongue and temper to get out of control.

DAY THIRTY-FOUR:

GOSSIP

We cannot talk about gossip without talking about the tongue. We cannot talk about the tongue without studying **James chapter three.**

James 3:1-18: *"My brethren, be not many masters, knowing that we shall receive the greater condemnation. For in many things we offend all. If any man offends not in word, the same is a perfect man, and able also to bridle the whole body. Behold, we put bits in the horses' mouths that they may obey us; and we turn about their whole body. Behold also the ships, which though they be so great, and are driven of fierce winds, yet are they turned about with a very small helm, whithersoever the governor listed. Even so, the tongue is a little member and boasted great things. Behold how great a matter a little fire kindle! And the tongue is a fire, a world of iniquity: so is the tongue among our members, that it defiles the whole body, and sets on fire the course of nature; and it is set on fire of hell. For every kind of beasts, and of birds, and of serpents, and of things in the sea, is tamed, and hath been tamed of mankind: But the tongue can no man tame; it is an unruly evil, full of deadly poison. Therewith bless us God, even the Father; and therewith curse we men, which are made after the similitude of God. Out of the same mouth proceed blessing and cursing. My brethren, these things ought not so to be. Doth a fountain sends forth at the same place sweet water and bitter? Can the fig tree, my brethren, bear olive berries, neither a vine, figs? So, can no fountain both yield salt water and fresh? Who is a wise man and endued with knowledge among you? Let him show out of a good conversation his works with meekness of wisdom. But if ye have bitter envying and strife in your hearts, glory not, and lie not against the truth. This wisdom descended not from above but is earthly, sensual, and devilish. For where envying and strife is, there is confusion and every evil work. But the wisdom that is from above is first pure, then peaceable, gentle, and easy to be entreated, full of mercy and good fruits, without partiality, and without hypocrisy. And the fruit of righteousness is sown in peace of them that make peace." (KJV, 2020).*

Now let us look at specific critical points in the passage of scripture. There is an old saying, "What goes around comes around!" This is so true when it comes to the things that we say. What we say today to someone may affect our lives years later. Especially, if you said something derogatory or hateful to someone that hurt them, then five years later, you needed a favor or assistance from a business, and you walked in to ask for their help. You find that the person you were hateful to now holds all the cards. This person is the manager who will have the ultimate decision authority of whether or not to help you. It is best always to be friendly, polite, and kind, whether or not you think the person you are showing this kindness to deserve it or not. You must remember that misrepresentations, envy, wrath, false statements, deceptions, and malice are the things the tongue can spew out, like dragons' breaths of fire to destroy another person.

The chapter says that any man cannot tame the tongue. It is hard to imagine that our tongues cannot be tamed or controlled. Considering that all species of beasts have been tamed by a man down through the generations, how is it that man has a "flaw" that cannot be corrected or controlled? So how could it be that a member of a man's body could be so evil that it cannot be tamed without the Holy Ghost to help? What we have to realize that salvation alone cannot control our tongues. It takes special prayer and help from the Holy Ghost/Holy Spirit in your life to have a lifestyle/personality change to control your tongue.

The most damage that our tongues can do besides "murder" other people are killing our blessings. In **James 3:11,** we are told that we cannot have both sweet and bitter water flowing from the same fountain. We cannot speak blessings and cursing simultaneously and expect God to ignore the bad things we say and bless us. We have to choose what we want, good or evil. One of the crucial things for you to remember is that you invite other spirits to come in and reside when you plant seeds of lying and deceitfulness in your life. Those spirits usually include bitterness, envy, strife, pride, arrogance, pessimistic viewpoint, confusion, evil thoughts, evil deeds, and other spirits that usually destroy your values and convictions like immoral, sexually related spirits. In the third chapter of James, Paul provides proof of why gossiping or being a busy-body is wrong. He tells us how it destroys the church members versus building them up, affecting the entire church.

This is not what God wants from us. He wants us to be pure, peaceable, gentle, kind, merciful, loving, longsuffering, genuine, honest, compassionate, and wise. James 3:18 ends by reminding us that "peacemakers" are continually recommending the divine wisdom of the fruits of righteousness to be sown in peace to others. It is better to uplift, encourage, enlighten, and bless others than to cut down, degrade, and destroy. Remember, the tongue is the one part of your body that can kill the spirit of a man or woman and destroy them and their lives without ever pulling a trigger or throwing a knife. Listed below are the scriptures for why discord or strife is usually present in our lives:

CAUSES OF DISCORD ARE USUALLY

HATRED:

<u>Proverbs 10:12</u>: *"Hatred stirs up strife: but love covers all sins."* (KJV, 2020).

PRIDE:

<u>Proverbs 13:10</u>: *"Only by pride cometh contention: but with the well-advised is wisdom." (KJV, 2020).*

CONTENTIOUS SPIRIT:

<u>Proverbs 26:21</u>: *"As coals are to burning coals, and wood to fire; so is a contentious man to kindle strife."*

ANGER:

<u>Proverbs 29:22</u>: *"An angry man stirs up strife, and a furious man abounds in transgression." (KJV, 2020).*

FOOLISH QUESTIONS:

I Timothy 6:4: *"He is proud, knowing nothing, but doting about questions and strife of words, whereof cometh envy, strife, railings, evil surmising."* (KJV, 2020).

ENVY & STRIFE:

James 3: 16: *"For where envying and strife is, there is confusion and every evil work."* (KJV, 2020).

The Bible teaches us that we should not ever strive with another person or sow discord; we should control all gossip. Let us take a look at those scriptures.

FORBIDDEN TO STRIVE OR SOW DISCORD:

<u>II Timothy 2:14</u>: *"Of these things put them in remembrance, charging them before the Lord that they strive not about words to no profit, but to the subverting of the hearers."* (KJV, 2020).

II Timothy 2:24: *"And the servant of the Lord must not strive, but be gentle unto all men, apt to teach, patient."* (KJV, 2020).

Psalms 120:7: *"I am for peace, but when I speak, they are for war."* (KJV, 2020).

Psalms 140:2: *"Which imagine mischief in their heart; continually are they gathered together for war."* (KJV, 2020).

Proverbs 15:18: *"A wrathful man stirs up strife, but he that is slow to answer appeases strife."* (KJV, 2020).

Proverbs 17:19: *"He loves transgression that loves strife and he that exalts his gate seeks destruction."* (KJV, 2020).

Proverbs 28:6: *"A fool's lips enter into contention, and his mouth calls for strokes."* (KJV, 2020).

Proverbs 26:21: *"As coals are to burning coals and wood to fire, so is a contentious man to kindle strife."* (KJV, 2020).

In the New Testament, Paul used an unusual term for a group of people going between the churches and church communities, stirring up strife. He called them "busy-bodies." (See the glossary for definitions and examples). See also definition for gossip. Let us take a look at the scriptures regarding busybodies. We should not get caught up in this form of disobedience to God. I will try to explain why this is considered disobedience in this lesson and other lessons to follow.

BUSY-BODIES ARE IDLE:

II Thessalonians 3:11: *"For we hear that there are some which walk among you disorderly, working not at all but who are busybodies."* (KJV, 2020).

BUSY-BODIES: MISCHIEVOUS, IDLE TALE-BEARERS:

I Timothy 5:13: *"And withal they learn to be idle, wandering about from house to house and not only idle but tattlers also and busybodies, speaking things which they ought not."* (KJV, 2020).

CHRISTIANS MUST NOT BE BUSY-BODIES:

I Peter 4:15: *"But let none of you suffer as a murderer, or as a thief, or as an evil-doer or as a busybody in other men's matters."* *(KJV, 2020).*

Paul taught that to be a busy body, gossiper, or one who bears false witness, is the same as being a talebearer, tattler, a person who enjoys slandering others, or someone who loves to go about whispering evil about other individuals as a way or method to control them. In **Proverbs 20:3,** the scripture states that busy-bodies (gossipers) are fools. There are two scriptures that we need to look at:

Proverbs 26:17: *"he that passed by, and meddleth with strife belonging not to him, is like one that taketh a dog by the ears."* *(KJV, 2020).*

This scripture talks about the person who delights in strife & willful provocation or the person who likes to start up strife between two individuals, not worrying about their families' consequences.

II Kings 14:10: *"Thou hast indeed smitten Edom, and thine heart hath lifted thee up: the glory of this, and tarry at home: for why shouldest thou meddle to thy hurt, that thou shouldest fall, even thou, and Judah with thee?"* *(KJV, 2020).*

It was apparent that Amaziah was full of pride by his statements about his victory over Edom. He did not give God any of the glory or even acknowledge God at all with his victory. When a man or woman gets to the point in his/her life that everything is something that HE/SHE did, not what God did for them…. then that individual has allowed their self-centeredness and pride to become their Idols. God is no longer the first place. God will not share you with anything or anyone!

These scriptures talk about the mischief that busy-bodies bring upon themselves. The main thing for us to remember is that Gossip provides a false witness or false report about someone else that is designed to hurt them, destroy their reputation or cost them a job or something in life that they need or want. Gossip is pure evil and not the desired fruit for your life. Do not let Satan slip you into this trap and become involved in gossip or tell-baring. Do not let Satan get your miracles or blessings! It is not worth it.

DAY THIRTY-FOUR ASSIGNMENT

ASSIGNMENT FOR TODAY:

In addition to any notes or thoughts that you had about today's lesson, I want you to make a list of the following things in your notebook and pray this list to God:

    a.   Make a list of people you need to stay away from who participate in gossip and strife.

    b.   If you do not have anyone you need to stay away from, pray that God will give you the wisdom and discernment to recognize this type of individual when they approach you.

    c.   If you are a gossiper or busy-body, then sincerely pray and ask God to help you to stop this inappropriate behavior and give you victory over this personality trait that you have acquired. God will help you.

    d.   If you listed people under #1, you need to pray and ask God to help you control yourself around these people not to get involved. Ask God to help you to walk away whenever they start sharing gossip. Or at least keep your mouth shut and not participate in the gossip if you are in a place where you cannot walk away, like work or church.

DAY THIRTY-FIVE:

JEALOUSY

Jealousy is an emotion or attitude whereby one is envious of the possession of another person. Most parents describe to their kids the giant ugly green-eyed monster that takes over evil people! Jealousy usually brings with it the spirits of envy and covetousness. **Envy** is an emotion displayed that causes pain or ill will to others. It is an emotion that is jealous of the good or blessings that others are enjoying. It is the inability to show joy or thankfulness when others win or get what they desire or deserve. (Google.com, 2020).

Envy is the base of all degrading and disgraceful passions. Jealousy stops God's blessings and keeps away our joy. It begins by making us envy or covet what our neighbors have and takes first place in our lives. When this happens, we push God out and replace him with something else in the top position. We develop another idol in our lives. It is usually the desire to obtain what we want (money), our obsession with money, a position, or promotion (greed) that becomes our idol.

When we let things come between God and us, especially things that generate the works of the flesh in our lives (envy, jealousy, covetousness, and greed/bitterness), then we destroy our relationship with God. He cannot even look upon us. The Bible says that God cannot look upon the works of the flesh. They are an abomination to him. If we have sin in our lives, God cannot bear to look at or enjoy a relationship with us. We must ask him to remove these sins from our lives and cover us with his blood and deliver us from all unrighteousness.

There are two excellent Old Testament examples of jealousy and the consequences of it in the Bible. The first story is about Joseph, and his brothers, who sold him into slavery because they were jealous, were so intense that they hated him.

Genesis 37:3-4: *"Now Israel loved Joseph more than all his children because he was the son of his old age: and he made him a coat of many colors. And when his brethren saw that their father loved him more than all his brethren, they hated him and could not speak peaceably unto him." (KJV, 2020).*

Jacob's coat made for Joseph to wear was beautiful long, full length, and had sleeves, all made of a patchwork of different colors. It was the type of coat that children of royalty wore. Jacob giving this unique coat to Joseph led his brothers to believe that Joseph was loved the most, making their anger run high. But Joseph's dream sent their anger and rage to the boiling point.

Then Jacob sent Joseph on a trip to Dothan (about 60 miles away) to check on his brothers. Jacob had no idea that their hatred had risen to this point. But the very sight of their "honored brother" in his coat of many colors coming to Lord over them sent them off the edge. They did the unthinkable! They sold him to a group of Ishmaelite merchants who were on their way to Egypt for 20 pieces of silver (that was 2/3 the price of a slave, equivalent to around $2.00 US dollar in that day).

They did not care about the money; they just wanted to be rid of him. Then they planned a scheme to deceive their father so that he would not know what they had done and try to rescue Joseph. They took his coat of many colors, killed an animal, and put the animal's blood on Joseph's coat. Joseph's brothers took his coat to their father, Jacob, telling him they could not find Joseph's body, but an animal must have eaten him because here was his coat! What an elaborate plan of conspiracy! Their hate was almost at the point of murder. They would have killed him if they thought that they could have lived with themselves. So, they did the next best thing. Get rid of him and make his father believe wild animals had killed him.

But God had a plan. He used what Joseph's brothers meant for evil to work a miracle and a way to guarantee that the children of Israel would not be lost from the earth due to the famine that was coming. When God was ready for Joseph to be used, he gave Pharaoh a dream. Joseph was called from the prison to interpret the Kings' dream. When that occurred, then Pharaoh promoted Joseph to run the plan that he had dreamed. See, when God gets ready to bring you from the *Pit to the Palace*, he will even create the job you are going to if necessary! Note that Joseph was around 17 years old when sold by his brothers. When he was called up from prison to the palace, he was 30 years old.

In those 13 years, Joseph probably wondered when God was going to deliver him. Jealousy drove Joseph's brother to do this horrible deed that he did not deserve, yet God made a way of escape. God kept his promise to be there and never to forsake him. Look at what it cost Joseph's brothers and his father. They all suffered as a result of this sin. Sin always takes you farther than you wanted to go, cost you more than you were willing to pay, and keeps you in bondage longer than you planned, all for nothing! Do not let Satan walk you into this trap; the consequences of jealousy ruling in our lives are not worth it.

The second story is about Daniel. He went to the lions' den because some of his colleagues were jealous of him. Daniel had an experience similar to Joseph's. The difference was Daniel was already in a position of authority in the palace when this happened to him. These men were jealous of the position that Daniel held and wanted him removed.

To accomplish Daniel's removal from his position, they developed a conspiracy plan that would put the king in such a position that he could not show favor to Daniel or change his mind. They knew that the king liked Daniel. Their conspiracy plan was to get Daniel framed for a crime that would force the King to put Daniel to death. When this happened, Daniel did not lose his faith in God. He did not stoop to the level of his accuser. Daniel knew that his God was going to deliver him one way or another. Daniel's God did not disappoint him, but he showed up and showed out! God proved Daniel out. So, the men that accused Daniel and their families were all thrown into the lion's den and killed. Jealousy cost them their lives and the lives of all of their family members! Satan never shows you what jealousy will cost you. Do not walk into this trap. Decide today that you are not going to allow this spirit to control you.

DAY THIRTY-FIVE ASSIGNMENT

ASSIGNMENT FOR TODAY:

In addition to any notes or thoughts that you had about today's lesson, I want you to make a list of the following things in your notebook and pray this list to God:

1) Make a list of the people that you have been jealous of in the past. List why you were jealous. You may have people in your current environment that you are jealous.

2) Look at this list and try to determine a common trigger between each person listed. Determine a common ground between these types of jealousy or a significant difference. If you can figure out what triggers you to be jealous of people, you can work on it. You are looking for things like weight, looks, money, status, positions, personality, etc.

3) Then pray over your list. Ask God to help you to get deliverance over these jealousies. You want deliverance before your jealousies do to you what they did to Joseph's brothers or Daniel's colleagues.

DAY THIRTY-SIX:

MUSIC CHOICES

Secular music (what the non-Christian community plays) has a different focus than Christian music. Take a look at the various types of secular music. (Rap, R and B, country or western, bluegrass, rock and roll, pop, and disco). What do they have in common? They pump you up to want something you cannot have or do not need or make you lust (sexually) after that person that you should not have in your life. All secular music will result in the works of the flesh becoming active and in control of your life.

What does Christian music focus on in your life? It promotes praising God and thanking him for his blessings on you. Christian songs have words to encourage you by reminding you of the things God has done for you. Some songs remind us of God's blessings to our ancestors and the children of Israel in the Bible. These songs build our faith and make us long to be in heaven.

Do you see the significant difference between the two types of music? Now, which one do you think God wants you to listen to each day? Of course, the music that honors and glorifies him. He wants us to listen to the music that puts good things into our minds, the music that uplifts us. Refer back to the Day-19 devotion topic on "Garbage In—Garbage Out." That lesson dealt mainly with filthy communications, pornography, and dirty movies. However, secular music falls into that category too.

Secular music is wrong because it promotes the works of the flesh in our lives. It causes us to desire the things of the world that are forbidden in **Galatians 5: 19-21**. Secular music encourages us to long for and lust after things and people we cannot have in our lives. Things and individuals or lifestyles that will pull us away from God's plan and purpose for our lives.... not help us move toward them. Let us take a close look at the works of the flesh. We need to study each one of these seventeen (17) things listed in Galatians so that we will know how to establish our standards and convictions for our lives and our home. A thorough study of each of these will also help us see why God does not want us involved.

What are the works of the flesh? The New Testament scripture that lists the works of the flesh is found in **Galatians 5: 19-21**. This list is extensive. The King James Bible translators utilized Old English words (hard to understand) for the Greek and Hebrew words when they translated the Bible in 1611. To keep you from being confused by these old English words, I provided you with a more modern definition of each of these works of the flesh. Each one is listed in the glossary at the back of this book to help you find them later. These definitions can also be found on Google.com (2020).

Galatians 5: 19-21: *"the works of the flesh are manifest, which are these; Adultery, fornication, uncleanness, lasciviousness, Idolatry, witchcraft, hatred, variance, emulations, wrath, strife, seditions, heresies, envying, murders, drunkenness, revellings, and such like: of the which I tell you before, as I have also told you in time past, that they which do such things shall not inherit the kingdom of God." (KJV, 2020).*

THE SEVENTEEN WORKS OF THE FLESH

Adultery: a sexual relationship with a person other than the person you are married. The act of violating one's marriage vows by engaging in pornography, prostitution, internet sex, petting, fondling, caressing, sexually inappropriate talk, communications, or behavior with a person other than the individual married.

Scriptures that give examples of adultery:
Matthew 5:27-28; 5:32; 15:19; 19:9; 19:18   John 8:3-4
Mark 7:21; 10:11-12; 10:19   Luke 16:18; 18:20
Romans 2:22; 13:9   James 2:11   Revelation 2:22

Fornication: This is basically the same as adultery. In some social settings, they call the inappropriate sexual acts between two NON-Married individuals as fornication and adultery as sex between a married person and someone other than his/her husband. In other areas, they use the words interchangeably.

Uncleanness: This is a condition of impurity. This category includes but is not limited to the prevalent acts of perversion in Paul's day under the Roman rule. The common types of uncleanness that Paul preached against were: sodomy, homosexuality/lesbianism, pederasty, bestiality, and all kinds of sexual perversion, especially those resulting in harm to the human body or abnormal use/abuse of the human body. This also included molestation, incest, and sexual abuse of minors.

Scriptures that give examples of uncleanness are found in:
Matthew 23:27   Romans 1:21-32; 6:19   II Corinthians. 12:21
Colossians 3:5   Ephesians 4:19; 5:3   I Thessalonians 2:3; 4:7

Lasciviousness: This is behavior that is lustful, unchaste, and lewd. Lasciviousness is also considered the promotion of or the partaking in actions, events, etc., that tend to produce lewd, obscene, and vulgar emotions (like heavy petting between non-married individuals) that makes one desire or lust after sex or lewd things. This is the primary reason most Christians have to avoid so many worldly pleasures.

Scriptures that give examples of lasciviousness:
Mark 7:22   Romans 13:13   II Corinthians 12:21
Galatians 5:19   Ephesians 4:19   I Peter 4:3
Jude 1:4   II Peter 2:7; 2:18

Idolatry: The act of image worship. In the Bible times, they worshipped idols made of wood, stone, gold, silver, bronze, and other precious stones. Today, people worship possessions and things that they hold to be dear to their hearts. An idol to a Christian is anything that takes first place in our hearts. God is to have first place, family second, and all others last. You can make an idol out of a car, boat, or even money. If your job and desires to make money always keep you out of the church, from reading, praying, making money your idol, or your career has become your idol, you need to look at this situation and make some changes.

Scriptures that give examples of idolatry:
I Corinthians 10:14   Colossians 3:5   I Peter 4:3   Ephesians 5:5

Witchcraft: This is the practice of sorcery, dealing with evil spirits, magic, magical incantations, enchantments, séances, casting of spells, and charms by casting evil spirits or using mind-altering drugs or potions. These are all evil, regardless of the desired outcome. In other words, it does not justify the use of these methods if one is seeking love, good, health, or blessings for themselves or others.

Scriptures that give examples of witchcraft are found in:
Luke 12:29   Rev. 9:21; 18:23; 21:8; 22:15

Hatred: A state of mind or attitude whereby one is not of a forgiving nature or refuses to let go of ought, grudge, or desire for revenge against an individual. This attitude is also characterized by bitterness, malice, ill will anger, abhorrence, hate, loathing, or dislike toward another person.

Scriptures that give examples of hatred:
Luke 23:12   Romans 8:7   Ephesians 2:15-16
James 4:4   Galatians 5:20

Variance: A person with a personality trait or character trait that loves dissensions, discord, quarreling, arguing, fighting, debating, and disputes. This also describes a person who thrives on chaos and confusion in groups or churches. They are categorized as a person who gets his/her way by stirring-up things.

A scripture that gives an example of variance:
Romans 1:29

Emulations: This is a personality trait or character trait that is demonstrated by extreme displays of envying, jealousy, and deviant behavior to put down another person for the sake of lifting one to the top. In other words, a person who is always stepping on others, hurting them to get the promotion, the publicity or the reward/raise, etc.   Some people call these individuals "zealous." However, their zeal goes above the bounds of motivation.

Scriptures that give examples of emulations:
John 2:17	Acts 5: 17; 13:45	Philippians 3:6
Colossians 4:13	I Corinthians 3:3	James 3:14-15
Hebrews 10:27	II Corinthians 7:7; 7:11; 9:2; 11:2	
	Romans 2:8; 10:2; 13:13	

Wrath: This is a personality trait or character trait that is very noticeable due to the person's anger, indignation, resentment, and the fierceness in which they seek revenge or the public destruction of another individual.

Scriptures that give examples of wrath:
Hebrews 11:27   Romans 2:8   Luke 4:28   Acts 19:28
II Corinthians 12:20   Ephesians 4:31   Colossians 3:8
Revelation 12:12; 14:8,10,19; 15:1,7; 16:1, 19; 18:3; 19:15

Strife: A person who has a personality trait or character traits that love to see contention, disputing, and strife. It is usually a person who loves to publicly display angry words or start arguments and sit back and watch them mushroom. A person who loves strife also loves revenge and display bitterness and hatred.

Scriptures that give examples of strife:
II Corinthians 12:20	Philippians 1:16; 2:3
James 3:14, 16	Romans 2:8

Seditions: This is characterized by "divisions" or cliques in a group or church. A person with a sedition spirit loves to cause divisions and strife in a group or church to control the situation or outcomes. A popular definition is a person with a spirit of sedition who loves to cause disorder, disarray, and strife in religious groups, government, and the home.

Scriptures that give examples of wrath:
Romans 16:17   I Corinthians 3:3

Heresies: False witnesses, accusations made against someone that are not true. Heresies are spreading gossip and rumors as facts, thereby defaming another person's character, integrity, or honesty. See devotion on gossip, busy-bodies, and lookup bearing false witness for more details

Envying: It is a character trait or emotion displayed by an individual that causes pain or ill will to others. It is an emotion that is jealous of the good or blessings that others are enjoying. It is the inability to show joy or thankfulness when others win or get what they desire or deserve. Envy is the base of all degrading and disgraceful passions in a person's life.

Scriptures that give examples of envying are found in:
Galatians 5:21   Matthew 27:18   Mark 15:10   Romans 1:29   Phil. 1:15
I Tim. 6:4   Titus 3:3   James 4:5   I Peter 2:1

Murders: A person with an attitude or personality trait that desires to mar or destroy others' happiness and peace. A murderous attitude is an attitude of hate, an attitude that desires to "kill" good things for others. This also means to be a person to physically kill…. murders other human beings.

Scriptures that give examples of envying:
Matthew 15:18   I John 3:15

Drunkenness: A state of being drunk or out of control of your everyday functions due to alcohol or mind-altering drugs that have caused a total loss of inhibitions.

Scriptures that give examples of drunkenness:
Luke 21:34   Romans 13:13

Revellings: Rioting, lascivious and boisterous feastings with obscene music and their sinful activities like orgies. This was a display of lewd behavior during the Roman rule (during Paul's day) over Israel. Revellings and other works of the flesh, like lewdness and lasciviousness, were common in those days. This was mainly due to the idol worship at the pagan temples.

Scriptures that give examples of revellings:
Romans 13:13   I Peter 4:3

Secular music destroys Christian standards by the sinful thoughts that flood into our minds. Listen closely to the secular music that you have been listening to over the past month. Compare each song with this list of the works of the flesh. You will find that every song will promote at least one of these 17 things that God says will not enter heaven. Why would you pump this garbage into your mind when you know that it will only cost you in the end? Why put words in your mind that will cause you to lust after and fight desires for things you cannot have? Why not listen to gospel music, praise, and worship, hymns, or contemporary Christian music? Listen to something that does not promote these works of the flesh yet encourages the spirit's fruits. Look this up in the Glossary. You have already had a lesson on this topic of "Garbage in—Garbage out" and the spirit's fruits in Day-19 devotion.

It is not that God is trying to place so many restrictions on us. He designed us to honor and glorify him; so, he wants our minds pure and clean. He does not want filth and lust in our minds controlling how we act or where we go. God has a purpose and a plan for us, and he wants us to desire that more than the pleasures of the flesh. God wants us to praise and worship him. How can you do that with the lyrics of secular songs dancing in your head? How can you praise God when all you can think about is sex, drugs, rock-n-roll, and what you want that you do not have at present? Where does the praise fit into our daily lives when you listen to secular music? Nowhere!

DAY THIRTY-SIX ASSIGNMENT

ASSIGNMENT FOR TODAY:

In addition to any notes or thoughts that you had about today's lesson; I want you to do the following:

1) Clean out your music stacks in your house and your car. Commit to listening to only Christian music.

2) Commit to God that you will keep the "works of the flesh" out of your life with his help!

DAY THIRTY-SEVEN:

PAYING TITHES

According to Google.com (2020), the definition of tithes is the "act of paying tithes, is the act of giving an offering to God. We accomplish this by providing this offering to the church we attend. Some people give to missionaries and evangelists to help them cover expenses and have the funds to take the gospel to other countries. Paying tithes is the term given to the process of giving to spread the gospel and to show appreciation to God for what he has blessed you. The standard amount to pay is usually 10%. Some people pay more, and some pay less. However, this standard has been established due to several scriptures in the Old Testament about 10% tithes of the increase, not just money.

Is it essential for us to pay tithes? Yes, it is our way of showing thanks to God for what he has given to us. When we give him 10% of the money that we make each pay period, we say, thank you, Lord, for all you have provided to us! God wants us to bless, honor, and adore him with all the things and money he gives to us. You must understand that God blessed you with a job and good health to maintain that job. Yes, you must pay tithes.

Is it essential to pay tithes during this challenge and in prison? Yes, very important; you need to start practicing being compliant with all of God's commandments. If you want to fulfill this challenge to the fullest extent, try complying with all of his commandments. You will be amazed at how God will help you meet your needs in this challenge. God loves a cheerful giver!

Even a person in prison can pay tithes. Each month when I went to the commissary, I would buy items in the amount of 10% of my earned income with my prison job. I would give to those that did not have or share things with others. On one occasion, a lady was leaving to go home, and she did not have clothes. My mother made arrangements with some of their church friends to buy her a suitcase and put five suits of clothes in it. That included underclothes and all of the toiletry items needed. This suitcase had three sets of sleepwear, a housecoat, and house shoes. Then they bought a pair of tennis shoes. When my mother showed up at the prison the week before she was discharged and asked to speak with the Warden, he was in shock. He wanted to know how my mother knew about this lady. Mother explained that Norma and I had told her about this lady (locked up 25 years) was to be released with no one in her family left alive. She needed help. Mother informed the Warden that everything she would need to go to the half-way house in California was enclosed in the suitcase.

Several times during my 25 ½ months of incarceration, my parents and their church friends provided clothes for people to have to go to the halfway house upon discharge from prison. On one occasion, I took my tithes and bought the yarn on commissary and made a lady from Georgia a dress. She loved my crocheting. She had seen a dress in a magazine that had been crocheted. This dress cost over $10,000. I am confident the high cost was because this dress was hand crocheted and not made with a machine.

This inmate asked me if I could make that dress without a pattern, just her measurements. I crotched her that dress and it was beautiful. All the inmates from our housing unit and other units gathered near the R & D (Receiving and Discharge) area to see her when she left that day. She looked great! The look on her face made the months of making that dress worth it! This lady had given her life to the Lord before coming to prison, worked on habits and issues she had while incarcerated, and left a changed person.

One month, I bought all the shampoo and toiletry needs for another inmate and gave her my entire check for the previous month, plus half of the money that momma put on my account for three months. You may be asking why I would do this for someone else, especially a criminal. It is not about who they are or who they once were; it is about planting seeds in someone else. I have had several people write to my mother, telling her what a blessing these gifts and acts of kindness were to them. All of these ladies but one has put their lives back together and settled down since their release. They are married and have their families in church now. My sacrifice was worth it for all these souls! Pay your tithes and plant seeds into others while incarcerated! God will honor you!

The other concept that we must discuss to understand the concept of paying tithes is to examine the principle of planting/sowing and reaping. When a farmer decides to plant a garden, he selects seeds for the produce he needs. If the farmer wants a patch of watermelons to sell to the local market, he chooses watermelon seeds. If he plants corn seeds or bean seeds instead, he will not produce watermelons. He will produce the plants for the seeds that he planted and nothing else. It does not matter how much he prays or how much he speaks to the plants; it will not matter because he will only produce what he planted.

If we want favor and blessings from God, then we need to plant love, kindness, acceptance, favor, blessings, and positive words in others' lives. If we want mercy and grace, we need to be merciful to others.

SCRIPTURES FOR TITHES

Listed below are the most popular scriptures in the Bible that support paying tithes and the 10% requirement. Let us review a few scriptures on this topic. Hopefully, this will help you to understand why most ministers preach that you should give 10% of your income to the church that you attend.

Malachi 3:10: *"Bring ye all of the tithes into the storehouse that there may be meat in mine house and prove me now herewith saith the Lord of hosts, if I will now open you the windows of heaven and pour you out a blessing that there shall not be room enough to receive it." (KJV, 2020).*

Leviticus 27:30: *"And all the tithe of the land, whether of the seed of the land or of the fruit of the tree, is the Lord's. It is holy unto the Lord." (KJV, 2020).*

II Chronicles 31:5: *"And as soon as the commandment came aboard, the children of Israel brought in abundance the firstfruits of corn, wine and oil, and the honey and of all the increase of the fields; and the tithe of all things brought they in abundantly." (KJV, 2020).*

HOW TITHES ARE USED:

Tithes are used to pay the pastors, visiting preachers, operating expenses, electric bills, insurance, cleaning supplies, books, music, literature for classes, and other program expenses. The tithes are used to cover all of the operating costs of any ministry or church. Most ministries then take a percentage of what is received and give it to the mission field. In the years of my father's ministry, he always took 10% off the top of all funds received at the church and planted them in home and foreign missions. This type of seed faith planting always brought blessings and favor to the church.

I Corinthians 9:13-14: *Do ye not know that they which minister about holy things live of the things of the temple? And they which wait at the altar are partakers with the altar? Even so hath the Lord ordained that they which preach the gospel should live of the gospel? (KJV, 2020).*

In this scripture, the apostle Paul explains to the church at Corinth that they are to pay the elders and the pastors from the church's money as part of the offerings. He is telling them that they should, in essence, raise funds needed to cover their needs, operate their churches, and pay for the full-time workers in the church. If tithing is not a part of New Testament Law, how are the churches to raise this money? If you attend a church, enjoy the nice clean space, enjoy the comfortable pews, the air conditioning or heat, and utilize the restrooms' services, SOMEONE has to pay.

There are supplies needed to take care of those facilities, pay insurance, taxes, mortgage payments, etc., plus the salary for someone to provide the cleaning and other services. If you are going to enjoy the bulletins, Sunday school literature, songs, music, and other handouts…. then someone has to put money in the church. Therefore, you need to put money into a church that you love to attend. The amount of 10% has become the standard since it is mentioned in the Bible so many times. However, you can give more or less as you feel led.

Mission work is also funded by the money taken into a church or donated to mission organizations. We all agree that the commission Jesus gave to the New Testament church was to "evangelize the world with the gospel of Christ." For that to be done, it takes money and supplies. Paying tithes like anything else that we do should be done in moderation and in private. It should not be done for a show. If we do it to be seen by others, praised by an organization or pastor, we have already received our reward for what we did, instead of letting God provide us with that reward. God loves a cheerful and honest giver. He loves those who give of the little that they have and do not wait until they have a significant offering to share.

CHEERFUL GIVER

Luke 21:1: *And he looked up and saw the rich men casting their gifts into the treasury. And he saw also a certain poor widow casting in thither two mites. And he said, 'of a truth I say unto you, that this poor widow hath cast in more than all:' For all these have of their abundance cast in unto the offerings of God, but she of her penury hath cast in all the living that she had. (KJV, 2020).*

Even though most of the scriptures on tithes are all in the Old Testament, it can still be backed-up or confirmed with various New Testament Scriptures. I realize that some of you have never heard of paying tithes, while others have been taught that it is not required under grace and New Testament law. Others have probably been vexed with the "TV Evangelist," begging for money on every program. I understand. There are times that no matter how much I like to hear a particular preacher, that I will turn him/her off when the "money scams" start. However, as mature Christians, we cannot let the misinformed people cause us to miss our blessings from the Lord.

Until you learn the joy of giving to individuals and organizations that cannot offer you anything in return, you have not experienced joy. The best Christmas' that I have ever had were the ones on the mission field, giving Christmas toys to orphans, serving Christmas lunch to the homeless, having Christmas day celebrations, and services at nursing homes, jails, or prisons. There is nothing like giving hope to those who are alone, feel abandoned, or desperate. Individuals that feel that all hope is lost need our love and support tremendously around the holidays. Give it a try this year, be a cheerful giver! You do not have to wait until Christmas or until you are released to go home. You can begin sharing hope each day on the inside!

DAY THIRTY-SEVEN ASSIGNMENT

ASSIGNMENT FOR TODAY:

In addition to any notes or thoughts that you had about today's lesson; I want you to do the following:

1) Determine how much in tithes that you owe since the first day of this challenge.

2) Make a promise/pledge to pay the balance before the end of this challenge, if possible.

3) Commit to paying at least 10% tithes from each check/pay period from now on.

DAY THIRTY-EIGHT:

LAUGHTER AND HAPPINESS

We cannot talk about laughter and happiness without talking about love. Love is the key ingredient needed to ensure happiness in a home. Where there are love and happiness, laughter will follow. If you have not had a chance to see the movies or read the books "***Love Comes Softly***" and "***Loves Abiding Joy***," written by Janette Oke, you need to either get these books or order the movies. I enjoyed the books, but the movies for these two books were excellent. You can purchase the CDs for the movies on www.amazon.com. Most prison libraries or chapel libraries have copies of all of these books and movies.

Both books describe true love, laughter, and happiness in the home in a fashion that I cannot in this book. It would take 300 pages to share those details with you if you can watch these two movies. I am not sure that I could give the topic adequate coverage in this book. However, these movies demonstrate the advantages of love and forgiveness perfectly. They are worth the rental fee or purchase price. In the meantime, study the 13th chapter of I Corinthians. This chapter is called the "love chapter." The word charity translates to LOVE.

<u>**I Corinthians: 13:1-13:**</u> *Though I speak with the tongues of men and of angels and have not charity, I am become as sounding brass or a tinkling cymbal. And though I have the gift of prophecy, and understand all mysteries, and all knowledge; and though I have all faith, so that I could remove mountains, and have not charity, I am nothing. And though I bestow all my goods to feed the poor, and though I give my body to be burned, and have not charity, it profited me nothing. Charity suffers long, and is kind; charity envies not; charity vaunted not itself, is not puffed up, Doth not behave itself unseemly, seeks not her own, is not easily provoked, thinks no evil; Rejoices not in iniquity, but rejoices in the truth; bears all things, believeth all things, hopes all things, endures all things. Charity never fails: but whether there are prophecies, they shall fail; whether there are tongues, they shall cease; whether there is knowledge, it shall vanish away. For we know in part and we prophesy in part; but when that which is perfect is come, then that which is in part shall be done away. When I was a child, I spoke as a child; I understood as a child, I thought as a child: but when I became a man, I put away childish things. For now, we see through a glass, darkly; but then face to face: now I know in part; but then shall I know even as also*

I am known. And now abides faith, hope, charity, these three; but the greatest of these is charity. (KJV, 2020).

CHARACTERISTICS OF LOVE

Most Bible dictionaries state that charity comes from the Greek word agape. Agape means a spontaneous and divine love that is eternal. Agape love is a love that is greater than gifts. It is a love that will cause one to give his/her life for the person that they love. When you study I Corinthians 13, you will find references to many other components or attributes that an individual needs in their lives to know and truly experience agape love. I want to take time to define for you these additional components.

PATIENCE:

I Corinthian 13:4-7: *Charity suffereth long, and is kind; charity envieth not; charity vaunteth, not itself, is not puffed up, Doth not behave itself unseemly, seeketh not her own, is not easily provoked, thinketh no evil; Rejoiceth not in iniquity, but rejoiceth in the truth; Beareth all things, believeth all things, hopeth all things, endureth all things. (KJV, 2020).*

The apostle Paul talks about a person who can take time to complete a task, deal with a difficult situation or person without grumbling or complaining. Paul says that a person who possesses patience and longsuffering in their lives is a person with the fruits of the spirit in their life. A patient person is kind and considerate of others and longsuffering!

KINDNESS:

I Corinthians 13:4: *Charity suffereth long and is kind. (KJV, 2020).*

Kindness is one of the fruits of the spirit. It is also a characteristic of a person who is capable of being kind to others or showing compassion as a virtue. According to Google.com (2000), to be kind is defined as an individual that is gentle, compassionate, loving, considerate, and benevolent (giving) to other people.

GENEROSITY:

I Corinthians 13:4: *Charity envieth not. (KJV, 2020).*

According to Goggle.com (2020), generosity is a personality or character trait whereby someone shares what they have with those who do not have what they need. This person may be someone who goes above and beyond. If you asked a generous person for a piece of the pie, she might bake two pies so that you have enough to share with others or give you the rest of the pie she has with her. A generous person would be someone who loves to give and who does not complain about giving. A generous person will also give of their time and money to help others too.

HUMILITY:

I Corinthians 13:4: *Charity is not puffed up. (KJV, 2020).*

This personality trait or virtue is evident in a Christian's life if their attitude and actions align with God's word. This individual will present with remorse for their sins; a true spirit of love and forgiveness will be present. However, pride does not exist at any level in their lives, homes, careers, or ministries. Where humility is present, arrogance and egos are not present!

COURTESY:

I Corinthians 13:5: *Is not easily provoked or behaves un-seemingly. (KJV, 2020).*

Courtesy is a virtue whereby a person prefers his/her neighbor above themselves always. A courteous person will always be considerate of others. They will take pride in doing the "little-considerate" things for their partners and close friends or colleagues.

UNSELFISHNESS:

I Corinthians 13:5: *does not seek her own. (KJV, 2020).*

An unselfish person is someone who is not selfish; they are the opposite of selfish. To understand unselfishness, you need to understand the definition of selfishness. Selfishness is described as a person with an attitude that only allows them to strive for, achieve, or pursue things that benefit themselves, never considering others. Self-centeredness is not God's plan for us; he wants us to be UNSELFISH, which means that we need to provide for others, in addition to our families. We need to consider the feelings, wants, desires, and needs of others, not just our feelings and desires all the time. A selfish person will not take into consideration the feelings of others nor the consequences of their actions.

GOOD TEMPER:

<u>I Corinthians 13:5</u>: *is not provoked, nor thinks no evil. (KJV, 2020).*

 A person who behaves or controls themselves and their tempers does not get angry easily or upset over trivial things. A person who is not easily offended by things other people say or does is said to be a person who controls their temper. A person with a good temper will remain quiet, calm, and in control of their tongues and tempers despite the outburst or rudeness of another individual. This is a challenging task to accomplish. It takes lots of praying and reading!

RIGHTEOUSNESS:

<u>I Corinthians 13:6-7</u>: *rejoices in truth and bears all things. A righteous person is a clean, honest, moral person with integrity and ethics. It is a person who has accepted Jesus as his/her personal Lord and Savior and has allowed God to take first place in their lives. (KJV, 2020).*

 A righteous person is someone who has all of the other seven virtues or characteristics that we have discussed above. These individuals are honest, demonstrate integrity, and do not exhibit malice, envy, or become involved in deceitfulness. A righteous person is always sincere, showing charity or love that NEVER FAILS. True love will never be void or useless. It will never disappear. If you love someone, you will always love them! Also, note that Paul closes this chapter stating that three things will always be eternal. *"They will always last forever: Faith, Hope, and Divine Love."* One other great point to remember is not to murmur.

<u>John 6:43</u>: *"Jesus therefore answered and said unto them, Murmur not among you."* *(KJV, 2020).*

<u>I Corinthians 10:10</u>: *"Neither murmur yea as some of them also murmured and were destroyed of the destroyer." (KJV, 2020).*

<u>Philippians 2:14</u>: *"Do all things without murmuring and disputing." (KJV, 2020).*

 Why is laughter important? It is essential for people to be happy and enjoy peace. When a family is cohesively connected spiritually, you will see a home full of joy and laughter. If a family prays together and studies God's word together, then they share their tears and their joy with each other. You need to find things to laugh about and things to be thankful for in your life. It makes it easier to deal with the difficult times when you can remember the good times. Spend time with your children, making memories!

How can you generate happiness in your life? The only way to true happiness is through a life that is rooted and grounded in Christ Jesus. You cannot know true happiness unless you know the Lord, who is the giver of love. He is the perfect example of love. To understand real joy and love, we must have God first in our lives. Make daily reading and praying a top priority in your life and watch your home's atmosphere change positively.

With a heart of thanksgiving and praise, set the tone for the atmosphere of your home. Determine today that you will know the joy of your salvation and have a positive home life full of love and forgiveness. Promise God that you will bring your children or grandchildren to grow up to know and love him. Read and pray and watch God bless you!

A person with God's character and the love of God in their lives will love others and enjoy generating happiness for them. A Happy person does not murmur, grumble, or complain. They praise God through all circumstances knowing that victory is on the way!

DAY THIRTY-EIGHT ASSIGNMENT

ASSIGNMENT FOR TODAY:

In addition to any notes or thoughts you had about today's lesson, I want you to review all previous lists. If you have any unfinished assignments, take time today to complete them. There are only two days left in this challenge. If you have any letters to finish that you were writing to individuals or God, finish them today also.

DAY THIRTY-NINE:

A POT OF GOLD AT THE END OF THE RAINBOW

As children, we have all heard the story of the pot of gold that awaits at the end of the rainbow. It has always been said that if you could leave when you see the rainbow come in the sky and drive or fly till you came to the end of the rainbow, you would find a little guy guarding a pot of gold coins! Oh, how delightful that was to a child. I remember asking Dad if we could chase the rainbow. Of course, it always seemed that God put the rainbow in the sky while we were on the way to church or a church function. My dad believed that absolutely nothing came before church.... especially chasing rainbows. So as a child, I always thought I was being cheated out of something. Then as I grew up, and I realized that it was just a myth or tale.

There is a pot of gold at the end of the rainbow with God. We may not always see, know, or understand what God has planned for us, but we can be assured that he has a plan. If we just allow him to lead us toward that plan for our lives, we will find a "pot of gold" at the end of that road. God has promised us ETERNAL LIFE if we follow his commandments. What greater pot of gold can you achieve than this? Paul said that it was better to put up riches in heaven than to seek riches here on earth.

So, what keeps us from searching for God's pot of gold (his will for our lives) than seeking to find a gold mine, a pot of gold, a winning lottery ticket, or a get rich quick scheme at every turn in our lives? The things we store up here on earth, we will leave one day and let someone else enjoy them. Why do we even do this? What is wrong with us? Why not put treasures up in heaven where there will be a reward forever for us? The main reason is our own selfish, self-centered attitude that lusts after materialism.

1) **Selfishness**: A selfish person is one with an attitude that only allows them to strive for, achieve, or pursue things that benefit themselves or provide what they feel they need or want. It is all about them, and no one else. They do not take into consideration the feelings of others or the consequences of their actions.

2) **Self-centeredness**: A self-centered person is a totally selfish individual. He/she is incapable of denying themselves anything for the benefit of another. See the definition of selfish.

3) **Materialism**: Remember, in a previous devotion, we discussed several examples of materialism and the evil attitudes and deceit that

it brings to a person's life in the Bible. I will not re-discuss that devotion today. However, if you do not remember it, please refer back to the lesson of *"Materialism and Idols."*

This behavior or attitude reminds us of the Sadducees, who were concerned about two things in their lives. It consisted of power or position and money. Even when it came to dealing with Jesus and questioning him, they only wanted to trick him so that they could discredit him. They were afraid that Jesus was going to be more popular than them and would have more of the people following him and giving their money to him than to the temple or the Sadducees. They destroyed the Messiah out of fear of losing control in their lives!

However, if we are not careful, Satan will lead us into this same trap, making us lust after and covet what everyone else has in their lives and homes. He will bog us down with so much debt and daily/weekly duties to keep up the things we are acquiring that we do not have time for God or his plan for our lives. Satan loves to take away our vision of the "Pot of Gold" that waits for us on the other side….at the end of our rainbow!

Whatever you do as you go forth with your Christian walk, do not let things or money control you. Do not let people with things and money control or manipulate you with their money. You remain in charge of your life and home under the direction of the Holy Spirit. This spirit of pride, materialism, and idolatry will keep you from finding your pot of gold at the rainbow that God has set out for your life. Do not let anyone cause you to miss what God has for you.

We must remember that we cannot measure our lives and successes by the measuring stick of the world. It sometimes shows as OK on their yardstick, and at times, it looks like we are losing, when in reality, we are winning. You must remember that the world's philosophy is that the person who wins in the end "is the one who dies with the most toys and money!" That is not God's definition of a winner. Anyway, what good can those things, toys, and money do for us when we are gone? NOTHING! Someone else will inherit it and spend it for you after you are gone!

God's measuring stick says that the one who wins is the one with souls to bring to the throne, the one with good works, missions, and a family devoted to the Lord to present to Jesus. It is not what we have, but it is what we have done for the Lord that counts the most in the end at the Judgment. We must live for Him, have our sins under the blood, and bring as many people with us to meet the Lord. This is our commission! This is what determines who wins!

DAY THIRTY-NINE ASSIGNMENT

ASSIGNMENT FOR TODAY:

In addition to any notes or thoughts that you had about today's lesson; I want you to do the following:

1) If you had a fairy Godmother offer you three wishes, what would they be?

   a)

   b)

   c)

2) Now, look back (after you have written your answer) to the request that you made on day nine (9) and compare it to this list. What have you learned about yourself? Have your priorities changed?

DAY FORTY:

SETTING GOALS AND CONTINUING YOUR WALK WITH GOD

I have left the most critical group of topics and questions to be discussed in this last lesson through strategic design. This lesson will complete your challenge, giving you a "well-rounded" exposure to the essential topics. This information will help you make an informed decision about your soul's future. I pray you will be able to complete this assignment and make a genuine commitment to Christ, asking him to be your Lord and Savior at the end of this lesson, if you have not already done so today.

The most important thing that you will do now after accepting Christ is to set goals and make plans to continue walking in the grace, mercy, and love of our Lord Jesus Christ!

1) **Setting goals**: You need to set goals in your personal Bible Studies and Daily Bible Reading. You would not think of proceeding forward with your career without establishing goals and setting target dates. Do not overlook this vital task in your relationship with God. Listed below are examples of goals that you might consider setting:

   a. Read through the Bible in one (1) year from now
   b. Read one (1) Christian authored book every 90-days
   c. Complete one (1) Bible study per month

2) **Dreams**: It is important to have dreams and desires. Dreams are essential to our mental health and keep us focused with our lives and careers. It is ok to dream about spiritual things too. If there is something that you would love to do for God, keep that dream close! Do not lose it. Even if you cannot see a way financially or physically to proceed with that dream, it is ok. If the dream fits into God's plan/purpose for your life, then he will make way for that dream to come true. Do not let anyone destroy your dreams. Do not ever let anyone tell you that you are not qualified to dream and plan at that level. God does not need qualifications. He needs a willing and teachable heart; then, he will supply the rest!

3)   Regardless of what happens in your life or what you experience over the next few years of your life……. Continuing to walk with God! Do not let anything or anyone stop you. You have accepted this 40-Day Challenge. You have experienced God at a new level in your life. You have felt his presence. He has made himself real to you in a new way. Do not let Satan take this experience away from you in the future. Do not let anyone else convince you that this challenge was not what you thought. Do not let them destroy the truth you have learned either. In the closing chapter of this challenge, we will cover the scriptures on deception and how not to be deceived. This should help you understand what God expects of you. Keep these handy for future review as needed. Do not forget them!

DECEITFUL APPEARANCES:

Appearances of people and their attitudes can be deceitful. You may only see the side of the person that he/she wants you to see. You need to pray that God will give you discernment of spirits. You will be able to recognize the real character of a man or woman. Sometimes, I realize a person's true attitude with only one sentence in an entire conversation. A person can cover how they feel some of the time, but not all of the time. If you ask the right questions, eventually, you will arrive at the truth. We have to remember not to judge a person by how he/she appears or dresses before us. Sometimes, God will use whoever is willing and available to bring you a word of knowledge from the Lord. You may not like their nationality, skin color, the way they dress, or what they are driving, but you still cannot judge them. Listen to what they have to say and then compare it with the word of God. If it is scriptural, accept it; if not, throw it down and forget it.

I Samuel 16:7: *But the Lord said unto Samuel, look not on his countenance or on the height of this stature; because I have refused him. For the Lord sees not as man sees; for man looks on the outward appearance, but the Lord looks on the heart. (KJV, 2020).*

Matthew 23:27: *Woe unto you scribes and Pharisees, hypocrites: for ye are like unto white sepulchers which indeed appear beautifully toward, but are within full of dead men's bones and of all uncleanness. (KJV, 2020).*

John 7:24: *Judge not according to the appearance, but Judge righteous judgment. (KJV, 2020).*

Ask God for wisdom and discernment as you end this study, and you are going to begin your walk with the Lord. It is not a great mystery or a secret that God wants to keep from you. God desires you to understand his word, know the Bible's truths, and enjoy an excellent relationship with Jesus Christ.

Decide that you are not going to be deceitful but a productive branch of the Vine. Jesus is the vine; we are the branches. We are to bring forth fruit to glorify and honor him. Make it your mission to be spiritually productive. Let God groom you and prune you if necessary. A vine to grow and produce many branches must be cut back and pruned each year. For the branches to produce more fruit each season, they have to be pruned and clipped too. Let God's hand begin to work in your life, filing off the rough edges and cutting away all of the dead branches so that you can produce fruit for him.

John 15:1-27: *I am the true vine, and my Father is the husbandman. Every branch in me that bears not fruit he takes away: and every branch that bears fruit, he purges it, that it may bring forth more fruit. Now ye are clean through the word which I have spoken unto you. Abide in me, and I in you. As the branch cannot bear fruit of itself, except it abide in the vine; no more can ye, except ye abide in me. I am the vine; ye are the branches: He that abides in me, and I in him, the same brings forth much fruit: for without me ye can do nothing. If a man abides not in me, he is cast forth as a branch, and is withered; and men gather them, and cast them into the fire, and they are burned. If ye abide in me, and my words abide in you, ye shall ask what ye will, and it shall be done unto you. Herein is my Father glorified, that ye bear much fruit; so, shall ye be my disciples. As the Father hath loved me, so have I loved you: continue ye in my love. If ye keep my commandments, ye shall abide in my love; even as I have kept my Father's commandments, and abide in his love. These things have I spoken unto you, that my joy might remain in you and that your joy might be full. This is my commandment, that ye love one another, as I have loved you. Greater love hath no man than this that a man lay down his life for his friends. Ye are my friends; if ye do whatsoever, I command you. Henceforth I call you not servants; for the servant knows not what his lord doeth: but I have called you friends; for all things that I have heard of my Father I have made known unto you. Ye have not chosen me, but I have chosen you, and ordained you, that ye should go and bring forth fruit, and that your fruit should remain: that whatsoever ye shall ask of the Father in my name, he may give it to you. These things I command you, that ye love one another. If the world hates you, ye know that it hated me before it hated you. If ye were of the world, the world would love its own: but because ye are not of the world, but I have chosen you out of the world; therefore, the world hates you. Remember the word that I said unto you, the servant is not greater than his lord. If they have persecuted me, they will also persecute you; if they have kept my saying, they will keep yours also. But all these things will they do unto you for my name's sake, because they know not him that sent me. If I had not come and spoken unto them,* *they had not had sin: but now they have no coat for their sin. He that hates me hates my Father also. If I had not done among them the works which none other man did, they had not had sin: but now have they both seen and hated both me and my Father. But this cometh to pass, that the word might be fulfilled that is written in their law. They hated me without a cause. But when the Comforter is come, whom I will send unto you from the Father, even the Spirit of truth, which proceeded from the Father, he shall testify of me: And ye also shall bear witness, because ye have been with me from the beginning. (KJV, 2020).*

Galatians 5:1-26: *Stand fast therefore in the liberty wherewith Christ hath made us free, and be not entangled again with the yoke of bondage…. but faith which works by love. Ye did run well; who did hinder you that ye should not obey the truth? This persuasion cometh not of him that calls you; a little leaven leavens the whole lump. I have confidence in you through the Lord that ye will be none otherwise minded: but he that troubles you shall bear his judgment, whosoever he is…. For, brethren, ye have been called unto liberty; only uses not liberty for an occasion to the flesh, but by love serve one another. For all the law is fulfilled in one word, even in this; Thou shalt love thy neighbor as thyself. But if ye bite and devour one another, take heed that ye are not consumed one of another. This, I say then, walk in the Spirit, and ye shall not fulfill the lust of the flesh. For the flesh lusts against the Spirit, and the Spirit against the flesh: and these are contrary the one to the other: so that ye cannot do the things that ye would. But if ye be led of the Spirit, ye are not under the law. Now the works of the flesh are manifest, which are these; Adultery, fornication, uncleanness, lasciviousness, Idolatry, witchcraft, hatred, variance, emulations, wrath, strife, seditions, heresies, envying, murders, drunkenness, revellings, and such like: of the which I tell you before, as I have also told you in time past, that they which do such things shall not inherit the kingdom of God. But the fruit of the Spirit is love, joy, peace, longsuffering, gentleness, goodness, faith, Meekness, temperance: against such; there is no law. And they that are Christ's have crucified the flesh with the affections and lusts. If we live in the Spirit, let us also walk in the Spirit. Let us not be desirous of vain glory, provoking one another, envying one another. (KJV, 2020).*

I strongly recommend that your first book to read now that you are through this challenge is *"The Vine"* by Bruce Wilkerson. Let his words challenge you to a closer relationship with Christ and a stronger desire to keep God's commandments. Approach this new walk or way of life with NEVER-THE-LESS faith! No matter what happens…you will trust God with all of your heart and serve him for the rest of your life. Do not forget to greet him every morning, "Good Morning, Holy Spirit!"

Now that your 40-day challenge is over, how do you feel? Have you learned anything these 40-days? Has God met you? Was the challenge worth it? Please write to us and share your comments and suggestions. We want to hear from you. We want to hear how God is moving in your life and the miracles that are happening. We promise to read and answer every letter sent to us at the ministry address listed on the book's inside front cover or listed in the conclusion.

DAY FORTY ASSIGNMENT

ASSIGNMENT FOR TODAY:

In addition to any notes or thoughts that you had about today's lesson, I want you to review all of the lists you made—mark each request answered by prayer or by your Bible reading and studies. Update your lists or create a new one for the items you have not found an answer to yet or have not completed. Keep reading and searching God's word! Set goals for reading through the Bible each year at least once, preferably two to four times per year!

CONCLUSION—SUMMARY OF THIS STUDY AND 40-DAY CHALLENGE

Did you find this challenge helpful? Was the format of this book easy to follow? Did you learn something from this book and this challenge? What have you decided? Are you going to continue to follow Jesus? Or have you decided that this is not for you? We would greatly appreciate your writing a letter to share your testimony, suggestions for changes, and your prayer requests. I realize that you are busy, which would be a sacrifice, but we would love the feedback. If you have suggestions for this book or future books, please do not hesitate to list those suggestions.

Called-Out Ministries, Inc.
P. O. Box 323
Repton, AL 36475-0323
Email: called-out@minister.com
Fax: **1-251-248-2709**

If you need to study materials, contact the companies we have listed in this book's appendix. If you still need materials after that, write to us; if you have a particular need not to find anything addressing, please write to us. If you are in prison or jail, write for the Bible study courses listed in the appendix. Get started studying God's word. The more of your free time that you can spend in God's word, the more you will see God move for you, not only on the inside but with your family on the outside. Do not underestimate the power of the word of God.

Do not forget to refer to the appendix to the "Read through the Bible" Outlines for reading through the Old Testament, New Testament, and the entire Bible in a specific time frame. Select an outline that you feel that you can keep up with and begin reading. I strongly recommend that you start with the New Testament first. If you are a slow reader, start with the read through the New Testament in 40-days.

If you cannot find a church in your area, write to us. We will try to help you locate one. Or if your prison or jail does not have a ministry or chaplain, write to us; we will try to find someone or a group in your area to start one.

LaWanda's next book has already gone to press. It will be published and ready in bookstores around December 2020. The title of her next book will be: "*Living a Christian Life in Prison.*" This book is a dynamic challenge about living the Christian life behind bars. It is a must-read for all prisoners. The principles discussed in this book are encouraging for anyone regardless of whether he/she is incarcerated or not. Do not miss this book.

If you are not incarcerated, this book can be a blessing to you because you can be in a prison of your own without bars. Your family situation and other circumstances in your life can have you more bound than an incarcerated person. I strongly encourage you to get the book: "*Living a Christian Life in Prison*" and finding out how to live your life to its fullest amid the prison you are in, whether it is a prison with or without bars. There are spiritual prisons that can be worse than physical prison. Read this book and let God give you "freedom." Then read "From the Pit to the Palace" before your release, so you are ready to go home!

Called-Out Ministries, Inc., will be redesigning their website in early 2021 to add an online purchase option for all books that donate the royalties to their organization. Since the four books I have written have been given to them, you will be able to purchase all four of my books from Called-Out Ministries. So, keep checking back to see when this website goes live.

www.called-outministries.org

ABOUT THE AUTHOR

LaWanda Nall, a native of southern Alabama, is a minister and speaker. She is the daughter of an Assembly of God Pastor and his wife. LaWanda had lived her life to the best of her ability to honor God through the years. She is not a perfect person, but a forgiven one. One who loves the Lord with all of her heart! LaWanda had a heart for missions. She is a registered nurse with a Master's Degree in Nursing Administration, who used her nursing career to further her missions work, domestic and international. LaWanda had been on assignments in over 23 countries. She was extremely active in sending support to Haiti and Mexico through a long-time missionary friend of the family, Don Jones and his family, and Lifeline Ministries in Joplin, MO.

LaWanda's desire for the past ten years was to get things together and be able to retire between 40-45 years of age so that she could do full-time missions. About the time she was almost to see this dream come true, she experienced the greatest trial of her life, being accused of committing a crime that she did not commit. She was wrongfully accused, false evidence placed in the courts against her, and people hired by State Farm Insurance Company and the Florida Department of Insurance to lie under oath in a federal court against her. It was a hard time. A trial that rocked her world and tested her faith in her Lord and Savior, more than words could ever say. It was not enough to be accused of something when not guilty. No, it didn't stop there. She was sentenced to federal prison and then "punished" within the system as people who fought against her joined evil forces and called in favors of friends of theirs to see that LaWanda suffered! But as always, God never forgets his own. God never leaves them forsaken and forgotten. LaWanda suffered more than any human being should be asked to suffer as she was beaten and sexually assaulted while incarcerated. On one occasion, she had been left to die, but God knew where she was and sent an angel (another inmate) to take care of her.

For months after LaWanda's release, she remained strong. She refused to let the things she had wrongfully experienced stop her. However, she had physical struggles because of the injuries encountered in prison. This resulted in six surgeries that had to be done immediately after her release. At the time of the first edition release, she faced two surgeries to correct the trauma that she sustained. Those surgeries and others have been completed since the publication of the first edition. LaWanda has remained true to her faith, refusing to believe anything other than the words of the song she wrote.

"Jesus, I love you; Master, I adore you; Savior, you are all that I need; Father, you are awesome; you gave your only son just for me! Jesus, I

love you; Master, I adore you, Savior, you are worthy of all of the honor and praise; Father, you are my greatest love, so I pledge to serve you for the rest of my life!" (Nall, 2007).

LaWanda has worked with many people within the prison systems, half-way houses, jails, and local churches to complete this course before publication. It has been tested in domestic and international fields. It has been amazing how God has used this study guide as a tool to help people who, under normal circumstances, would have never wandered into a church or stopped to ask a Pastor for guidance and or help to find a way to find purpose and direction for their lives. Most have had to change to a new lifestyle after release.

This manuscript impacted so many people's lives before publication that there is no way to find the words to explain the changes that have occurred without sharing personal information about those individuals. Our prayer is that you will read this book, work through the assignments, and experience such a change in your heart and life that you will want to share it with others. Do not put your copy up on the shelf. After you finish this book, pass it on to someone else. Share this fantastic news of the gospel of Christ with others. Challenge them to take this 40-day challenge or test!

LaWanda has, at the time of the publication of this second edition, completed another manuscript, which is in the final edit stage. *Living a Christian Life in Prison*, her second book outlines and details the struggles you will face while incarcerated. LaWanda shares her struggles with her faith during this time and which topics she found must be tackled to live a practical Christian life in prison. *From the Pit to the Palace*, her third book outlines her struggles during and immediately after prison. She discusses the battles she had to fight once exonerated to claim her ministry and nursing career. She shares with you steps for holding on to that faith even in the darkest trials of life, knowing that God will **ALWAYS** be there with you. Other devotional book manuscripts are in the process and will be released during 2021 and 2022. A list is located at the end of this book.

As you read through this book, remember that LaWanda and her family waited for the Jury's verdict to come in on 28 May 2004 at the Federal Court House in Pensacola, FL, singing this chorus from a song LaWanda had written: **"*Nevertheless, God I will serve you. Nevertheless, I go to prison; I will serve you; nevertheless, I walk through the fire. I know that you will be the God that delivers. Nevertheless, Lord, I will never leave you.*"** LaWanda had no idea that the words of this song and two others that she had written about the Shofar Horn and Jesus I Love you, would be the words that helped her keep her faith during this trial and the two and half years incarcerated.

LaWanda Nall is an internationally known speaker in the nursing field and the religious community. She was the closing Sunday Morning Speaker at the First Assembly of God General Council in Romania in 1996. LaWanda was the first woman to speak in public in that country in the religious community and the first woman preacher on national TV in Romania. She has preached and taught in churches all over the United States and on International Missions. Even though she had been involved in medical missions in over 23 countries, her faith was tested severely. She sums this trial into one comment.

"Jesus just had to see if I was for real or if it was lip service. I had told him I would go anywhere he wanted me to go, and I would help whoever he wanted me to help! God tested that promise. I should have been more specific when I prayed. However, God had a few people sitting in three prisons that he wanted to be touched and lives that needed to be changed forever. There were some key souls in those three county jails that they decided to drag me through too! I do not regret it....89 souls, later.... However, do not tell God you're willing unless you mean it.... he might just take you up on your offer!"

The first version of this book significantly impacted our ministries' outreach to the prison system. Over 60,000 inmates went through the first book in "Life Skills Courses," with over 33,000 giving their lives to Christ while incarcerated because of this book. We are expecting this second version to exceed this outreach. With the support of Called-Out Ministries, Inc., and their publishing company, we will reach more people with the royalties of this second version that we could achieve with the first version. All of the royalties of all book sales have gone back into books for prisoners. LaWanda has not taken a dollar from the sales of any of the Christian books she has written.

Read this book with an open heart and mind. Let God work a *new work* in your heart. Then sit down and write to LaWanda and tell her what God has done for you! The supporters of her minister need to see these books' impact across the United States for Jesus! Other Christians are motivated to donate books and pray for the prison ministry when they hear your testimonies. She adds testimonies frequently to the Called-Out Ministries' website.

LAWANDA NALL

SALVATION AND COMMITMENT CARD

Complete this page, tear it out or make a photocopy and complete it. If you do not have access to a copy machine, you can put it on regular paper and mail it to us.

Name: _____ ID#: _____

Name of Church you attend: _____

Pastor's Name: _____

City where church located: _____

Name of Prison/Jail: _____

Housing Unit: _____

Address: _____

_____

Phone: _____ Fax: _____

Email address: _____

Sex: _____ Age: _____ Date of Birth: _____

Date of Incarceration: _____

Expected Date of Release: _____

Date you accepted Jesus Christ as your personal Lord and Savior:
_____ Was your commitment to Christ a result of reading this book: _____

If you were already a Christian at the time you read this book, tell us why you decided to take this challenge and complete this study:

_____

_____

_____

_____

_____

_____

If you accepted Jesus as a result of this book, please share your testimony with us. Tell us how this book helped you.

_____

_____

_____

_____

_____

_____

_____

Additional Comments:

_____
_____
_____
_____
_____
_____
_____
_____
_____
_____
_____
_____
_____
_____
_____

You may write on a separate piece of paper and attach it to this page if you need more space. You can also answer all of these questions on regular paper if this book is not your copy but borrowed from the prison library. The back if you need more space.

Make sure that you mail your commitment card to us at:

Called-Out Ministries, Inc.
P. O. Box 323
Repton, AL 36475-0323

Fax: 251-248-2709

called-out@minister.com

At present, we are only accepting money orders, cashier checks, business and personal checks for book orders, or donations of books through the ministry. Credit card purchases will need to be completed through Amazon.com until our website is ready in spring 2021.

REFERENCE

Campbell, W., Atkins, E., & Atkins, T. (2000). *Shackles-Praise You.* [Song-As recorded by Mary, Mary "Thankful Album"]. Nashville, TN: Columbia Records.

Google.com (2020). *Definitions.* Retrieved from https://www.google.com/ [add in the word you are searching for under the search tab]

Kent, C. (2013). *When I lay my Isaac down.* Colorado Springs, CO: NavPress

KJV. (2020). *King James Bible online.* Retrieved from https://www.king jamesbibleonline.com

Merriam-Webster.com (2020). *Definitions.* Retrieved from https://merriam-webster.com/ [add in the word you are searching for under the search tab

Thomas, D. (1988). *He'll do it again.* [Song-As recorded by Karen Wheaton (1989]. Logan, WV

Rogers, R. (2007). *Into the deep: One man's story of how tragedy took his family but could not take his faith.* Chicago, IL: Tyndale Publishers

LAWANDA NALL

APPENDIX AND
RESOURCES SECTION

READ THROUGH THE BIBLE IN ONE YEAR

Genesis: January 1-10, read three chapters per day.
                    January 11-15, read four chapters per day.

Exodus: January 16-25, read four chapters per day.

Leviticus: January 26-31, read four chapters per day.
                    On February 1, read the last three chapters.

Numbers: February 2-13, read three chapters per day.

Deuteronomy: February 14-13, read three chapters per day.
                    February 24, read the last four chapters.

Joshua: February 25-28, read three chapters per day.

                    March 1-4, read three chapters per day.

Judges: March 5-8, read four chapters per day.
                    On March 9, read the last five chapters.

Ruth: March 10, read the book of Ruth.

I Samuel: March 11-19, read three chapters per day.

                    March 20, read the last four chapters.

II Samuel: March 21-26, read four chapters per day.

I Kings: March 27-31, read four chapters per day.
                    April 1, read the last two chapters of this book.

II Kings: April 2-8, read three chapters per day.
                    April 9, read the last four chapters of this book.

I Chronicles: April 10-18, read three chapters per day.
                    April 19, read the last two chapters of this book.
II Chronicles: April 20-30, read three chapters per day.

May 1, read the last three chapters of this book.

Ezra:	May 2-3, read five chapters per day in this book.
Nehemiah:	May 4-8, read three chapters per day. May 9, read the last four chapters of this book.
Esther:	May 10-11, read five chapters per day.
Job:	May 12, read four chapters per day. May 13, read the last two chapters of this book.
Psalms:	May 14-23, read ten Psalms each day.
Proverbs:	May 24-30, read four chapters each day. May 31, read the last three chapters.
Ecclesiastes:	June 1-3, read four chapters per day.
Solomon:	June 4-5, read four chapters per day.
Isaiah:	June 6-27, read three chapters per day.
Jeremiah:	June 28-30, read three chapters per day. July 1-10, read three chapters per day.
Lamentations:	July 11, read the book of Lamentations.
Ezekiel:	July 12-23, read four chapters per day.
Daniel:	July 24-26, read four chapters per day.
Hosea:	July 27-29, read four chapters per day. July 30, read the last two chapters.
Joel:	July 31, read the book of Joel.
Amos:	August 1, read five chapters. August 2, read the last four chapters.
Obadiah:	August 3, read the book of Obadiah.
Jonah:	August 3, read the book of Obadiah.

Micah: August 4, read four chapters and on
August 5, read the last three chapters.

Nahum: August 6, read the book of Nahum.

Habakkuk: August 7, read the book of Habakkuk.

Zephaniah: August 8, read the Book of Zephaniah.

Haggai: August 8, read the book of Haggai.

Zechariah: August 9-11, read four chapters per day.
August 12, read the last two chapters.

Malachi: August 13, read the book of Malachi.

Matthew: August 14-20, read four chapters per day.

Mark: August 21-24, read four chapters per day.

Luke: August 25-30, read four chapters per day.

John: August 31, read three chapters.
September 1-6, read three chapters/day.

Acts: September 7-11, read four chapters/day.

Romans: September 12-15, read four chapters/day.

I Corinthians: September 16-19, read four chapters/day.

II Corinthians: Sept. 20-22, read three chapters/day.
September 23, read the last four chapters.

Galatians: September 24, read the book of Galatians.

Ephesians: September 25, read the entire book.

Philippians: September 26, read the entire book.

Colossians:	September 27, read the entire book.
I Thessalonians:	September 28, read the entire book.
II Thessalonians:	September 29, read the entire book.
I Timothy:	September 30, read the entire book.
II Timothy:	October 1, read the book of II Timothy.
Titus:	October 2, read the book of Titus.
Philemon:	October 2, read the book of Philemon.
Hebrews:	October 3-5, read three chapters/day. On October 6, read the last four chapters.
James:	October 7, read the book of James.
I Peter:	October 8, read the book of I Peter.
II Peter:	October 9, read the book of II Peter.
I John:	October 10, read the book of I John.
II John:	October 11, read the book of II John.
III John:	October 11, read the book of III John.
Jude:	October 12, read the book of Jude.
Revelations:	October 13-18, read three chapters/day. October 19, read the last four chapters.

READ THROUGH THE BIBLE IN 40-DAYS

<u>Genesis</u>:	Day 1-2, read the entire book.
<u>Exodus</u>:	Day 3-4, read the entire book.
<u>Leviticus</u>:	Day 5, read the book of Leviticus
<u>Numbers</u>:	Day 6, read the book of Numbers
<u>Deuteronomy</u>:	Day 7, read the book of Deut.
<u>Joshua</u>:	Day 8, read the book of Joshua
<u>Judges</u>:	Day 9, read the book of Judges
<u>Ruth</u>:	Day 10, read the book of Ruth
<u>I Samuel:</u>	Day 11, read the book of I Samuel
<u>II Samuel</u>:	Day 12, read the book of II Samuel.
<u>I Kings</u>:	Day 13, read the book of I Kings.
<u>II Kings</u>:	Day 13, read the book of II Kings
<u>I Chronicles</u>:	Day 14, read the book of I Chronicles.
<u>II Chronicles</u>:	Day 14, read the book of II Chronicles.
<u>Ezra</u>:	Day 15, read the book of Ezra
<u>Nehemiah</u>:	Day 15, read the book of Nehemiah
<u>Esther</u>:	Day 16, read the book of Esther.
<u>Job</u>:	Day 17, read the book of Job.
<u>Psalms</u>:	Day 18-19, read the entire book

Proverbs: Day 20, read the book of Proverbs.

Ecclesiastes: Day 20, read the book of Ecclesiastes.

Solomon: Day 21, read the book of Solomon

Isaiah: Day 22, read the book of Isaiah.

Jeremiah: Day 23, read the book of Jeremiah.

Lamentations: Day 23, read the entire book.

Ezekiel: Day 24, read the book of Ezekiel

Daniel: Day 25, read the book of Daniel

Hosea: Day 25, read the book of Hosea

Joel: Day 26, read the book of Joel.

Amos: Day 26, read the book of Amos.

Obadiah: Day 26, read the book of Obadiah.

Jonah: Day 27, read the book of Micah.

Nahum: Day 27, read the book of Nahum.

Habakkuk: Day 27, read the book of Habakkuk.

Zephaniah: Day 27, read the book of Zephaniah.

Haggai: Day 28 read the book of Haggai

Zechariah: Day 28, read the book of Zechariah

Malachi: Day 28, read the book of Malachi.

Matthew: Day 27, read the book of Matthew.

<u>**Mark**</u>:	Day 28, read the book of Mark.
<u>**Luke**</u>:	Day 29, read the book of Luke.
<u>**John**</u>:	Day 30, read the book of John.
<u>**Acts**</u>:	Day 31, read the book of Acts.
<u>**Romans**</u>:	Day 32, read the book of Romans.
<u>**I Corinthians**</u>:	Day 33, read the book of I Corinthians.
<u>**II Corinthians**</u>:	Day 33, read the entire book.
<u>**Galatians**</u>:	Day 34, read the book of Galatians.
<u>**Ephesians**</u>:	Day 34, read the book of Ephesians.
<u>**Philippians**</u>:	Day 35, read the book of Philippians.
<u>**Colossians**</u>:	Day 35, read the book of Colossians.
<u>**I Thessalonians**</u>:	Day 36, read the entire book.
<u>**II Thessalonians**</u>:	Day 36, read the entire book.
<u>**I Timothy**</u>:	Day 37, read the book of I Timothy.
<u>**II Timothy**</u>:	Day 37, read the book of II Timothy
<u>**Titus**</u>:	Day 38, read the book of Titus.
<u>**Philemon**</u>:	Day 38, read the book of Philemon.
<u>**Hebrews**</u>:	Day 38, read the book of Hebrews.
<u>**James**</u>:	Day 39, read the book of James.
<u>**I Peter**</u>:	Day 39, read the book of I Peter
<u>**II Peter**</u>:	Day 39, read the book of II Peter.
<u>**I John**</u>:	Day 39, read the book of I John.

II John: Day 39, read the book of II John.

III John: Day 39, read the book of III John.

Jude: Day 40, read the book of Jude.

Revelations: Day 40, read the book of revelations.

READING THROUGH THE BIBLE
WITH CD AND APPS

Locate the Bible on CDs either at a Christian book store or on Amazon.com. Once you have selected a company and type of CD's you prefer, spend 30 minutes per day listening to the Bible on CD minimum. I listen to an entire CD every morning and one every night. They play while I am in the bathroom, getting ready those two times per day. You can design a system that will work for you. It is very easy to go through the New Testament in 30 days and the Old Testament in 45 days with the CDs.

You can also download Bible apps that you can read on your cell phone. Several of the Bible apps have audiobook options where the app will read the Bible to you. These are all free for android and apple phones and iPads.

RECOMMENDED BIBLES AND STUDY GUIDES

Listed below are some of the more popular study Bibles and study guides. This is not an all-inclusive list. There are other Bibles and study guides out there. However, we recommend that you choose only the King James Version (KJV), New King James Version (NKJV), or New International Version (NIV) to prevent confusion with your studies since you are just starting in this Christian walk.

1) Rick Warren's Bible Study Methods
2) Max Lucado Devotional Bible
3) Life Application Study Bible by Tyndale Publishers
4) Charles Stanley Life Principles Bible
5) Dake's Annotated Reference Bible
6) Thompson Chain Reference
7) The Expositor's Study Bible by Jimmy Swaggart
8) The New Scofield Reference Bible
9) The Bible Story Book Series—See *Day-13* devotion for order information

LAWANDA NALL

RECOMMENDED BOOKS

TO READ

1. "The *purpose-driven life"* by Rick Warren
2. *"The purpose-driven church"* by Rick Warren
3. *"The Blood"* by Benny Hinn
4. *"The Anointing"* by Benny Hinn
5. *"The Healing"* by Benny Hinn
6. *"Good Morning, Holy Spirit"* by Benny Hinn
7. *"In the Eye of the Storm"* by Max Lucado
8. *"Facing your Giants" by* Max Lucado
9. *"When God Whispers your name:* by Max Lucado
10. *"Six Hours One Friday"* by Max Lucado
11. *"When I lay my Isaac Down"* by Carol Kent
    (Carol Kent's second book and a devotional are excellent reference readings, too).
12. All Books, including devotionals by O. S. Hawkins.
13. *"Secrets of the Vine"* by Bruce Wilkerson
14. *"The Jabez Prayer"* by Bruce Wilkerson
15. *"When Godly People do Ungodly Things"* by Beth Moore
16. *"Breaking Free"* by Beth Moore
17. *"Believing God"* by Beth Moore
18. *"Jesus, The One and Only"* by Beth Moore
19. *"Out of the Fire"* by Beth Moore
20. *"Hadassah, One Night with the King"* by Tommy Tunney
21. *"God's Favorite House"* by Tommy Tunney
22. *"The Road Home"* by Tommy Tunney
23. *"Silent No More"* by Rod Parsley
24. Any of the books, devotionals, or prayer journals
        by Charlie O' Neal (available on Amazon.com)
25. Any books written by Perry Stone (available on Amazon.com)

RECOMMENDED BIBLE
STUDY COURSES

Please note that all of these companies offer Bible Study courses to prisoners free of charge while incarcerated. If you are not an inmate, you may get some for free, and for others, you will have to pay a small fee to cover their cost of printing and postage. But these are great courses to take to enrich your life with the word of God.

1) Gospel Express
   P. O. Box 17
   Lynn, NC 28750

2) Gospel Echoes Team
   P. O. Box 55
   Goshen, IN 46527-0555

3) Good News Jail & Prison Ministry Grading Center
   P. O. Box 98
   Bristol, VA 24203-0098

4) International prison Ministry
   P. O. Box 130063
   Dallas, TX 75313-0063

5) Set Free Prison Ministry
   P. O. Box 5440
   Riverside, CA 92517

6) Source of Light Ministries International, Inc.
   1011 Mission Road
   Madison, GA 30650-9939

7) Stinkdamp Bible Study
   P. O. Box 3475
   Rancho Cucamonga, CA 91729

8) Ten Mile Bible School
   P. O. Box 85
   Burlington, KY 41005

9) Son Shine Ministries, Int'l
   P. O. Box 456
   Zale, TX 76098

10) Country Wide Ministry
    P. O. Box 1030
    Dellslow, WV 26531

11) Crossroads Bible Institute
    2976 Ivanrest SW, STE 125
    Grandville, MI 49418

12) HIS Place foundation
    3508 Broadmoor Blvd
    San Bernardino, CA 92404

13) Lamp & Light Publishers
    26 Road 5577
    Farmington, NM 87401

14) Mount Hope, Inc.
    P. O. Box 1511
    Hagerstown, MD 21741

15) Project Philip
    P. O. Box 1008
    Chino, CA 91708-1008

16) Prison Fellowship
    P. O. Box 17500
    Washington, DC 20041

17) Christ Truth Ministries
    P. O. Box 610
    Upland, CA 91786

18) Lamplight Studies
    P. O. Box 290088
    Brooklyn, NY 11229

19) Prisoners for Christ
    P. O. Box 1530
    Woodinville, VA 98072

20) Gospel Ministries Bible Course
    P. O. Box 126
    Pitman, NJ 08071-0126

Numerous other prison Bible study courses are available. There are approximately 68 ministries with courses for inmates and their families. I have listed only the most popular. These organizations will provide courses to people in prison and their families free of charge. Even if you are not an inmate....contact them and increase your knowledge of the Christian faith's fundamentals.

Numerous Bible study courses can be located on the internet. Many Bible schools and colleges are offering Bible study courses for the cost of the books and supplies only to Christian to encourage them to study God's word. Feel free to contact the major Protestant Organizations or go online to search for their web sites to get information on these types of courses and study materials for Sunday School Teachers, etc.

1) Assemblies of God   www.ag.org

2) Church of God   www.churchofgod.cc

3) Four Square   www.foursquare.org

4) United Methodist   www.umc.org

5) Lutheran   www.elca.org

6) Southern Baptist   www.sbc.net

7) Independent Baptist   www.independentbaptist.com

8) Evangelical Association   www.evangelicalchurch.org

9) Gospel Express   www.gospelexpressonline.org

10) Prison Mission Fellowship   www.pmabcf.org

LAWANDA NALL

GLOSSARY OF TERMS

The list below is one of the most common terms used in this book in alphabetical order for your convenience. All definitions are from the Random House Webster's Dictionary, (c) 1993. For the words that are not found in this dictionary, the definitions listed below are the author's explanation of the most "common" or standard interpretation of those words in the Christian community.

1) **Abhorrence**:   To detest someone or something; to regard with a repugnant, horrid, despicable, vile, or disgusting attitude.

2) **Abstain:**   to not affiliate with, participate in, or have anything to do with a particular function, event, activity, or person.

3) **Adultery**: a sexual relationship with a person other than the person you are married. The act of violating one's marriage vows by engaging in pornography, prostitution, internet sex, petting, fondling, behaviors, sexually inappropriate talk, or communications with a person other than the individual married. *(Adultery is one of the works of the flesh that should NOT be present in our lives and will not be allowed to enter into heaven.)*

4) **Arrogant**: an individual with an overbearing, egotistical attitude making it appear that he/she feels that they are superior to all others around them.

5) **Bitterness**: an attitude or personality trait whereby an individual harbors negative feelings toward someone else who has inflicted pain in their life. Bitterness is the root of hatred, which is one of the works of the flesh.

6) **Busy-Bodies**: a term that Paul used to describe a group of people going amongst the churches and the church communities stirring up strife. Paul called them gossipers and people with heresies. See definition for strife and heresies. (works of the flesh), wholly forbidden for a Christian. God will not tolerate, look upon, or allow in heaven.

7) **Calvary:** The place where Jesus was crucified between two thieves.

8) **Challenge**: A petition, wager, bet, or agreement between two individuals where they agree that based upon the outcome, one will win, and the other releases all rights.

9) **Christian**: a person who demonstrates Christ-like behavior, attitudes, and decisions based on what is morally and biblically correct instead of what is best for them as an individual. A person who demonstrates the fruits of the spirit in their life and does not demonstrate any of the works of the flesh. A person who is a follower of the teaching of Christ.

10) **Christ-Centered:** A lifestyle choice whereby one has Christ at the center of their life, home, and career. It is a choice because he/she loves their Lord and Savior.

11) **Chosen:** An individual or group of people that have been personally selected for a project, reward, or promotion. God chose us before we were born to serve him and to love him.

12) **Commitment:** A pledge or promise that is made by one person to another. Usually, commitments are made in writing, like loans, contracts, or employment agreements. We make a commitment to the Lord in prayer.

13) **Confused**: A state of mind where one cannot figure out what he/she believes or the inability to sort out the facts. A person can be confused about the facts or confused about what they believe. This is usually due to a lack of knowledge. To prevent spiritual confusion, one must read and study the Bible to not be confused by false doctrines and teachers.

14) **Contentment**: This is a condition or state where a person feels happy with their surroundings and is satisfied with life.

15) **Contrite**: one who shows complete remorse for the wrong that he/she has done. If you come before the Lord with a contrite spirit, then you go before him in the humblest state humanly possible with genuine remorse for your sins.

16) **Convictions:** These are your standards or guidelines that you have determined that God wants/desires of your life. When you pray and establish your standards and convictions, please note that the minimum

must include having the "fruits of the spirit" present in your life and NONE of the "works of the flesh" present. Look up the definition of each of these.

17) **Covetousness**: A feeling or emotion that is a cousin to jealousy. It is a feeling of envy of the personal possession or prosperity or relationships of another person. To covet another person's possession is not only a sin but leads to the implementation of other spirits into your life, like envy.

18) **Cross:** The symbol of the Christian Faith. This is the term applied to the apparatus that Jesus was crucified upon as he hung between two thieves.

19) **Crucifixion:** The act of killing someone in a hideous method. Usually, slow death is filled with extreme pain and agony.

20) **Depravity**: This is a state or condition whereby something or someone has been made bad, wrong, evil, immoral, or corrupt. This is accomplished by hanging around with a group or individual with different standards and convictions or by feeding your mind immoral, violent behavior (ex: TV/pornography) data.

21) **Deceitfulness:** The act, state, or attitude where a person plans to deceive another by causing them to believe something false by twisting facts to "deceives" them into making the wrong conclusions or assumptions.

22) **Deprivation:** A state of being depraved or the act of depriving someone. To deny an individual, deceive that person, strip away, or steal from them a prized possession.

23) **Devotions**: A time set aside by a husband and wife to read and pray each evening with their children. An individual may also set aside a time of personal devotions.

24) **Discontentment:** A state of not-being satisfied or content. An emotional state where one is not satisfied with their life, home, job, church, etc.

25) **Dishonesty:** The opposite of truthfulness and integrity. It is a condition whereby one feels that telling the truth about something will cost him/her more than they want to pay. One may be dishonest in dealings with a spouse or taxes, etc.

26) **Disobedience:** The act of not obeying. It is the opposite of obedience. *See Obey and Obedience.*

27) **Dissatisfaction:** The opposite of satisfaction. Not happy or dissatisfied with a product or spouse, or home.

28) **Drunkenness:** A state of being drunk or out of control of your everyday functions due to alcohol or mind-altering drugs that have caused a total loss of inhibitions. *(Drunkenness is one of the works of the flesh that should NOT be present in our lives and will not be allowed to enter into heaven.)*

29) **Egotistical:** An attitude where one feels that they are superior to others or thinks that they can do anything or they are always the best person for the job…. etc. An egotistical person is arrogant and usually very difficult to deal with or be around.

30) **Emulations:** This is a personality or character trait that is demonstrated by displays of envying, jealousy, and deviant behavior to put down another person for self-gratification. A person who is always stepping on others, hurting them to get the promotion, the publicity, or the reward. Some call these individuals "zealous." Their zeal goes above the bounds of motivation. *(Emulations is one of the works of the flesh that should NOT be present in our lives and will not be allowed to enter into heaven.)*

31) **Evil heart:** A heart that is not good; this type of heart is called a "black heart" in some societies. It is characterized by desires for revenge, hatred, murder, others' destruction, selfishness, and other traits found in the seventeen (17) works of the flesh listed in Galatians, the fifth chapter.

32) **Envy/Envying:** A character trait or emotion displayed by an individual causes pain or ill will to others. It is an emotion that is jealous of the good or blessings that others are enjoying. It is the inability to show joy or thankfulness when others win or get what they desire or deserve. Envy is the base of all degrading and disgraceful passions in a person's life. *Envying is one of the works of the flesh that should NOT be present in our lives and will not be allowed to enter into heaven.)*

33) **Faith:** A state or emotional condition where one learns to live divinely implant acquired or an inwardly or wholehearted confidence or a state where an individual learns to have trust and reliance in God regardless of what the circumstances appear to be at the moment. *(Faith is one of the fruits of the spirit that we should have active in our lives at all times).*

34) **Fasting:** A set-aside time for sacrificing something that is important to you, like sacrificing TV for a week, or boating or fishing, etc., or fasting of favorite foods for a designated period of time. See the devotion on fasting.

35) **Flesh:** the physical body. In the spiritual rim…the, ADAM nature of man is referred to as the flesh in the scriptures.

36) **Forgiveness:** The ability to not hold a grudge, seek revenge, or teach someone else a lesson or the desire to ensure that others learn the lessons that you think they deserve. Forgiveness is a trait where you can genuinely forget the pain someone else has caused you and not seek revenge.

37) **Fornication:** This is basically the same as adultery. In some social settings, they call the sexual acts between two NON-Married individuals as fornication and adultery as sex between two individuals who are married to someone other than the person they are having sex with inappropriately. Some countries use these words interchangeably. *(Fornication is one of the works of the flesh that should NOT be present in our lives and will not be allowed to enter into heaven.)*

38) **Fruits of the Spirit:** There are nine fruits of the spirit listed in Galatians 5:22. These are the attitudes and behaviors that God desires out of all of us daily. The nine fruits of the Spirit are love, joy, peace, longsuffering, gentleness, goodness, faith, meekness, and temperance. These are the character traits that God says will inherit eternal life.

39) **Gentleness:** A personality trait or character trait that one possesses that allows them to remain gentle, soft-spoken, kind, even-tempered cultured, and refined in his/her conduct. *(Gentleness is one of the fruits of the spirit that we should have active in our lives at all times).*

40) **Giver:** A person who loves to do nice things for others. Someone who obtains pleasure for helping others, giving, sharing, loving, and showing compassion to those in need. They are always seeking something to do for someone else, not looking to see who can do something for them.

41) **Goodness:** An emotion or character trait where an individual consistently stays in a state of being kind, considerate, compassionate, virtuous, benevolent, generous, and demonstrates a Christ-like attitude/conduct. *(Goodness is one of the fruits of the spirit that we should have active in our lives at all times).*

42) **Greed:** An attitude or emotion where one feels that he/she cannot get enough. The problem with greed is that most people do not know when to stop. Before long, they are being deceitful, envious, and even commit murder.

43) **Hatred:** A state of mind or attitude whereby one is not of a forgiving nature or refuses to let go of ought, grudge, or desire for revenge against an individual. This attitude is also characterized by bitterness, malice, ill will anger, abhorrence, hate, or dislike toward another person. *(Hatred is one of the works of the flesh that should NOT be present in our lives and will not be allowed to enter into heaven.)*

44) **Heresies:** Heresies are false witnesses and accusations made against someone that are not true. It means to spread gossip and rumors as facts, defaming another person's character, integrity, or honesty.

45) **Idolatry:** The act of image worship. In the Bible times, they worshipped idols made of wood, stone, gold, silver, bronze, and other precious stones. Today, people worship possessions and things that they hold to be dear to their hearts. An idol to a Christian is anything that takes first place in our hearts. God is to have first place, family second, and all others last. You can make an idol out of a car, boat, or even money. If your job and desire to make money keep you out of the church and from reading and praying…., then it is your idol. *(Idolatry is one of the works of the flesh that should NOT be present in our lives and will not be allowed to enter into heaven.)*

46) **Impurity:** A state of uncleanness in one's life. See the definition of *uncleanness.*

47) **Integrity:** A person with integrity is someone who will not compromise his/her standards or convictions for anyone or any job or obtain anything in life. It is total obedience to God with unwavering faith and commitment to God.

48) **Jealousy:** An emotion or attitude whereby one is envious of the possession of another person.

49) **Jesus:** The Son of God; his only son. He was conceived of by the Holy Ghost. The virgin Mary was the human chosen to carry this God-man child, the Savior of the world.

50) **Joy:** an emotion or state of mind where one experiences gladness, delight, excitement, etc. over blessing received, gifts, rewards, the birth of a child, etc. *(Joy is one of the fruits of the spirit that we should have active in our lives at all times)*

51) **Kind:** to be kind means to be gentle, compassionate, loving, considerate, or benevolent (giving) to another person.

52) **Kindness:** A person who is capable of being kind to others or showing compassion as a virtue. Look at the definition of a kind person.

53) **Lasciviousness:** This is behavior that is lustful, unchaste, and lewd. Lasciviousness is also considered the promotion of or the partaking in actions, events, etc. This tends to produce vulgar emotions like heavy petting between non-married individuals) or viewing things that make one desire or lust after sex or lewd things. This is the primary reason most Christians have to avoid so many worldly pleasures; just so he/she will not commit lasciviousness. *(Lasciviousness is one of the works of the flesh that should NOT be present in our lives and will not be allowed to enter into heaven.)*

54) **Laziness:** It is a character trait or personality trait of an individual displayed by their defiant refusal to work or be productive. This character trait is prevalent in individuals on welfare or that have learned to "milk the system" or to "play the system" to get what they want for nothing. It is an attitude that makes one sit behind and want everyone else to bring to them what they need, without cost to them. This is an attitude that God hates. A lazy person will also be disobedient to God. God hates disobedience as much as idolatry.

55) **Lewd:** Any actions, behavior, dress, or attitude that promotes a sexually provocative response from another individual or promotes sexually impure thoughts and actions. Examples are lewd dress, pornography, and sexually inappropriate communications. See also lasciviousness.

56) **Longsuffering:**   A virtue or character trait whereby an individual displays patience, endures offenses, injuries, and provocations by others without murmuring, rumbling, or complaining. An individual with this character trait does not show resentment or seek revenge when he/she suffers because of others' actions. *(Longsuffering is one of the fruits of the spirit that we should have active in our lives at all times).*

57) **Love:**   Love is a feeling or emotion that expresses how one feels about another person. A feeling that shows kindness, patience, and long-suffering with another individual. Here are many types of love; the kind of love a parent has for a child, the love between a husband and wife; the love between two friends or colleagues. There is divine love also. It is a firm, tender, compassionate type of love where someone is willing to give EVERYTHING, including his/her life, for the person that he/she loves. This is what Jesus did for us...he gave his life for us. *(Love is one of the fruits of the spirit that we should have active in our lives at all times).*

58) **Lust:**   Impure sexual thoughts or desires.

59) **Lying:**   The act of telling something that is not true; a false statement that is said as a statement of fact.

60) **Madness:** An emotion that one feels when angry at another individual. Madness, agitations, and rages can also be a mental illness.

61) **Malice:** It is a deliberate act to induce harm or discomfort on another individual. You may have revengeful thoughts that lead to you taking malicious actions against another person. It usually involves lying, deceit, and inflicting harm on another.

62) **Meekness:** A condition or character trait whereby one under pressure displays a pleasant attitude with gentleness, kindness, and even balanced tempers and passions. This individual would be patient in suffering injuries, persecutions, and would never feel a need for revenge. *(Meekness is one of the fruits of the spirit that we should have active in our lives at all times).*

63) **Murders:** A person with an attitude or personality trait that desires to mar or destroy others' happiness and peace. A murderous attitude is an attitude of hate, an attitude that desires to "kill" good things for others. This also means to be a person to physically kill…. murders other human beings. *(Murders is one of the works of the flesh that should NOT be present in our lives and will not be allowed to enter into heaven.)*

64) **Obey:** To follow, to do as instructed, or commanded with a positive attitude; to complete the task given entirely and thoroughly to the best of one's ability.

65) **Obedience:** The act of obeying one's commands. This is something that God requires out of all Christians. No exceptions. Obedience is a requirement for eternal life.

66) **Peace:** a feeling, state, or condition where a person is at ease, relaxed, non-stressed, or in perfect harmony with their environment or themselves. It is a state of quiet, rest, and security during turmoil, strife, and temptations. *(Peace is one of the fruits of the spirit that we should have active in our lives at all times)*.

67) **Pledge:** A pledge is a promise or public commitment to complete an assignment or do something for someone. If we pledge to serve the Lord for the rest of our lives, we make a public commitment and promise to him.

68) **Polygamy:** The act of taking more than one wife. This is illegal in all States in the United States except Utah. It is a common practice still in the Middle East. In most Muslim countries, a man can have up to four wives at one time.

69) **Prayer:** a petition or request that is made to God. Can be spoken audibly, thought, whispered, mentally spoken, or written.

70) **Rapture:** The term used by the Christian community for the event that all Christians are looking forward. It is referred to as a "catching away" of the Christians ready in Revelation. The rapture is the event that all true Christians are longing for and praying about daily if they are sincere. It is the event that marks the closing or coming to an end of this evil world as we know it today.

71) **Resentment:** An attitude whereby one person hates or despises another person. You can resent another individual. This means that you openly criticize, degrade, or manipulate that person for your good.

72) **Revenge:** *See vengeance.* Revenge is the act of seeking vengeance.

73) **Revellings:** Rioting, lascivious and boisterous feastings with obscene music and their sinful activities like orgies. This is a prevalent way to display lewd behavior during the Roman Rule over Israel…during Paul's days. *(Revellings is one of the works of the flesh that should NOT be present in our lives and will not be allowed to enter into heaven.)*

74) **Sacrifice:** It is valuable or important to us that we give up for the Lord. It is something that we learn to do without because we love God. Jesus was our sacrifice for our sins. He died in our place. In the Old Testament, they sacrificed (killed) animals and offered them on an altar before the Lord to sacrifice for their sins. We no longer are required to do this under grace.

75) **Salvation:** The gift that God has given to us. The blood of his Son Jesus was shed for our sins. He died in our place so that we could live.

76) **Satisfied life:** This is a condition or state where you are happy with what you have done, where you live, what you have, and what you are doing.

77) **Savior:** Our Savior is Jesus Christ. A savior is someone who gives their life or their most valuable possession to save you from death, destruction, or some horrible fate. The Christian faith is the only religion where the "Savior" or leader is still alive. It is the only faith with a risen savior and a living God.

78) **Seditions:** This is characterized by "divisions" or cliques in a group or church. A person with a sedition spirit loves to cause divisions and strife in a group or church to control the situation or outcomes. A popular definition is that a person with a spirit of sedition is an individual who loves to cause disorder, disarray, and strife in religious groups, government, or the home. *(Seditions is one of the works of the flesh that should NOT be present in our lives and will not be allowed to enter into heaven.)*

79) **Self-centered:** A self-centered person is a selfish individual. He/she is incapable of denying themselves anything for the benefit of another. See the definition of selfish.

80) **Selfish:** A person with an attitude that only allows them to strive for, achieve, or pursue things that benefit themselves or provides for them what they feel that they need or want. It is all about them, and no one

else. They do not take into consideration the feelings of others or the consequences of their actions.

81) **Secular**: Worldly, non-religious. This term was used to describe music and activities usually. Most things are classified as secular or religious.

82) **Son of God:** The son of God, Jesus Christ. He was born of the virgin Mary, engaged to Joseph. However, Joseph was not the father of Jesus. The Holy Ghost came upon Mary, and she conceived without having ever known a man sexually and bares a son. Jesus was God and Man.

82) **Standards**: see convictions….

83) **Strife**: A person who has a personality trait or character traits that love to see contention, disputing, and strife. It is usually a person who loves to publicly display angry words or start arguments and sit back and watch them mushroom. A person who loves strife also loves revenge and display bitterness and hatred. *(Strife is one of the works of the flesh that should NOT be present in our lives and will not be allowed to enter into heaven.)*

84) **Stubbornness**: A person's character or attitude may be described as stubborn if he/she is not willing to accept instructions, not ready to change, or be flexible. A person who is challenging to deal with is considered stubborn.

85) **Supplication**: to humbly request, petition, or entreat the Lord for your needs

86) **Taker:** A person who is the opposite of a giver. A person who does not understand the joy of giving, sharing, and compassion. An incredibly selfish, self-centered individual. Most of the time, these people are unhappy and discontent with everything they get in life, including mates.

87) **Temper:** A condition or state where a person lets external factors, other individuals, and things cause them to lose all self-control, temperance, patience, and meekness, thereby displaying rude behavior, noted with screams, shouts, and inappropriate communications during this outburst or display.

88) **Temperance:** It is a personality trait or character trait whereby one displays self-control in all things. Moderation with regards to any type of indulgence for self-pleasure is always maintained. This includes

drinking, eating, play, and other passionate pleasures. SELF-CONTROL is the best word to describe a person with temperance. *(Temperance is one of the fruits of the spirit that we should have active in our lives at all times).*

89) **Thanks, or Thanksgiving:** To give thanks means to praise someone for what they did for you. To give thanks to God is to praise him for his blessing on your life and for giving you eternal life. God desires for us to be thankful at all times.

90) **Thankful:** It is the act of expressing one's gratitude for a kind act or deed done on their behalf. God desires for us to have a spirit of thankfulness in our lives.

91) **Thankfulness:** A condition or attitude where one is grateful or thankful for something that has been done for them.

92) **Tithes:** Tithes is 10% of our earning or material increases that we give to the Lord through our church. It is used to further the gospel of Christ or meet the elderly, homeless, or those in need.

93) **Trials:** periods or times of testing. Most people feel that a "trial" is when something terrible or something unplanned happens to them. Most of the time, they categorize it as "unfair."

94) **Trinity:** The religious term used to describe the God-Head or the organizational structure of Heaven. It is God, the Father; Jesus, the Son; and the Holy Spirit—the gift he has given us to be with us always.

95) **Trust:** This is a state that you reach when you feel someone you know and love can be accountable for whatever you assign him or her. Trust is earned. The easiest and quickest way to earn someone's trust is to base your relationship with that person on TRUTHFULNESS at all times.

96) **Truthfulness:** This is a sincere attitude, behavior, or speech that includes speaking the truth, only the truth and nothing else. Truthfulness does not include non-verbal communications of a different response than the truth. Truthfulness does not have a life filled with deceit to control situations, individuals, or promote success. Truthfulness is a virtue that guarantees that you are speaking, living, nodding, etc., to the truth.... nothing else.

97) **Unbelief:** a condition where individuals decide that they do not have any faith in the person or program discussed. It is a lack of faith in religious matters.

98) **Unchaste**: Unchaste mainly refers to sexual immorality or any immodest, unclean, or impure behavior.

99) **Uncleanness**: This is a condition of impurity. This category includes but is not limited to Paul's day's prevalent acts under the Roman rule. The common types of uncleanness that Paul preached against were: sodomy, homosexuality, lesbianism, pederasty, bestiality, and various kinds of sexual perversion, especially those resulting in harm to the human body or abnormal use/abuse of the human body. This also included molestation, incest, and sexual abuse of minors. *(Uncleanliness is one of the works of the flesh that should NOT be present in our lives and will not be allowed to enter into heaven.)*

100) **Unfair:** Something that happens that is not customary or standard. When something is done to another person that violates that individual's personal space, his or her rights, or anticipated benefits and rewards, it is said to be unfair.

101) **Un-forgiveness:** The opposite of forgiveness. *See the definition of forgiveness.*

102) **Unthankful or ungrateful**: Both are a spirit or attitude that an individual displays that is the opposite of being thankful. It is an ungrateful, spiteful, defeatist attitude that shows a lack of contentment and peace in one's life.

103) **Variances:** This is a person with a personality trait or character trait that loves dissensions, discord, quarreling, arguing, fighting, debating, and disputes. This is a person who thrives on chaos and confusion in groups or churches. They are categorized as a person who gets his/her way by stirring-up things. *(Variances is one of the works of the flesh that should NOT be present in our lives and will not be allowed to enter into heaven.)*

104) **Vengeance:** The act of getting even with someone for something that they did to you. This may include inflicting pain, discomfort, public humiliation, or destruction of one's career, life, or marriage. This act is usually one of hatred and bitterness. It is a self-destructive spirit.

105) **Witchcraft**: This is the practice of sorcery, dealing with evil spirits, magic, magical incantations, enchantments, séances, casting of spells, and charms by casting evil spirits or using mind-altering drugs or potions. These are all evil, regardless of the desired outcome. In other words, it does not justify the use of these methods if one is seeking love, good, health, or blessings for themselves or others. *(Witchcraft is one of the works of the flesh that should NOT be present in our lives and will not be allowed to enter into heaven.)*

106) **Works of the Flesh**: There are 19 works of the flesh listed in Galatians. This list begins at Galatians 5:19. They are adultery, fortification, uncleanness, lasciviousness, idolatry, witchcraft, hatred, variance, emulations, wrath, strife, seditions, heresies, envying, murders, drunkenness, and revellings. Each one of these is defined in this glossary. This SHOULD NOT be present in a Christian's life. *(Actually, the Bible says that these works of the flesh are an abomination and will not be allowed to enter into heaven.)*

107) **Wrath**: This is a personality trait or character trait that is very noticeable due to the person's anger, resentment, and fierceness. They seek revenge or the public destruction of another individual. *(Wrath is one of the works of the flesh that should NOT be present in our lives and will not be allowed to enter into heaven.)*

"JESUS, I LOVE YOU!"

This is a song written by LaWanda Nall in 2002 and copyright protected in (c) 2009 and 2020. The music for this song is available through Called-Out Ministries, Inc.

Start this song by singing the chorus first,

and then sing verse one.

CHORUS:

Jesus, I love you, Master I adore you, Savior, you are all that I need, Father, you are awesome, you gave your only son, and you did that just for me. Jesus, I love you, Master I adore you, Savior, you are worthy of all of the honor and praise. Father, you are my greatest love, so I pledge to serve you for the rest of my life.

VERSE ONE:

On Earth, we pledge our love to another, making promises and taking vows to honor and adore. Sometimes, one will break these vows, but I found a love where he never changes his mind.

Repeat the Chorus, and then sing verse two.

VERSE TWO:

There is no greater love than the love of the Father. He gave his only son. The beauty of this love is he did this just for you and me.... even before we were born.

www.ingramcontent.com/pod-product-compliance
Lightning Source LLC
Chambersburg PA
CBHW060015100426
42740CB00010B/1494